Biographies

IN AMERICAN FOREIGN POLICY
Joseph A. Fry, University of Nevada, Las Vegas
Series Editor

The Biographies in American Foreign Policy Series employs the enduring medium of biography to examine the major episodes and themes in the history of U.S. foreign relations. By viewing policy formation and implementation from the perspective of influential participants, the series seeks to humanize and make more accessible those decisions and events that sometimes appear abstract or distant. Particular attention is devoted to those aspects of the subject's background, personality, and intellect that most influenced his or her approach to U.S. foreign policy, and each individual's role is placed in a context that takes into account domestic affairs, national interests and policies, and international and strategic considerations.

The series is directed primarily at undergraduate and graduate courses in U.S. foreign relations, but it is hoped that the genre and format may also prove attractive to the interested general reader. With these objectives in mind, the length of the volumes has been kept manageable, the documentation has been restricted to direct quotes and particularly controversial assertions, and the bibliographic essays have been tailored to provide historiographical assessment without tedium.

Producing books of high scholarly merit to appeal to a wide range of readers is an ambitious undertaking, and an excellent group of authors has agreed to participate. Some have compiled extensive scholarly records while others are just beginning promising careers, but all are distinguished by their comprehensive knowledge of U.S. foreign relations, their cooperative spirit, and their enthusiasm for the project. It has been a distinct pleasure to have been given the opportunity to work with these scholars as well as with Richard Hopper and his staff at Scholarly Resources.

Volumes Published

Lawrence S. Kaplan, *Thomas Jefferson: Westward the Course of Empire* (1999). Cloth ISBN 0-8420-2629-0   Paper ISBN 0-8420-2630-4

Richard H. Immerman, *John Foster Dulles: Piety, Pragmatism, and Power in U.S. Foreign Policy* (1999). Cloth ISBN 0-8420-2600-2 Paper ISBN 0-8420-2601-0

Thomas W. Zeiler, *Dean Rusk: Defending the American Mission Abroad* (2000). Cloth ISBN 0-8420-2685-1   Paper ISBN 0-8420-2686-X

Edward P. Crapol, *James G. Blaine: Architect of Empire* (2000). Cloth ISBN 0-8420-2604-5   Paper ISBN 0-8420-2605-3

David F. Schmitz, *Henry L. Stimson: The First Wise Man* (2001). Cloth ISBN 0-8420-2631-2   Paper ISBN 0-8420-2632-0

Thomas M. Leonard, *James K. Polk: A Clear and Unquestionable Destiny* (2001). Cloth ISBN 0-8420-2646-0   Paper ISBN 0-8420-2647-9

James E. Lewis Jr., *John Quincy Adams: Policymaker for the Union* (2001). Cloth ISBN 0-8420-2622-3   Paper ISBN 0-8420-2623-1

Catherine Forslund, *Anna Chennault: Informal Diplomacy and Asian Relations* (2002). Cloth ISBN 0-8420-2832-3   Paper ISBN 0-8420-2833-1

Lawrence S. Kaplan, *Alexander Hamilton: Ambivalent Anglophile* (2002). Cloth ISBN 0-8420-2877-3   Paper ISBN 0-8420-2878-1

Andrew J. DeRoche, *Andrew Young: Civil Rights Ambassador* (2003). Cloth ISBN 0-8420-2956-7   Paper ISBN 0-8420-2957-5

ANDREW YOUNG

ANDREW YOUNG

Civil Rights Ambassador

ANDREW J. DeROCHE

IN AMERICAN FOREIGN POLICY

Number 10

SR BOOKS

A Scholarly Resources Inc. Imprint
Wilmington, Delaware

Scholarly Resources Inc.
104 Greenhill Avenue
Wilmington, DE 19805-1897
www.scholarly.com

Library of Congress Cataloging-in-Publication Data

DeRoche, Andrew.
    Andrew Young : civil rights ambassador / Andrew J. DeRoche.
      p. cm. — (Biographies in American foreign policy ; no. 10)
    Includes bibliographical references (p.) and index.
    ISBN 0-8420-2956-7 (alk. paper) — ISBN 0-8420-2957-5 (pbk. :
alk. paper)
    1. Young, Andrew, 1932– 2. African American legislators—
United States—Biography. 3. Legislators—United States—
Biography. 4. United States. Congress. House—Biography.
5. African American diplomats—Biography. 6. African American
civil rights workers—Biography. 7. United States—Foreign
relations—20th century. 8. United States—Foreign relations—
Africa. 9. Africa—Foreign relations—United States. 10. United
States—Race relations—Political aspects. I. Title. II. Series.
E840.8.Y64D47 2003
973.92'092—dc21

                                         2003008099

Acknowledgments

Andy Fry has been an incredible editor, reading every chapter draft carefully and offering helpful suggestions. I followed most of them— and probably should have followed them all. Thanks also to Rick Hopper at Scholarly Resources, who has been enthusiastic about this project from the start. Tom Zeiler first suggested I contact Rick and Andy about a possible Andrew Young biography and, more generally, has fostered my development as a scholar of foreign relations.

My interest in Andrew Young began when he spoke at the baccalaureate ceremony at Princeton University in 1989, and I must credit John and Mary Lemkemeier for making me attend that speech. The late Howard Schonberger at the University of Maine guided my initial research in 1991 and confirmed for me that Young was an important figure. At the University of Colorado in 1993, Bob Schulzinger wisely suggested that I write my dissertation on Zimbabwe first and save the Young biography for a second book. Bob has continued to be helpful and supportive ever since.

Chris Riggs read every chapter and provided thoughtful comments. Jaime Bertrand perused the first few chapters and asked some excellent questions. Several parts of this book have been presented at conferences, and they benefited from the input of Piero Gleijeses, Cary Fraser, Robert Pratt, Michael Krenn, and Bill Stueck. Jack Grobler helped me gain some understanding of African reactions to Andrew Young. Carol Muldawer told me many stories about him, and so did Louise Suggs. Dennis Willard hosted me in Virginia; Charles and Suzanne Forlidas, in Atlanta.

Writing this book while maintaining a heavy teaching load has been a challenge. I could not have done it without great friends and family. There could be no better housemates than Rob Rehder and Jackson. Thanks to new friends Pam Ranallo, Val Kisiel, Jan Joost, and Becca Stuebe. Thanks to old friends Jim, Mitch, Boca, Lumpy, Eric, and John K. Thanks, most of all, to my parents, Mary and Wayne Corkum.

This book is dedicated to the people of South Africa and Zimbabwe.

About the Author

Andrew J. DeRoche, who earned his doctorate at the University of Colorado in 1997, is the author of *Black, White, and Chrome: The United States and Zimbabwe, 1953–1998* (2001). He is currently researching the role of Kenneth Kaunda in relations between Africa and the United States. He teaches history at Front Range Community College in Longmont, Colorado, where he lives with his cat, Jackson.

Contents

Preface

On January 30, 1977, Andrew Young became the U.S. Permanent Representative to the United Nations, and began the period in his career during which he would exercise his greatest influence on American foreign relations. Young accepted the position as ambassador to the UN because he hoped to take Martin Luther King's vision regarding racial equality onto the international stage. He intended to infuse the ideals of the civil rights movement into U.S. foreign policy, advocating human rights around the globe. The new link between race and foreign relations was underscored by the fact that Young was sworn in by Thurgood Marshall, who had won key civil rights court cases as a lawyer in the 1950s and was the first black Supreme Court justice. Young's ascension to the post of UN ambassador not only brought King's ideology to the world, but it also represented the unprecedented blending of the visions of two of the most influential American thinkers of the twentieth century: William Edward Burghardt Du Bois and Woodrow Wilson.

Du Bois championed racial equality at home and decolonization abroad, while Wilson fought for an international organization to resolve conflicts and ensure free trade. At the Versailles Peace Conference in the spring of 1919, Wilson worked doggedly to create the League of Nations, which he hoped would facilitate key components of his internationalist ideology. Meanwhile, Du Bois encouraged black soldiers returning from Europe to fight for racial equality at home. He exclaimed, "We are cowards and jackasses if now that that war is over, we do not marshal every ounce of our brain and brawn to fight a sterner, longer, more unbending battle against the forces of hell in our own land."* Also during that spring, Du Bois chaired a Pan-African conference in France to coordinate the struggle against colonialism in Africa. Du Bois attempted to meet with Wilson to discuss decolonization, but his request was denied.

*W. E. B. Du Bois, "Returning Soldiers," in Daniel Walden, ed., *W. E. B. Du Bois: The Crisis Writings* (New York: Fawcett, 1972), 259–61.

Rosalynn Carter, Jimmy Carter, Andrew Young, Jean Young, and Thurgood Marshall, White House, January 1977. *Courtesy of Jimmy Carter Library*

Wilson rejected any notion of racial equality at home or abroad. As president he approved a new policy in 1913 to segregate black government workers in Washington, DC, and at Versailles he vetoed a resolution against racism that the Japanese delegates had proposed adding to the treaty. Not only were the ideologies of these two great Americans mutually exclusive in 1919, but in their nation's capital the two men literally could not even sit in the same room. Things got worse before they got better. Wilson essentially worked himself to death in an unsuccessful effort to persuade Americans to join the League of Nations, which they never did. Du Bois became so frustrated with the slow rate of progress against racism in the United States that he spent his last years in exile in Ghana.

Over time, however, remarkable changes gradually occurred. In the aftermath of World War II, Americans embraced Wilsonian internationalism and played key roles in the formation of the United Nations. In the 1960s, the movement led by King made great strides toward racial equality, while many nations in Africa fought successfully for independence. The new international landscape in 1977 meant that one person, Andrew Young, could advocate the ideologies of both Wilson and Du Bois. Young shared Wilson's faith in internationalism and free trade, and Du Bois's antipathy to racism and colonialism. As UN ambassador, and throughout his entire career, Young combined their visions and championed human rights, peace, and economic development.

Chronology

1929

January 15   Martin Luther King Jr. is born in Atlanta, Georgia

1932

March 12   Andrew Jackson Young Jr. is born in New Orleans, Louisiana

1936

Jesse Owens wins four gold medals at the Olympics in Berlin, Germany

1941

December 7   Japan attacks Pearl Harbor

1947

May   Young graduates from Gilbert Academy, New Orleans

1948

August   After attending Dillard University in New Orleans for a year, Young transfers to Howard University in Washington, DC

1951

May   Young receives his B.S. in biology from Howard University

September   Young begins working for the Connecticut Council of Churches and enrolls at Hartford Theological Seminary

1954

May 17   U.S. Supreme Court rules that segregation in public schools is unconstitutional, in *Brown v. Board of Education of Topeka*

June 7   Jean Childs and Andrew Young marry in Marion, Alabama

1955

January	After graduating from Hartford Seminary with a Bachelor of Divinity degree, Young accepts a position as minister in Thomasville, Georgia
August 3	Andrea Young is born in Thomasville
December 1	Montgomery bus boycott begins

1957

February 13	Southern Christian Leadership Conference (SCLC) is formed
March 6	Ghana gains independence from Great Britain
July 19	Lisa Young is born in Thomasville, Georgia
August	Young begins work for the Youth Division of the National Council of Churches in New York City
September	Federal troops intervene to integrate schools in Little Rock, Arkansas

1960

February 1	College students begin the sit-in movement in Greensboro, North Carolina
March 21	South African police kill 69 nonviolent protesters at Sharpeville
April	Student Non-Violent Coordinating Committee forms at Shaw University in Raleigh, North Carolina
June 30	The Congo celebrates independence from Belgium

1961

June 6	Paula Young is born in New York City
August	Young starts work for the Citizenship School Program in Atlanta

1962

	Rebellions against Portuguese colonial regimes in Angola and Mozambique escalate
July	When Martin Luther King Jr. is jailed in Albany, Georgia, Young serves as his mediator with the local police
December	At an SCLC planning session for the upcoming demonstrations in Birmingham,

	Alabama, King accepts Young's offer to serve as negotiator with the white business community

1963

April 3	Civil rights campaign in Birmingham begins
May 10	A settlement between the SCLC and white business leaders is announced
June 11	President John F. Kennedy calls for a civil rights bill
August 28	King gives his "I Have a Dream" speech during the March on Washington
November 22	President Kennedy is assassinated in Dallas, Texas

1964

April	Young is named executive director of the SCLC and persuades King to stage protests in St. Augustine, Florida
June 9	During march in St. Augustine, Young is beaten by Ku Klux Klan members
June 12	In South Africa, Nelson Mandela is sentenced to life in prison for high treason
July 2	President Lyndon Johnson signs the Civil Rights Act of 1964
August	American ships are involved in incidents in the Tonkin Gulf off the coast of Vietnam, and Congress approves the Tonkin Gulf Resolution
October 24	Zambia gains independence from Great Britain
December 10	King receives the Nobel Peace Prize in Oslo, Norway

1965

January	Demonstrations by SCLC begin in Selma, Alabama
February	Malcolm X is assassinated in Harlem, and Young attends his funeral
March 6	U.S. marines are sent to base at Danang in Vietnam
March 7	A first attempt to march from Selma to Montgomery is violently stopped by Alabama state troopers

March 21	The second attempt to march to Montgomery begins
March 25	Marchers complete 54-mile walk and hold rally at state Capitol
August 6	President Johnson signs Voting Rights Act
August 11	Riot begins in Watts, Los Angeles
November 11	Ian Smith declares Rhodesia's independence from Great Britain

1967

April 4	King delivers "Beyond Vietnam" speech in New York City
July	Young condemns the Vietnam War in addresses before the National Council of Churches convention in Green Lake, Wisconsin

1968

April 4	King is assassinated in Memphis, Tennessee
April 29	Poor People's Campaign opens in Washington, DC
June 24	Poor People's Campaign ends

1970

November 3	Young loses his first bid for a seat in the U.S. Congress

1971

November	The Byrd Amendment, allowing chrome imports from Rhodesia, becomes law

1972

November 7	Young is elected to represent Georgia's Fifth District in the U.S. Congress
December	Soldiers of the Zimbabwe African National Union (ZANU) move from Mozambique into Rhodesia and begin guerrilla warfare

1973

February 15	Andrew Jackson Young III is born in Atlanta
July 26	Young's amendment prohibiting Portugal from using U.S. aid to support its wars in Angola and Mozambique is approved

1974

April 25	A coup d'état occurs in Lisbon, Portugal
November	Voters reelect Young to Congress
December	Young visits South Africa and meets jailed activist Robert Sobukwe
December	Robert Mugabe and Joshua Nkomo are released from prison in Rhodesia

1975

June	Robert Sobukwe's two children move into the Youngs' home in Atlanta
November	Young visits Zambia, Kenya, and Nigeria
December	Young calls for U.S. membership in the African Development Fund and denounces CIA involvement in Angola

1976

January 27	Congress prohibits further CIA activities in Angola
April 27	Henry Kissinger endorses majority rule for Rhodesia in a speech in Zambia
June 16	South African police and military attack students in Soweto
July	Young supports Jimmy Carter at the Democratic National Convention
September	Young and Charles Diggs initiate the founding of TransAfrica
October	Discussions of Kissinger's Peace Plan for Rhodesia begin in Geneva
November	Jimmy Carter is elected president, Young is reelected to Congress
December	Geneva Conference ends without agreement

1977

January 11	Young introduces bill to overturn the Byrd Amendment
January 30	Young sworn in as U.S. Ambassador to the United Nations
February	Young visits fifteen African countries, most notably, Nigeria
March 18	Carter signs the bill repealing the Byrd Amendment
April	Young forms the Gang of Five to negotiate Namibia's independence

May	Young attends majority rule conference in Mozambique, then visits South Africa
August 4	Tanzanian President Julius Nyerere meets with President Carter
August	Young tours the Caribbean
September 1	Young discusses the Anglo-American Peace Plan with Ian Smith in Rhodesia
September 12	Stephen Biko is killed by police in South Africa
November 4	The UN imposes a mandatory arms embargo against South Africa

1978

January 30–31	Young meets with Robert Mugabe and Joshua Nkomo at Malta
March 3	Ian Smith and Bishop Abel Muzorewa sign internal settlement in Rhodesia
March	President Carter visits Liberia and Nigeria
April	Young and Secretary of State Cyrus Vance discuss Anglo-American Plan with Mugabe and Nkomo in Dar es Salaam, Tanzania
July 10	During interview for *Le Matin* (Paris), Young remarks that there are political prisoners in the United States
July 13	Representative Larry McDonald's motion to impeach Young is defeated
October	Rhodesian forces bomb refugee camps in Zambia
December	Young attends conference on southern Africa in Khartoum, Sudan

1979

April	Abel Muzorewa is elected prime minister of Rhodesia–Zimbabwe
May	Young visits Australia and meets with Aborigines
June 7	Carter announces that he will maintain sanctions against Rhodesia and will not recognize Muzorewa regime
July 26	Young meets in New York with Zehdi Terzi, the Palestine Liberation Organization's representative to the UN
August 15	Young resigns from his post as ambassador to the UN

	December 17	Final settlement regarding Rhodesia is reached at Lancaster House in London

1980

	April 17	Mugabe sworn in as first prime minister of Zimbabwe
	August 27	Carter receives Mugabe at the White House
	November	Ronald Reagan defeats Carter in presidential election

1981

	October	Young is elected mayor of Atlanta

1982

	December	Young cohosts conference on Central America and the Caribbean in Atlanta

1983

		Nigeria opens a consulate in Atlanta
	September	Robert Mugabe visits Atlanta

1984

	March	Young leads trade delegation to South Korea
	March	French President François Mitterrand visits Atlanta
	November 21	TransAfrica begins protests at South African Embassy

1985

	April	Young visits his daughter in Uganda
	May 22	Young advocates sanctions against South Africa in his testimony before the Senate Foreign Relations Committee
	September	Samora Machel, president of Mozambique, meets with Young in Atlanta
	October	Young wins second mayoral term, then visits the USSR and China

1986

	January	Carter and Young conduct an agricultural mission to the Sudan, Tanzania, Zambia, and Ghana
	July	Young tours Japan to celebrate the new direct flights from Atlanta to Japan

| August | During visit to Angola, Young criticizes Reagan's policy |
| October 3 | Congress approves the Comprehensive Anti-Apartheid Act |

1987

January	Young attends an African-American Institute conference on development in southern Africa in Botswana and delivers speeches in Zimbabwe
April	Young denounces Reagan's support for the contras during a trip to Nicaragua
August	Young visits Guatemala to consider helping train their police force

1988

April	Atlanta is chosen as the U.S.-nominated site for the 1996 summer Olympics
July	The Democratic National Convention is held in Atlanta
August	Young attends Olympics in Seoul to lobby for 1996 Games

1989

| May | Young leads trade delegation to the USSR France opens a consulate in Atlanta |

1990

February	Nelson Mandela is released from prison
June	Mandela visits Atlanta
August 7	Zell Miller defeats Young in the Georgia Democratic gubernatorial primary
September 18	International Olympic Committee chooses Atlanta as the site for 1996 Games

1992

| November | Bill (William Jefferson) Clinton wins presidential election |

1994

May	South Africans elect Nelson Mandela as prime minister
September 18	Jean Young dies
October	President Clinton appoints Young to oversee the Southern Africa Development Fund

1995

December	Atlanta Chamber of Commerce names Young as chairperson

1996

March 24	Carolyn Watson and Andrew Young marry in Cape Town
July 19	Summer Olympics begin in Atlanta

1997

January	GoodWorks International opens for business

1998

May	The National Summit on Africa's regional meeting takes place in Atlanta

1999

March	GoodWorks hosts banquet for Olusegun Obasanjo, president of Nigeria
August	Georgia State University names its School of Policy Studies after Young
November	The National Council of Churches names Young its president

2000

February	The National Summit on Africa takes place in Washington, DC, with Young as master of ceremonies
May 18	Africa Growth and Opportunity Act is signed by President Clinton

2001

March 10	A street in downtown Atlanta is renamed Andrew Young International Boulevard

2002

March 12	Andrew Young turns 70
June 20	Young hosts the Leon Sullivan Dinner in Washington, DC, and takes over as chairman of the Leon Sullivan Summit

2003

July 12–19	The 6th Leon Sullivan Summit convenes in Abuga, Nigeria, with Young as chairman

1

From New Orleans to New York

1932–1960

Andrew Jackson Young was born on March 12, 1932, in New Orleans, to Daisy Fuller Young and Dr. Andrew Young. The Youngs had married the previous year and moved into a house on Cleveland Street, in a diverse community near Straight College. Before starting a family, Daisy Young had been a teacher. She stayed at home to raise Andy and his younger brother Walter. Dr. Young, a dentist, provided them with a middle-class lifestyle. Their house on Cleveland Street featured frequent guests, and Andy's favorite was his Uncle Walter, who had no children of his own and therefore showered his nephews with affection. The Youngs' home was a happy and comfortable place to grow up in, but these parents made certain that their boys understood the importance of three things: religion, work, and education.

The Youngs attended Central Congregational Church, which conducted its services in the New England Congregational style. The minister delivered serious sermons, and the parishioners refrained from singing African-American spirituals or displaying excessive emotion. It was a far cry from the Baptist faith practiced by most southern blacks. Yet the Youngs' religion did contain a strong humanitarian element that Andy carried with him throughout his life. People all across New Orleans knew his maternal grandmother as someone who provided a good meal to anyone in need, and Andy's mother carried on this tradition by taking casseroles to ailing or elderly members of the church. Daisy Young's active involvement with the church also included teaching Sunday School, and her husband served as a deacon. Andy did his part by reading from the Bible to his blind grandmother every day for four years.

Andy spent a lot of time at his father's dental office, and this experience influenced his development in several respects. Dr. Young required Andy to introduce himself to all the patients, so from his earliest days he learned not to be shy around strangers. Often his father sent him on errands to buy supplies for the office, planting the seeds of a work ethic and sense of responsibility. Perhaps most important, Andy accompanied his father on several trips into rural Louisiana to provide dental care to poor people, as part of a program initiated by Governor Huey Long. Traveling in the southern backwoods in the 1930s was extremely dangerous for a black man, and Andy learned a lot from watching his father navigate that treacherous terrain. He later described his father's strategy: "Self-control, unflagging courtesy, and compassion toward those who were rude were his guides."[1]

Andy's formal education began at age six when he entered the Valena Jones Elementary School, where he was placed into the third grade because he already could read and write. He realized that in order to survive among older and bigger boys he would need to make friends, so he introduced himself around. His suggestion that they pool their lunch money and purchase food at a market across the street rather than eat cafeteria food was a big hit, an early example of the ability to gain popularity and approval that would serve him so well in activism and politics. During his years in elementary school he read avidly in his spare time, particularly the *Pittsburgh Courier*, where he learned about black soldiers fighting in World War II and Negro League baseball stars such as Satchel Paige.

His biggest hero, though, was Jesse Owens. In fact, his earliest memory was of Owens winning four gold medals at the 1936 Olympics in Berlin. He and his father watched Owens's heroics on the *Movietone News* at the Orpheum Theater, and Andy knew even then that it represented much more than an athletic accomplishment. Dr. Young had already explained to him why he had to sit in the back of buses, and he had heard Nazi slogans and "Heil Hitlers" inside a German cultural center just one hundred yards from home. Andy understood that Owens's triumph had "defeated Adolph Hitler's dreams of a German master race and the notions of white supremacy and racism in general."[2]

Owens certainly inspired African Americans as they confronted discrimination in the United States in the 1930s and 1940s. Living in New Orleans and touring Louisiana with his father, Andy often encountered segregation and other forms of racism. His father explained racism as a sickness in others and would not allow Andy to feel inferior. His father's philosophy, combined with the loving support of the Youngs' extended family, fostered Andy's healthy self-esteem. He needed that quality at school, where the challenges of being younger and smaller got even worse in 1943 when he graduated from elementary school. The public schools offered no eighth grade for black children, so eleven-year-old Andy went right into ninth grade at the prestigious Gilbert Academy.

Dr. Young wanted Andy to be able to protect himself against older classmates, so he taught him some of the basics of boxing. He stressed the importance of remaining calm and thinking rather than relying on emotions. Later, he arranged for one of his patients to give boxing lessons to Andy and his brother Walter. The patient, a local boxing legend named Eddie Brown, gladly provided the instruction in exchange for his dental work. Andy never really pursued boxing, but when his father arranged for some very special track training he took to it very quickly. Again, in exchange for dental work provided by his father, Andy learned how to run dashes from former Olympic star Ralph Metcalfe, then coaching at Xavier University. Andy later speculated, "Daddy figured if we didn't take to boxing, we better learn how to run."[3]

Although he loved running and was faster than most boys his age, he was simply too small to compete in track or his other favorite sport, basketball, while at Gilbert Academy. Nevertheless, he enjoyed high school very much. The discrimination of the day meant that students at black schools such as Gilbert benefited from the skills of very talented black teachers and administrators who could not get jobs elsewhere. Gilbert Principal Margaret Bowen drilled manners, personal hygiene, and politeness into her charges. One English teacher, a Miss Blakely, specialized in Shakespeare. Andy's other favorite English teacher, Mrs. Moses, emphasized black poetry and literature when that was still uncommon, thus helping to make up for the whitewashed history classes that ignored all black achievement. Much of Andy's significant learning came outside the formal school setting—on the streets of New Orleans. The Cleveland Avenue neighborhood where he grew up exposed him to tremendous human diversity. Among the other families on the block were Irish, Italian, German, Cajun, and African American folk. The religions included Catholicism and several varieties of Protestantism, and politics ranged from extreme American patriots to Nazis.

Living in the midst of such a "jambalaya" as a youth helped prepare Andy for his future work as an activist, politician, and diplomat. As he explained it, "When you grow up with the world in
your community you are prepared to deal with difference, diversity, and conflict."[4]

After his school days at Gilbert, Andy waited for the streetcar
on Canal Street in the shopping district and watched the colorful
population of New Orleans pass by. A particularly enlightening
experience was the occasional haircut at Levi Hartman's barber-
shop on notorious Rampart Street. Many of the other customers
were World War II veterans, and they often spoke of places they
had been in Europe where there was no segregation or discrimination. As for that most famous of all New Orleans institutions, Mardi
Gras, the Youngs did bring the boys to watch the parade but made
sure to criticize strongly the accompanying drinking and hysterics
that they deemed immoral. Another key venue for Andy's education was the Dryades Street YMCA, which his parents wholeheartedly supported. The director, William Mitchell, required the
members to take his classes, in which he discussed admirable figures from black history. He also taught them about Africa, and he
was the first person Andy knew who had visited that mysterious
continent. Mitchell brought several African students back to the
United States to attend school here, an action Andy replicated later.

In 1947, Andy graduated from Gilbert Academy. Because he
was only fifteen, his parents insisted that he start college at Dillard
University, which was only a few blocks from their new house. His
year at Dillard resembled his experience at Gilbert in many respects,
and, if anything, Dillard had even stricter rules governing student
conduct. Sadly, from Andy's perspective, the short walk to Dillard
lacked the excitement of the streetcar rides and people-watching
that had enlivened his high school days. After a year at Dillard,
Andy eagerly transferred to Howard University in Washington, DC.

Young's years at Howard were bittersweet, however. By his
senior year he had finally grown tall enough to have an opportunity to participate on the track team, and he emerged as their
number-one sprinter. He won several races that year and also com-
peted on the varsity swim team. His athletic success was not du-
plicated in the classroom, however. He earned only one "A" at
Howard—not surprisingly, considering his future jobs, it was in a
public-speaking course. Compounding his mediocre scholarly
record, he found the social scene at Howard disappointing. Many

of his fellow students were elitist, and it was the first time he had ever encountered people who refused to say "hello."

As had been his experience growing up in New Orleans, much of his important education at Howard took place outside the hallowed halls. Many of his classmates were World War II veterans utilizing the GI Bill, and they regaled him with stories of their escapades in Europe or Asia. But a fellow student from Nigeria, Emmanuel Odeku, impressed Young most. Odeku displayed tremendous discipline, sleeping only a few hours a night, and completing his studies at Howard in only two years. He went on to earn a medical degree from McGill University, became the only neurosurgeon in West Africa, and was the dean of Nigeria's medical school in the early 1960s. People like Odeku showed Young the great potential of Africa. "His courage and commitment are one reason I continue to have hope that Nigeria, despite its tumultuous history, will fulfill its destiny as one of the world's most prosperous and influential nations," Young wrote in his memoirs.[5]

In May 1951, Young graduated from Howard with a Bachelor of Science degree in Biology. His parents and brother attended the ceremony, and then the whole family piled into the car and headed back to New Orleans. Along the way they stopped in Kings Mountain, North Carolina, for a summer conference organized by the Congregational Church. Now that Young had completed his studies at Howard, his parents expected him to go to graduate school—and probably to become a dentist. His own biggest goal, as his years at Howard ended, was to try out for the 1952 Olympic track team. The Kings Mountain conference led to a future that involved neither dentistry nor sprinting.

His roommate at Kings Mountain was a young white minister named John Heinrich, who was about to take his wife and newborn baby to Zimbabwe (then Southern Rhodesia) as a missionary. That Heinrich would take his young family to a distant land in order to teach people earned Young's respect and sparked serious thoughts about his own future. He and Heinrich never discussed what Young should do, nor did they discuss religion. Still, Heinrich's religious faith and commitment to help others convinced Young that perhaps he could find a more meaningful existence than running track and stumbling through dental school. These thoughts fermented further a few days later when Young and some of the other young men skipped a conference session and climbed Kings Mountain instead. Young ran the whole way up, and in the fifteen or twenty minutes he enjoyed at the top alone, he had a spiritual awakening of sorts. "On Kings Mountain I began to think about a personal religious purpose around which I could organize my life," he recalled.[6]

It was not immediately clear what that actually meant in specific terms such as additional education or career options. It was clear that he was not going to be a dentist, but he was afraid to break the news to his parents during the remainder of their drive back to New Orleans. In the days after arriving at home, Young could not bring up the subject and he did not know what to do next. A friend asked him to drive out to Texas for a religious retreat at Lake Brownwood. Happy to escape his parents' house, Young agreed to go. At the retreat, for the first time, he discussed race relations with white people in real depth, and he realized that it was their religious faith that had them questioning segregation and other forms of discrimination. At Lake Brownwood, he first thought seriously about becoming a minister.

Back in New Orleans after the retreat, Young received an invitation from the National Council of Churches' Youth Department to participate in a training program at Camp Mack in Indiana. The sessions would prepare him and his colleagues to spend six months working in the National Council of Churches' United Christian Youth Action program. The only African American at Camp Mack, Young befriended an African named Eduardo Mondlane, and they talked at length about their views on life. Mondlane would later lead the liberation struggle in his native Mozambique, and he was the first of many such leaders whom Young met through his work for the National Council of Churches. Camp Mack also provided Young with his first inkling of the theories of nonviolence. One of the people who organized the Youth Action program, Don Bowman, lent him a book on Mohandas Gandhi. After finishing that volume, he read several of Gandhi's articles and his autobiography. He realized from this initial study of Gandhi how spirituality could be applied to a political situation and began to ponder ways in which Gandhi's methods could be used to fight segregation in the South.

After completing the training in Indiana, Young journeyed to Connecticut for his six months of service. The Connecticut Council of Churches provided him with a room at the Hartford Theological Seminary. During the fall of 1951, while he completed his stint for Youth Action, he took two courses at the seminary: the Philosophy of Religion and the New Testament. For the first time, studying stimulated his mind the way sprinting or swimming had stimulated his body. Late in the semester he applied for admission as a full-time seminary student, and just before going home for Christmas, the dean informed him that he was accepted, in spite of his poor grades at Howard.

While in New Orleans for the holiday break, Young had told his parents of his decision. His father, extremely upset, refused to pay any of the costs of seminary training. Determined to succeed despite his father's anger, Young obtained a partial scholarship and took on three part-time jobs: working in the cafeteria and library and cleaning furnaces. He may not have had his parents' approval, but he certainly had their work ethic. Young never regretted his decision; he eagerly ingested the seminary's exciting new ideas about theology and basked in the colorful glow of its very diverse population. As he later wrote, "The school was famous for its expertise in non-Western cultures and attracted many students from Africa, the Far East, and the Mideast. My first real interest in world affairs began in the multinational atmosphere at Hartford Seminary."[7]

After his first exciting semester as a full-time seminary student in the cosmopolitan environment at Hartford, he spent the summer of 1952 in a very different setting—a small town in rural Alabama. Thanks to some behind-the-scenes finagling by his mother, the family's minister in New Orleans arranged for Young to serve as minister for the summer at a church in Marion, Alabama, in the cotton belt not far from Selma. Upon arriving in Marion, he was offered room and board by the Childs family. Norman and Idella Childs had five children, and Young was particularly impressed by the books and photos he saw in the room of their daughter Jean, who would soon be home from college. When he met Jean in person, Young was even more impressed, and the couple fell in love during a magical summer in Marion.

That fall both returned to school, Andrew to Hartford and Jean to Manchester College in Indiana. They persevered through the year, then shared a wonderful experience together in the summer of 1953. Jean won a fellowship to spend six weeks working in refugee camps in Austria, and Andrew borrowed money from his parents to accompany her. Jean worked with children, and Andrew helped build a community center for the refugees, most of whom were from Romania or Yugoslavia. After six weeks of work, the couple toured

Germany and Italy. Seeing some of the results of the Marshall Plan, after extensive contact with people fleeing the Soviet bloc, gave Young valuable insight into the dynamics of the Cold War and a sense of the good that the United States could do around the world.

The time in Europe also underlined the degree of racial injustice in the American South. As rare visiting African Americans, Andrew and Jean were the subject of considerable curiosity in Austria, and whenever Young got his hair cut, crowds would gather to watch and take locks of hair as souvenirs. This curiosity was never hostile, though, and in Europe they experienced no formal racial discrimination. Andrew later remembered, "We were permitted to eat in restaurants, stay in hotels and youth hostels, freely explore museums, and purchase tickets to concerts without reference to a 'colored' section."[8] The lack of institutionalized racism in Europe was a refreshing change from Louisiana or Alabama. Furthermore, many individual Europeans held progressive views on race relations and joined with Young in the struggle against racial injustice in the years ahead.

The fall of 1953 found Andrew and Jean once again apart, as they returned to their respective programs of study. During Christmas break, he proposed. On June 7, 1954, the young couple was married in Marion. The whole wedding party then drove to New Orleans so Andrew's mother could give a reception, too. The newlyweds moved to Thomasville, Georgia, where Andrew served as summer minister. They returned to Hartford for the fall semester so that he could complete his studies, while Jean taught at an inner-city school. In December, Young received his Bachelor of Divinity degree and was ordained into the ministry. In January of 1955 they went back to Thomasville, Georgia, where he began his first full-time job.

Not surprisingly, considering that he was just twenty-two, Young learned a lot about the ministry and a lot about himself. Conducting services at the Congregationalist Church in Thomasville required little adjustment on his part, but his job also required him to preach at a church in rural Beachton. The parishioners there worshiped in a style more akin to Baptists, with lots of spirited singing. Young quickly adapted, throwing out his written notes and improvising like a jazz singer. In order to gain respect and get closer to his flock, when he visited farm families he often joined them in the fields picking cotton or peanuts. In many respects, though, he and Jean asserted themselves during their years in Thomasville.

Despite the grumblings of church elders, Young played guard on the YMCA basketball team. For her part, Jean rejected the traditional role of minister's wife. She taught in the segregated Thomasville elementary school and wore shorts in public. Any antagonism evaporated in August of 1955, however, with the birth of the Youngs' first child, Andrea. The community showered her with love, and the Youngs never had to look far for baby-sitters or day care. The display of warmth and unity in Thomasville deeply impressed Young, and he would see it mirrored countless times throughout the South during his civil rights activism in the 1960s.

The movement for African-American freedom, in fact, began in earnest very soon after Andrea's birth. In December 1955, the arrest of Rosa Parks sparked the Montgomery bus boycott, led by a young minister named Martin Luther King Jr. Jean had attended school in Alabama with King's wife Coretta, which gave the Youngs even more incentive to follow the dramatic events closely. With a new baby and major responsibilities in Thomasville, they did not participate directly in the Montgomery events, but they did organize a voter-registration drive during the summer of 1956. This work attracted the attention of the Ku Klux Klan, whose members came to Thomasville in large numbers, intending to intimidate Young. Concerned for his family's safety, he instructed Jean that if Klan members approached the house, she should sit in the upstairs window with a shotgun while he talked with them. Jean refused to point a gun at another human being, however, and scolded him for not practicing the nonviolence that he preached. He relented, they spent the night with friends, and the Klan left town without bothering them directly. Most important, his wife's commitment to pacifism and nonviolence profoundly impressed Young in a way that books and lectures on the subjects never had.[9]

The Youngs' voter-registration work helped President Dwight Eisenhower win Georgia and re-election in November of 1956. Early the following year, his administration reluctantly, and perhaps inadvertently, began to foster a connection between the civil rights movement in the South and the struggle against colonialism in Africa. In March 1957, Vice President Richard Nixon attended the celebration of Ghana's independence from Great Britain. Nixon brought little in the way of concrete support for President Kwame Nkrumah's new nation, and the vice president was outshone at the ceremony by Martin Luther King. To Nixon's credit, however, he returned to Washington determined to make Africa and civil rights

higher priorities for the administration. He kept his word—meeting
with King at the White House and engineering the creation of a
separate African Bureau at the State Department.

Not long after King returned from Ghana's independence celebration, he and Young met for the first time. They both delivered
speeches at Talladega College in Talladega, Alabama, and then participated in a panel discussion. Afterward, Young attempted to engage King in a serious exchange regarding Gandhi's nonviolence,
but the exhausted King would talk only about his children. He did
invite Young to visit him in Montgomery, but he must not have
been overly impressed with his fellow minister, because, four years
later, when King was asked if he knew Young, he replied, "I cannot
for the world place Andrew Young!"[10]

In May 1957, Young drove to Washington for a prayer pilgrim-
mage on behalf of the civil rights bill being debated in Congress.
The bill passed, establishing a civil rights division in the Justice
Department. He promptly returned to Thomasville, because Jean
was in the late stages of pregnancy, and in July their second daughter, Lisa, was born. In the meantime, Don Newby of the National
Council of Churches (NCC) offered Young a job in New York City.
He wanted Young to serve as associate director of their Youth Department, in part because, of the six hundred executives in the
NCC's national headquarters, only one was black. Young decided
to accept and believed that in working with predominantly white
church leaders across the country he could provide education regarding racial issues, an important step in ending discrimination.
Young's willingness and ability to engage whites in the process of
resolving racial disputes became traits that served him well in the
civil rights movement in the 1960s and later as a politician and
diplomat.

In August of 1957, Young started his new job in New York City,
which he considered "a microcosm of the world, and all the world's
cultures, crammed into much too small a space."[11] After two years
in rural Georgia, he enjoyed the excitement of riding the subway
and going to work in a skyscraper near the new United Nations
building. In many ways, the atmosphere resembled the multicultural New Orleans of his youth, though on a much larger scale. In
addition to living in a thrilling place, the Youngs had moved to
New York at a very exciting time. Ghana's independence the previous spring inspired liberation movements across all Africa, and
Andrew and Jean followed the developments closely. With several
African friends from his years at Howard and Hartford, Young had

a personal interest in the progress in such places as Kenya and Nigeria. He later elaborated: "Africa's emergence from centuries of colonialism made us as African Americans feel part of a world movement for the liberation and self-determination of subjugated peoples."[12]

At the same time, people around the world watched events in the southern United States closely. Just after Young moved to New York, a crisis erupted in Little Rock, Arkansas, when black students tried to integrate Central High School. Against his personal inclinations, President Eisenhower eventually used troops to enforce order and facilitate integration. Little Rock was not only another important act in the unfolding drama of the civil rights movement, but also a watershed in the importance of race in U.S. foreign relations. The crisis sparked intense international scrutiny of racial injustice in the South, and from that time forward, world opinion represented a constituency that influenced American policymakers as they grappled with the civil rights movement.[13]

Simply being in New York in the late 1950s would have exposed Young to the exciting freedom struggles around the world. As it turned out, his job with the National Council of Churches (NCC) frequently involved him directly with international relations. Many of the constituent churches of the NCC, including the Methodists, Baptists, Presbyterians, and Young's United Church of Christ, sponsored major overseas missionary operations. The missionaries ran schools, hospitals, churches, presses, and farm projects. Because of these extensive activities around the globe, NCC meetings often devoted considerable time to discussions of international affairs.

The NCC staffers, including Young, met occasionally with Secretary of State John Foster Dulles, who briefed them on the reasoning behind the Marshall Plan and other foreign assistance in the struggle against communism. Dulles respected the role of the NCC, and religion in general, in foreign relations. In the late 1930s, he attended conferences arranged by the World Council of Churches, once delivering the keynote address. In the early 1940s, he chaired a committee sponsored by the Federal Council of Churches, diligently churning out publications on the subject of Christianity's role in war and peace. Dulles believed throughout the rest of his life that religious principles should play a key role in the construction of the international political structure.[14] His thinking may well have influenced Young, for whom religion and diplomacy were often intertwined.

In 1958, Young participated in an international youth gathering in Switzerland, and got to know a young theologian from Berlin named Ernest Lange. They hit it off, and Lange hosted Young during several of his later trips to Germany for World Church Council sessions. During one visit, Lange took him to the East Berlin Technical University to address the students. Not surprisingly, these eastern bloc students knew all about the harassment of Paul Robeson for his pro-Soviet statements and the lynching of Emmet Till. They had basically assumed that life for African Americans in the South was no better than in the days of slavery, and they were fascinated by Young's descriptions of the blossoming civil rights movement. School officials warned Young not to discuss overtly political issues. Although he tried to stick mostly to scriptures and spirituals, it was a struggle for him to find material that was apolitical. "The more I talked, and the more I searched for an innocuous approach to this Bible study, the more I realized how well the Bible speaks to the needs of oppressed people everywhere and in all times," he recalled.[15]

While representing the NCC's Youth Department at World Council sessions in Geneva, Young took part in the Program to Combat Racism. This operation sent aid to the liberation movements in South Africa and Zimbabwe (then Southern Rhodesia), but limited this aid to food, medicine, and educational supplies for refugees. The liberation movements dispatched representatives to the World Council gatherings to describe the conditions in their countries and request more support. During these discussions, Young met many representatives from the African National Congress and other groups fighting the white regimes of southern Africa and was struck by their serious and thoughtful natures. They were not the crazy terrorists portrayed in the press and they often provided Young with insightful and enlightening assessments of international relations.

One representative from Mozambique, in particular, presented an extremely compelling explanation of why he and his fellow rebels were becoming frustrated with the Western world. They had recently received a large shipment of medicine from Canada, for which they were very thankful. Soon afterward, they shot down a plane that had been attacking them, only to find that it was made in Canada. He pointed out to Young and the others in attendance that if the West did not provide the colonizers with modern weaponry, then he and his fellow soldiers would not need the bandages and medicine. Western Christians were simultaneously sending them medical supplies while keeping the Portuguese military "supplied" with guns and napalm. This lesson by the soldier from Mozambique profoundly influenced Young, and, years later as a member of Congress, he fought to end U.S. military assistance to Portugal. After he left Congress to serve as ambassador to the United Nations, he encountered many of the people he had met at the World Council sessions, who by then had risen to positions of power in African nations.

Before serving in Congress and at the United Nations, however, Young spent the 1960s in the eye of the storm of the civil rights movement. He and Jean had moved to New York in 1957, with the understanding that they would return to the South within five years. In 1961, after about four years in New York, they headed back to Georgia to join in the expanding fight for racial equality. This decision provided Young with incredible opportunities and challenges.

So as Young headed south to join the civil rights movement in 1961, his philosophy of international relations was beginning to crystallize. For him, the most important issue in the world was the fight against racial discrimination, whether in Alabama or Angola. He and other civil rights activists saw themselves taking part in a global battle against oppression, seeking citizenship rights for all people from Birmingham to Johannesburg. Young believed that Christianity and Gandhian nonviolence could facilitate the realization of racial justice around the globe. Americans, particularly those participating in the civil rights movement, could assist in the worldwide struggle. According to Young's evolving worldview, everyone deserved citizenship and freedom from oppression. Driving south in 1961 to begin working toward that vision, he was well on his way to becoming a civil rights ambassador.

Notes

1. Andrew Young, *An Easy Burden: The Civil Rights Movement and the Transformation of America* (New York: HarperCollins, 1996), 13.

2. Andrew Young, *A Way Out of No Way: The Spiritual Memoirs of Andrew Young* (Nashville: Thomas Nelson, 1994), 146.

3. Young, *An Easy Burden*, 25.

4. Ibid., 22.

5. Ibid., 43–44.

6. Young, *A Way Out of No Way*, 21.

7. Young, *An Easy Burden*, 62.

8. Ibid., 74.

9. Young, *A Way Out of No Way*, 40–43.

10. Young, *An Easy Burden*, 131.

11. Ibid., 110.

12. Ibid., 113.

13. Cary Fraser, "Crossing the Color Line in Little Rock: The Eisenhower Administration and the Dilemma of Race for U.S. Foreign Policy," *Diplomatic History* 24, no. 2 (Spring 2000): 233–64.

14. Richard Immerman, *John Foster Dulles: Piety, Pragmatism, and Power in U.S. Foreign Policy* (Wilmington, DE: Scholarly Resources, 1999), 14–15, 20–22.

15. Young, *An Easy Burden*, 121–22.

2

Civil Rights in a Global Context

1961–1969

The escalating struggle for civil rights attracted Andrew Young and his wife Jean back to the South in 1961. The specific spark came from a television program called "The Nashville Sit-in Story," which examined the activities of John Lewis, Diane Nash, James Bevel, and other members of the Student Nonviolent Coordinating Committee (SNCC). The compelling work being done by these young African Americans convinced Young that it was time to join the fight. Their nonviolent tactics, furthermore, reinforced his conviction that the battles for justice by people of color around the world were linked. He was convinced that "Gandhi's monsoon, the independence of India, was stirring up tornadoes in America."[1]

Young arranged for the United Church of Christ to oversee a citizenship education program for African Americans in Savannah, Georgia, funded by a grant from the Field Foundation. In August 1961 he moved to Atlanta, where his office was located at the headquarters of the Southern Christian Leadership Conference (SCLC). He had frequent contact with Martin Luther King and the other SCLC leaders, but administered his own separate budget. Although this allowed him autonomy, he still made a conscious effort not to step on any toes. He "figured that as a Congregationalist among Baptist preachers with large egos, the best approach for me was to stay low key."[2]

In addition to Young, the staff of the Citizenship Education Program (CEP) included Septima Clark and Dorothy Cotton. The trio hoped to begin voter-registration efforts in 188 counties across the South that had black majorities but few registered blacks. They conducted week-long training sessions at their facility in Dorchester, Georgia, about thirty miles south of Savannah. Taught informally, with lots of discussion, the curriculum featured black history, literacy, and civics, which was conveyed by examining real-world documents such as tax forms and drivers' license applications. In addition to practical training, Young and his associates also introduced the students to the philosophy of nonviolence, particularly Gandhi's ideas. Participants in these early sessions came from all over the South, and among a group from Mississippi was a future hero of the civil rights movement, Fannie Lou Hamer. When Hamer returned to Mississippi, she lost her job and her home due to her activism. Young sent $100 to help her find a place to live, and after her untimely death in 1977, he delivered the funeral eulogy. She was just one in a long line of rural African Americans who impressed him deeply.

Early in 1962 the CEP staff went to Albany, Georgia, to provide training to student activists who were waging a difficult fight for racial equality. The Albany movement featured exceptionally spirited singing, most notably by sixteen-year-old Bernice Johnson Reagon, who later earned fame and preserved the songs of the struggle with her group, Sweet Honey in the Rock. The students at Albany probably thought of Young at twenty-nine as old, but when they did the limbo, he could go as low as any of them. In general, he got along well with the young SNCC activists.

While Young continued to devote most of his time to citizenship training, by mid-1962 he had begun to take on some duties in King's SCLC. When King and Ralph Abernathy, later president of SCLC, were jailed in Albany in July, they relied on his daily visits to keep them informed. During those seven weeks, Young was regularly called into the office of the Albany police chief, Laurie Pritchard. Pritchard eventually told Young that he knew segregation was morally wrong and that it went against the teachings of Catholicism, to which he had recently converted. He insisted that he was only doing his job, which required him to enforce local law. He stuck by this opinion, and the SCLC left Albany without achieving a victory. Nevertheless, this initial example of Young's exceptional ability to communicate with the white opposition foreshadowed better days ahead. Young later gave Pritchard a positive recommendation that helped him secure a job in North Carolina.

The absence of federal government support contributed to the SCLC's failure to overturn Albany's discriminatory laws in 1962. In general, during his first two years in office, President John F.

John F. Kennedy, Julius Nyerere, and G. Mennen Williams, White House, July 1963. *Courtesy of John F. Kennedy Library*

Kennedy refrained from significant civil rights initiatives. While conducting voter registration work, Young and his colleagues received no direct assistance from the Kennedy administration. To some extent, though, Kennedy shared Young's worldview regarding race. From the beginning of his presidency, Kennedy sent signals in support of the liberation of southern Africa. As his first appointment, he named Michigan Governor G. Mennen "Soapy" Williams as Assistant Secretary of State for Africa. After an eloquent address, in which he asserted that "Africa was for the Africans," Williams was punched in the nose by a white supremacist in Zambia (then Northern Rhodesia). Despite such hostility, Williams condemned the white regimes of southern Africa throughout his tenure at the State Department and urged Kennedy to support decolonization.

In addition to Williams's strong words in favor of liberation, the Kennedy administration supplied little concrete support for the rebels in the Portuguese colonies of Angola and Mozambique. In late 1961, the Central Intelligence Agency (CIA) began providing the Angolan guerrilla forces (UNITA) led by Holden Roberto with aid and put Roberto on the payroll. Early in 1962, the agency increased the aid, and Roberto received CIA payments into the 1970s. Early 1962 also saw a modicum of U.S. encouragement for the guerrilla soldiers in Mozambique. The leader of the Front for the Liberation of Mozambique (FRELIMO), Dr. Eduardo Mondlane, met with Attorney General Robert Kennedy. Mondlane's intelligence and anticommunist convictions persuaded Kennedy to pay for the costs of Mondlane's trip and expand aid to Roberto.[3] Young probably knew absolutely nothing about Kennedy's meeting with Mondlane, but surely he would have been happy about the U.S. support for the old friend he had met at Christian summer camp in Indiana.

Providing limited aid to the guerrillas in Angola and Mozambique was one way that the Kennedy administration supported freedom and independence in Africa. Kennedy's hosting numerous presidents of new African nations, such as Julius Nyerere from Tanzania, on state visits to the White House raised African morale. Another, much more substantial example of Kennedy's African activism was the Peace Corps. The enthusiastic work by Peace Corps volunteers endeared Kennedy and the United States to people in new nations such as Nigeria, Malawi, and Kenya. Furthermore, the Peace Corps provided African Americans with an opportunity to help the recently independent states of Africa to prosper, and more than six hundred blacks served in Africa in the program's first ten years. For these volunteers and many other African Americans such as Andrew Young, the existence of a strong connection between the struggles against racism in Africa and the United States was crystal clear by 1962.

Some black leaders contended that the decolonization of Africa would inspire the civil rights movement to greater heights. Speaking in Ghana in 1962, the African-American poet Langston Hughes proclaimed, "Black Africa today is sending rejuvenating currents of liberty over all the earth reaching even as far as Little Rock, Birmingham, and Jackson, Mississippi."[4] Others, such as the participants in the American Negro Leadership Conference on Africa (ANLCA), emphasized the central role that the U.S. government could play. After attending the ANLCA's first session in the fall of 1962, King met with Kennedy and urged him to increase diplomatic pressure to end colonialism throughout Africa and to support the civil rights movement in the South. But as of late 1962, Kennedy did not seem to see the same connections between the struggles in Africa and the United States that King and Young saw.

Events in Birmingham soon opened his eyes to the interplay between civil rights and foreign relations.

In December 1962 at the Dorchester facility near Savannah, Georgia, King orchestrated a planning session for a campaign that SCLC would oversee in Birmingham, Alabama. At another turning point in his life, Young offered to act as a go-between with Birmingham's leading white business people. He had some solid contacts in that community from his work with the National Council of Churches. He later recalled his reasoning: "I did not view the white business leaders in Birmingham as bad people; they were people in a bad situation. My attitude was influenced by my understanding of Christianity and Gandhi. . . . I was determined to be respectful and keep them always focused on the issues rather than give them any reason to form negative perceptions of me."[5]

King gladly accepted Young's offer, and he played a key role as events unfolded in Alabama in the spring of 1963. Mediating between SCLC and white officials became one of Young's special skills, and the ability to negotiate with whites later served him well in Congress, as Ambassador to the UN, and as mayor of Atlanta. Although other members of SCLC sometimes jokingly derided him as an "Uncle Tom," they also came to appreciate his crucial contribution. Hosea Williams, one of the more radical of King's assistants, characterized Young as "probably the greatest mind in the country for dealing with white people."[6]

After a spirited holiday season highlighted by dancing and Jean's homemade macaroni and cheese, Young and his colleagues went to Birmingham early in 1963 to lay the groundwork for the coming struggle. He continued to assist with citizenship training, but spent his hectic days mainly scurrying from press conferences to strategy talks to negotiations to mass meetings. When King made the fateful decision to head a march in spite of a ban, and go to jail on Good Friday, tremendous responsibility for keeping the SCLC campaign on track fell to Young. That night he addressed a mass meeting for the first time, and on Easter Sunday he helped lead a march to the jail.

As the campaign continued week after week, Young maintained his frenetic pace. He hustled from workshops to demonstrations to the jail, then quickly showered and donned a suit for his negotiations with the Birmingham Board of Trade. The boycott of downtown stores was taking effect, and gradually the business community became willing to make concessions on such issues as hiring more blacks. Meanwhile, international attention remained transfixed by the ongoing confrontations with Sheriff Bull Connor's police dogs and fire hoses, which he ordered his subordinates to use to quell the protests. The SCLC staff escalated the offensive in early May, when they first utilized hundreds of children in the marches, thus filling the jails without jeopardizing family incomes.

During the second major march of children, one of the police dogs viciously bit into the stomach of a young boy. A photographer captured the gruesome image, and it landed on front pages around the world. President Kennedy remarked the next day that the photo made him ill. Indeed, this was the beginning of Birmingham's impact on Kennedy's racial policies, both domestic and foreign. He had attempted to keep foreign and domestic race issues separate, but that was no longer possible. African papers followed developments closely, with many of the white editors in southern Africa pointing out that the United States was hardly qualified to advise them on improving race relations. Perhaps more important to Kennedy was the Soviets' broadcasting more than fourteen hundred radio announcements that were critical of American race relations in the second half of May alone. Such messages could severely damage the reputation of the United States in the Third World. King pointed out that Kennedy was "battling for the minds and the hearts of men in Asia and Africa—some one billion men in the neutralist sector of the world—and they aren't gonna respect the United States of America if she deprives men and women of the basic rights of life because of the color of their skin."[7]

Obviously there were ramifications for U.S. foreign policy, but that was not all. The Birmingham campaign, in fact, made a major impact at three levels: local, national, and international. In great part due to Young's skillful negotiating, an agreement to desegregate Birmingham's lunch counters within ninety days and to begin hiring black store clerks was reached on May 10. In an address to the nation on June 11, in reaction to the Birmingham situation, Kennedy identified civil rights as a moral issue and also as one that affected the American reputation abroad. For these reasons, he declared that it was time to pass tough legislation to guarantee basic citizenship to all Americans. Eventually the legislation that his administration proposed was embodied in the landmark Civil Rights Act of 1964. Although Kennedy did not live to see it become law, he had initiated a broad-based and very sincere effort for its passage. Secretary of State Dean Rusk was the first member of the administration to testify in favor of the bill before Congress in the fall of 1963.[8]

In addition to supporting the domestic component of Kennedy's June appeal, Rusk clearly comprehended the international dimension. Very positive comments had been received from foreign leaders such as Tanzanian President Julius Nyerere, who informed Kennedy that he "appreciated your efforts in connection with the reinvigorated demand by the Negro Citizens of America for full equal rights."[9] With such reactions in mind, Rusk ordered that copies of the president's speech be sent to every U.S. embassy, along with in-depth guidelines. Essentially he wanted U.S. ambassadors to admit to the seriousness of the racial situation in the South and then emphasize the positive steps that the administration had undertaken. His Assistant Secretary for Africa, G. Mennen Williams, wanted to go much further.

Williams seized on the president's speech as an opportunity to champion a tougher policy toward South Africa, arguing that after hearing Kennedy's moralistic note, black Africans would expect something concrete. He suggested that the United States support a complete arms embargo by the United Nations against the Pretoria regime. Rusk resisted going that far, but the president himself suggested a unilateral U.S. arms embargo, to take effect at the beginning of 1964. On August 2, 1963, Kennedy's ambassador to the United Nations announced the embargo.[10] The struggle for civil rights in the United States, led by King and Young and their colleagues, finally had moved the U.S. government to take a stand against racial discrimination abroad. "The action in Birmingham sparked the conscience of the nation. It also sparked similar protests as far away as South Africa. The global human rights movement was born in Birmingham," contended Young.[11]

In the Cold War context of 1963, however, not all officials in the U.S. government looked kindly on the civil rights movement in the South or the liberation movements in the Third World. As King helped to plan the march on Washington that summer, he learned that J. Edgar Hoover and his Federal Bureau of Investigation (FBI) believed the SCLC to be under heavy communist influence. Since the early 1950s, the CIA had worked feverishly to remove Third World leaders whom they classified as communist: Jacobo Arbenz Guzmán in Guatemala, Fidel Castro in Cuba, Patrice Lumumba in the Congo, and Nelson Mandela in South Africa. In the case of Mandela, the CIA's collaboration with the apartheid government cast a shadow of racism across their supposedly anticommunist policy.[12] The FBI's onslaught against King and the SCLC continued long after 1963 and fit the same disturbing pattern.

In a June 22 meeting in the White House garden, Kennedy specifically requested that King purge two suspected communists from the SCLC staff—Stan Levison and Jack O'Dell. He claimed that the FBI intended to share its evidence with Southern senators such as James Eastland, who would then use it to discredit King and block civil rights legislation. King wanted evidence, and he sent Young to New Orleans to meet with Assistant Attorney General Burke Marshall. Marshall had no evidence to show Young, but insisted that O'Dell must resign. King reluctantly agreed, and O'Dell left the SCLC. Young felt anguished by it and brought O'Dell back onto the SCLC staff in 1970. But at a critical point in the movement in 1963, the SCLC had lost a skilled adviser through the same dynamics that victimized leaders of liberation movements in the Third World.

Young had decided not to participate in the August 28 march on Washington, but King called him and asked him to come. Andrew and Jean witnessed the famous "I Have a Dream" speech from seats at the base of the Lincoln Memorial, and they were thankful they had attended. In the months that followed the march, Young did get a chance to relax with his wife and three daughters, often meeting the Kings and the Abernathys at a YMCA pool to swim. He also returned to the citizenship training sessions, which had moved to South Carolina, where he was on the day Kennedy was assassinated. By the end of 1963, Young's position in the SCLC had become that of unofficial executive director, whose primary function was behind the scenes and out of the spotlight. He perceived his role as a "playmaker on the team; it was my job to keep the ball moving . . . to see that each one of my team of stars got the ball enough."[13]

In the spring of 1964, Wyatt Walker left the SCLC, and King officially named Young as the new executive director. His first challenge came in St. Augustine, Florida, where his colleague Hosea Williams was coordinating a campaign against segregation and economic discrimination. Young visited St. Augustine to assess the situation for King and attended a mass meeting to help Williams organize a march. As soon as he walked into the church, Williams announced that Andrew Young would be leading that night's procession to the Old Slave Market. Trapped by the clever Williams, Young had no choice but to march. As the column approached the Old Slave Market, the Ku Klux Klan assaulted them. Hooded thugs punched Young, cracked him on the head with a blackjack, knocked him to the ground, and kicked him relentlessly. He regained consciousness and led the demonstrators through the Old Slave Market and back to the church. He then went outside and broke into tears.

After personally experiencing the brutality of the Klan and seeing the courage of the protesters in St. Augustine, Young lobbied successfully for a major SCLC campaign there. King marched, spoke, and went to jail. Demonstrations lasted two months and included swim-ins at segregated pools and beaches. On June 9, Federal Judge Brian Simpson gave the SCLC a major boost by ruling in their favor in *Young v. Davis*. Young had filed a suit against Sheriff Davis on behalf of the SCLC. Simpson lifted the ban on marches and prohibited the use of several common punishments inflicted on civil rights activists in southern jails such as padded cells and sweatboxes. He exposed St. Augustine's "gun club" as actually a KKK klavern. This important case facilitated later SCLC efforts in Selma and Charleston. On the night of June 9, Young led another march into the Old Slave Market, and was again battered to the pavement by Klansmen wielding blackjacks. After making his way back to the church, he told reporters, "We are going to continue protesting unjust discrimination."[14]

The demonstrators sustained the fight all through June, maintaining pressure on the city of St. Augustine and keeping the reality of racist brutality in the news for the whole world to see. The courage of these and thousands of other activists paid off on July 2, 1964, when President Lyndon Johnson signed the Civil Rights Act. Three days later, SCLC staffers and St. Augustine officials reached an agreement that integrated all public accommodations. Young's efforts had contributed to a victory on the local and national level. Furthermore, he had been tested under fire. "The beatings I took in St. Augustine helped me establish my movement credentials. Now I had been to jail, I had been beaten, and I had guided the movement to a reasonably successful conclusion."[15] The blows he absorbed in the Old Slave Market guaranteed him the future respect of people around the world, from voters in Atlanta to Aborigines in Australia.

In late July, SCLC leaders toured rural Mississippi to observe the Freedom Summer project, which had been organized by the Student Nonviolent Coordinating Committee. Although Young disapproved of SNCC's widespread efforts in rural Mississippi as too dangerous, he was again inspired by the courage and heart of the common folk. That did not mean that he embraced all of their culture. During a stop at a general store, King and Abernathy bought an entire jar of pickled pigs' feet. As they proceeded to consume its contents, they tried in vain to get Young to sample one. Aversion to pigs' feet was another example of the difference between the middle-class Congregationalist from New Orleans and his Baptist buddies from Alabama and Georgia. Young, however, certainly relished the opportunity to eat more familiar fare during a subsequent stop at a rural restaurant, partaking of a huge feast of fried catfish. "When we were done, there was nothing left to those catfish but the heads, tails, and backbones. They looked like fish from a Felix the Cat cartoon," he observed.[16]

Relaxed times such as the catfish feast never lasted long. As King and Young toured Mississippi, violence erupted in the North. Riots broke out in New York City, then spread to Philadelphia and Rochester, where more than three hundred and fifty people were injured. Young led a delegation that toured Rochester to survey the damage and consider possible options for SCLC action. In a sermon at the Central Presbyterian Church there, he suggested that black anger in Rochester actually signified relatively good race relations. He argued that the existence of opportunities for African Americans had stirred their demands for even more. If Rochester could continue to improve its race relations, it would serve as an example for the rest of the world, as distant as Africa and as near as Mississippi. He concluded: "Mississippi cannot learn to live together as brothers until Rochester solves some problems . . . before Africa and Asia and the colored peoples of the world can develop any confidence and rapport and love and brotherhood for the nations of the West, it will be necessary for Mississippi to show the way, to show that the problems of race and poverty can be dealt with in a democratic society."[17] Clearsightedly, Young had connected the urban unrest in the North, the civil rights struggle in the South, and U.S. relations with Asia and Africa.

The efforts of the SCLC in Birmingham and the resulting Civil Rights Act improved the standing of the United States in the Third World, but there was still much to be done. At the SCLC convention in the fall of 1964, Young delivered a very rational analysis of the need for a voting rights bill. Getting such legislation passed would require at least as much activism as had preceded the Civil Rights Act, so he and the other SCLC leaders began discussing a campaign in rural Alabama, in the heart of several counties with incredibly low black voter registration. Before they launched their operation in Alabama, they journeyed to Olso, Norway, where King received the Nobel Peace Prize. This tremendous honor provided

King with an unprecedented opportunity to put the civil rights movement in a global context.

En route to Norway, the SCLC entourage stopped in London, where King spoke to more than three thousand people at St. Paul's Cathedral. He proclaimed, "In our struggle for freedom and justice in the U.S., which has also been so long and arduous, we feel a powerful sense of identification with those in the far more deadly struggle for freedom in South Africa." King acknowledged that the more extreme repression in South Africa had necessitated Mandela and the African National Congress's opting for violent means such as sabotage. At the same time, he pointed out how the international community could use nonviolence to help resolve the conflict. King suggested that people around the world should join in "a massive movement for economic sanctions" against the apartheid regime.[18] His message left a deep impression on Young, who played a key role in the fight for sanctions in the 1970s and 1980s.

In Oslo, King and his group stayed at the Grand Hotel, where their spontaneous singing in the lobby was a big hit. At the medal-presentation ceremony, King delivered a short statement, which Young had helped him prepare. King's major speech was the formal Nobel Lecture at Oslo University, and in it he returned to the links among the struggles of people of color around the world. He asserted that from India to Africa to the southern United States, "the freedom movement is spreading the widest liberation in human history."[19] After the ceremony, Norwegian students serenaded King with "We Shall Overcome," demonstrating another aspect of the international impact and appeal of the civil rights movement.

The Oslo trip included some controversial moments, with Abernathy making a scene because he was not allowed to ride in King's limousine and Bayard Rustin, one of King's advisers, openly inquiring at the U.S. Embassy about where he could find Norwegian prostitutes. Young, to the contrary, impressed U.S. Ambassador Margaret Tibbets with his logistical skills. She recalled that he was the only one of King's staffers who seemed organized. Tibbets was a no-nonsense Yankee diplomat from Maine, and Young's ability to interact smoothly with her again demonstrated his talent for getting along with people from all backgrounds.[20]

Soon after returning to the States from the Nobel trip the SCLC staff opened their campaign in Selma, Alabama, with King speaking in commemoration of emancipation on January 2, 1965. Young moved into the home of Selma resident Amelia Boynton and began laying the groundwork. On January 11, he took time out from Selma preparations to join Abernathy for a meeting with Federal Bureau of Investigation (FBI) official Cartha DeLoach. Young and Abernathy confronted DeLoach about the FBI's efforts to slander King and requested to see the sources of the bureau's information. DeLoach denied that the FBI was leaking negative rumors about King to the press and refused to disclose the bureau's sources. Young and Abernathy were furious with DeLoach, who later bragged to his boss, J. Edgar Hoover, that he had made the meeting "as unpleasant and embarrassing as possible" for King's assistants.[21] Once again, the FBI's aggressive and mean-spirited covert operations against King and the SCLC resembled the CIA's secret undertakings against Third World leaders. All were supposedly justified by anticommunism, which was part of the reason that Young sought to de-emphasize anticommunism in U.S. foreign relations in the 1970s.

Back in Selma, the demonstrations began, and by early February, King and Abernathy were once again in jail. Young took charge of logistics, delegating duties to other staffers and keeping open the lines of communication between King and the outside world. Malcolm X arrived in Selma and tried unsuccessfully to visit King in jail. He talked with Young, who had met him several times in Atlanta and New York. Malcolm was assassinated a few weeks later, and Young attended the funeral. Young characterized Malcolm as " a serious and sincere advocate for his belief in the need for blacks to develop a new sense of pride."[22] Although they had certainly not been close friends, their relationship of mutual respect was another very compelling example of Young's ability to work with and comprehend all sorts of persons.

The demonstrations in Selma continued, with a major march planned for Sunday, March 7. At the last minute, King decided he could not participate that day, so Young flew over from Atlanta to cancel the event. He found several hundred people ready to march. He conferred with John Lewis and Hosea Williams, and they all agreed that the demonstration should take place. They called King, who approved but insisted that Andy and Hosea could not both march at the same time because of the danger. They flipped a coin, and Hosea won the right to be in one of history's most famous showdowns. As the civil rights activists marched peacefully across the Edmund Pettus Bridge, they were brutally attacked by state troopers brandishing clubs and firing tear gas. Lewis was among the casualties, having sustained another in a long line of concussions.

In the aftermath of the violence, Young briefed King. They decided to plan another march across the bridge on Tuesday, March 9. The graphic scenes from Selma were broadcast around the world, ironically interrupting a documentary on the "Nuremberg Trials of Nazi Leaders." The eyes of the world again focused on the South. When King asked people to go to Selma and support the movement, they responded in huge numbers. The ultimate goal was a march from Selma to Montgomery, similar to some of Gandhi's great marches. The SCLC leaders decided that they needed more time to organize such a massive endeavor properly. So on the ninth, after crossing the bridge and praying, they returned to Selma. The day had gone smoothly, but that night a white minister from Boston, James Reeb, was beaten so severely that he eventually died from his injuries. A few nights later, President Lyndon B. Johnson requested that Congress pass voting rights legislation. He contended that the United States had waited over one hundred years for equality, and "the time for waiting is gone." Aware of the positive international ramifications of such a speech, his staff sent copies to the presidents of all African nations.[23]

Meanwhile, the SCLC leaders finalized their plans for the march to Montgomery. They decided to begin on March 21 and complete the 54-mile journey in five days. Jean insisted on joining her husband for the opening day, and brought daughters Lisa and Andrea. Lisa gladly rode on her father's shoulders for some of the way, but Young could not spend much time with his family. He repeatedly ran from the front to the back of the mile-long procession, dealing with various problems and trying to keep everyone singing the same song. At the end of the first day's seven miles, Young's family, King, and most of the other participants went home. Young played a key role in keeping the core group moving for the next three days. On day five, King and many celebrities returned for the dramatic walk into Montgomery.

Roy Wilkins, head of the National Association for the Advancement of Colored People (NAACP), joined for day five and witnessed a memorable scene. As the marchers approached the capitol building, they could see Governor George Wallace in the window. Young presciently yelled up at Wallace: "We come to warn that someday some of you in the statehouse are going to be in the cotton patch, and some of us in the cotton patch are going to be in the statehouse." In the 1970s, Young would be among the first Southern African Americans since 1901 to take a seat in the national government, although he probably would not have predicted it in 1965. He did believe in the power of nonviolence, however, and eloquently expressed his faith by again shouting up at the governor: "We come to love the hell out of the state of Alabama."[24] As he said this, he may have been thinking about the death threats that had been made against King that day, which fortunately proved idle. King capped off the historic occasion with a rousing address, and the successful trek from Selma to Montgomery boosted the president's efforts to pass voting legislation.

Johnson's ongoing support for civil rights impressed black African leaders such as the president of Kenya, Jomo Kenyatta. In April he informed Johnson, "In view of the wide interest and sympathy roused by incidents in the southern part of your country and the close connections between the Negro people and the people of Africa, I am writing to offer you my support in your government's efforts to remove all forms of discriminatory practices."[25] Kenyatta obviously agreed with King and Young that the civil rights struggle in the United States was part of a world movement for freedom and equality.

While African-American leaders such as Young and black African leaders like Kenyatta praised Johnson's domestic policy, they were beginning to oppose aspects of his foreign policy. Vietnam would soon overshadow all other international issues, but the first Johnson initiative that drew fire occurred in the Dominican Republic. Voters there had elected reformer Juan Bosch to the presidency in 1962, but he was soon ousted by a military coup. When Bosch attempted to regain power with a coup of his own in late April 1965, U.S. Ambassador John Barlow Martin warned Johnson that there were over fifty Communists among Bosch's supporters. Although Martin's evidence of communist influence was dubious, his plea was heeded. Johnson sent 33,000 U.S. marines into the Dominican Republic to crush the rebellion.

The intervention reflected the stridently anticommunist orientation advocated by Thomas Mann, the key formulator of Johnson's relations with Latin America. Young later denounced the U.S. action in the Dominican Republic as an example of racism. He pointed specifically at Mann and his upbringing in Texas, arguing that Mann viewed Hispanics as "wetbacks." Although Mann justified intervention as anticommunist action, Young contended that it had really been his negative view toward people of color that motivated the action. He believed that individuals "with that kind of background would not react comfortably to a mass movement amongst colored people." The intervention, Young concluded, was unnecessary, and a peaceful transition could have been negotiated.[26]

Although differences with the Johnson administration over foreign relations intensified and added to the stresses of Young's work with King, the summer of 1965 did afford Young a few chances to relax with his family. On several occasions, they went waterskiing on Lake Allatoona, north of Atlanta. By the time Young got to join them, Jean and the girls had conducted several trial runs. With his pride on the line, he studied books about waterskiing in the days leading up to the great challenge. With lots of effort and some luck, he got up on the skis during his first try. For the time being, his ego was secure, but that was not enough. Jean and the girls could all ski on two skis, so as he jokingly recalled, "To establish my superiority, I quickly learned to use just one."[27]

Bayard Rustin, Andrew Young, William Ryan, James Farmer, and John Lewis, 1965.
Courtesy of Library of Congress

Meanwhile in Washington, another monumental accomplishment of the civil rights movement was achieved. In great part due to the events in Selma, Congress passed the Voting Rights Act, and Johnson signed it into law on August 6, 1965. The act forbade literacy tests and empowered the federal government to register voters in districts where discrimination persisted. Young took pride in having played a key role in the events that secured the passage of the Voting Rights Act. The act dramatically increased the black vote, which helped elect Young to the U.S. Congress in 1972. The black vote was also a key to Jimmy Carter's victory in 1976, which provided Young the opportunity to serve at the United Nations.

Finally, his election as mayor of Atlanta in the 1980s reflected tremendous African-American support. Although he could not have realized it at the time, approval of the Voting Rights Act in August 1965 paved his way to spending nearly two decades in governmental positions.

A few days after Johnson signed the Voting Rights Act, the SCLC held its ninth annual convention. As keynote speaker, Young delivered an address entitled "An Experiment in Power." He described the past successes of the SCLC, particularly its efforts to gain civil rights legislation. He proposed gradually expanding SCLC's assault on injustice—first to the North, then around the world. While acknowledging that it would be a tremendous challenge, Young saw no need to abandon the nonviolent tactics that had worked in the South. Optimistically he contended that "if we are true to Gandhi and seek to attack issues rather than people, we can hope to inspire even our opposition to new moral heights, and thereby overcome."[28]

Young identified the U.S. intervention in Southeast Asia as a key issue with which the SCLC would have to grapple: "Our concern for the war in Vietnam . . . is only natural." He objected to spending money on a foreign war when the war on poverty at home had barely begun. He asserted, "We can never have the funds needed to make peace and prosperity so long as we spend so much to make war." He had begun to envision a political strategy to stop the fighting. He firmly rejected the notion of the SCLC's abandoning civil rights projects to join demonstrations against the war and, instead, recommended escalating efforts to register black voters. These new votes could help rid Congress of key promilitary legislators and facilitate the substitution of a policy of increased foreign aid for armed intervention. Rather than going to Washington to demonstrate against the war, Young advocated an effort to replace military-minded lawmakers "with men of good will . . . to vote a Marshall Plan for Asia, Africa and Latin America."[29] The South was a logical place to implement his plan, since many of the Pentagon's staunchest supporters in Congress during the 1960s hailed from Dixie.[30]

In his conclusion, Young returned to his main theme, that the SCLC should broaden its vision: "We must see that our work extends beyond the South and into the North, and when we have completed our work there we must go from New York to London and Paris and from there to Brazzaville and Johannesburg until the rights of man are secure the world over."[31] With these words, Young foreshadowed his future role in U.S. relations with southern Africa, and particularly his work against apartheid in South Africa.

The day after Young's speech, King issued a statement to the convention that condemned the Vietnam War as immoral and called for negotiations. Thus began an internal debate among SCLC leaders over how to deal with the Vietnam conflict. For the rest of 1965 and throughout 1966, the debate remained essentially a private one. Relatively moderate leaders like Young dissuaded King from an open break with Johnson over Vietnam, citing the president's assistance on civil rights legislation and expressing the hope that he would offer similar help in the future. On the other end of the spectrum of SCLC opinion, James Bevel espoused vocal denunciation of the war. King heeded the advice of the moderates, refraining from public criticism of Johnson. Rather than protest the fighting in Vietnam, the SCLC attempted to redress the complex problems in the slums of Chicago.

In January 1966, the SCLC rented a tenement apartment in the Windy City for $150 per month. King intended to move in, but Young ended up spending more time there and feared being knifed by a drug addict. He felt "that it would be one thing to be killed by the Klan in the South—that was an acceptable martyrdom—but to be murdered by a junkie in Chicago seemed to me the ultimate absurdity."[32] Fortunately, he avoided such a fate, and facilitated the limited SCLC success in Chicago. A federal grant helped tenants improve their apartments, and a few were able to convert from renting to owning. Operation Breadbasket, led by new SCLC staffer Jesse Jackson, provided jobs for blacks in local grocery stores and persuaded owners to stock black-made products. The Chicago campaign also manifested some Southern spirit, especially in the churches. Young witnessed this as he preached in about fifty Baptist churches during his stay there.

Despite the existence of healthy grassroots enthusiasm and the hard work of Jackson, Young, and many other SCLC leaders, the Chicago campaign resulted in very little measurable progress. Violence flared often during the summer of 1966, and the key issue of discriminatory housing practices could not be easily resolved. When Young and King negotiated an agreement with Mayor Richard J. Daley and the housing board in August, it was condemned as too little, too late. The SCLC's experience in Chicago exemplified the immense difficulties involved in taking the civil rights struggle to the North.

On the bright side, the summer of 1966 provided Young with an opportunity to visit Europe again and to get to know more African nationalists. The United Church of Christ selected him to serve on the board of the World Council of Churches' Program to Combat Racism. He and Jean attended the annual meeting near Geneva, and Andrew met Sam Nujoma, the leader of the liberation forces in Namibia who would become that country's first president. Following a brief vacation in Paris, Young jumped back into the fray and pushed himself hard through the autumn. After the annual SCLC retreat near Savannah, he collapsed on a bathroom floor at the airport and passed out from exhaustion. His friend Fred Bennet found him, put him on a plane to Atlanta, and called Jean. She took her husband from the airport to the hospital, where the doctors prescribed rest.

Young's response was to take off the next day on a flight to Israel, where he began hammering out the logistics for a pilgrimage of five thousand people to the Holy Land. Young persuaded leaders in Israel and Jordan to allow the entourage to pass from Israel to Jordan through Jerusalem. They also agreed to build an amphitheater on the Sea of Galilee from which King would deliver a speech. Both Arabs and Jews would benefit from the tourist money, and King hoped it would be a real boost to peace in the region. Unfortunately, Egyptian jets were shot down over Gaza the day Andrew and Jean left Tel Aviv, and ultimately the Six-Day War in June 1967 ended King's plans for a pilgrimage. Nonetheless, Young's efforts had introduced him to the complexities of the Middle East.

Overall, 1966 had been a challenging year. As Young surveyed matters in December, he deemed SCLC "opposition to the war in Vietnam . . . clear." He recognized that King preferred an occasional statement against the war to an all-consuming protest movement. President Johnson was not an ideal ally, but Young did not advocate a "categorical break with the Federal Government." The administration could play a key role in helping the needy, and the SCLC planned to continue its political strategy to encourage such a role. Simultaneously they could gradually expand their movement in the North and onto the international stage.[33]

While Young hoped to continue a positive relationship with the Johnson administration, the escalating Vietnam conflict rendered that extremely difficult. In January 1967, the SCLC's most outspoken critic of the war, James Bevel, left the group to focus full-time on protesting. During a February vacation in Jamaica, King decided to criticize openly U.S. intervention in Southeast Asia, and he delivered his first major public antiwar speech at the end of the month. Meanwhile, Young denounced Johnson's policy in Atlanta on February 1. He labeled the war a catastrophe and decried it on both economic and moral grounds. Economically, the war consumed funds that could have gone to the war on poverty. Morally, war defied the commandment "Thou shalt not kill." Driving this point home, he concluded that "mass murder is no way to solve problems."[34]

Other international issues weighed on Young's mind in early 1967, particularly events in southern Africa. To wealthy friends of Robert Kennedy, he professed particular concern "about our relationship to South Africa, Angola, and Rhodesia. . . . We are beginning to see a role in relation to the African nationalists and we must have a nonviolent alternative—mainly because the countries are prepared to thwart violence and the U.S. will keep them supplied with arms."[35] As a congressman and ambassador in the 1970s, Young took a very active role in revising U.S. policy toward the liberation struggles in southern Africa. During his tenure with the SCLC, however, the war in Vietnam overshadowed all other foreign relations topics.

Young himself had denounced the war as far back as 1965, and he had spoken out against it publicly in early 1967, but he was not recognized nationally as the spokesperson for the civil rights movement. In that sense, Young's view on the war was not particularly important. King's view, of course, was another story, and he was determined to go public with his antiwar stance. The key question for the SCLC in the spring of 1967, therefore, was how strongly and in what forum King should criticize U.S. policy. One potential option was participation in an upcoming demonstration in New York known as the Spring Mobilization. King sent Young to meet with the planners of the demonstration to discuss his possible role. The session was very disappointing. "Only one person there seemed even rational. . . . It was the wildest bunch of kooks I had ever run across," Young remarked.[36]

Young advised King not to associate himself with such a ragtag collection of radicals, because it would definitely hurt SCLC's standing with the government and with moderate supporters of civil rights. Instead, Young suggested that King speak out in a more familiar setting that they could control. King agreed, so Young contacted influential New York religious leaders John Bennet and Abraham Herschel. They organized a forum and speech by King at Riverside Church in Manhattan across from the National Council of Churches' headquarters. At Riverside on April 4, 1967, King delivered "Beyond Vietnam," which Young had helped him write.

King argued that African Americans were being sent eight thousand miles to fight for freedoms they did not enjoy in Georgia or Harlem. He pointed out that the war was damaging U.S. credibility in the Third World and advocated an end to the bombing and the beginning of real negotiations. King repeated this message in another address at the UN Plaza on April 15, after he and Young had participated in an antiwar march. King had spoken out strongly against the war, and Young's advice and support had been instrumental. Stan Levison, a King adviser whom many considered a Communist, criticized Young for pushing King too far to the left on Vietnam. However, King and Young thought their approach would be acceptable to the government and SCLC's moderate allies.[37]

As quickly became evident, many of those moderates deemed King's denunciation of U.S. policy a serious mistake. Fellow civil rights leader Roy Wilkins considered King's stance a tactical error, and influential black journalist Carl Rowan severely rebuked him. Some former supporters of the SCLC turned hostile. Young did his best to answer these criticisms, compiling a pamphlet of editorials and letters supporting King's position from a variety of positions and mailing it to the SCLC membership. In the pamphlet he explained, "Although the SCLC engages its primary attention in civil rights, its board unanimously supports Dr. King's right to speak as well as of his position on the war."[38] The criticisms continued, including an editorial in the *Atlanta Constitution*. Young responded to the editor: "We here at SCLC have been engaged in quite a struggle of the conscience. Perhaps our sensitivities have misled us, or maybe our information is wrong, but from our reading of history we have no alternative but to oppose the war in Vietnam."[39]

Many of the attacks on King contended that he was naive about international relations and should therefore stick to domestic issues. In fact, he understood the situation in Vietnam quite well, having read the insightful work of the brilliant French-American scholar Bernard Fall and talked at length with Swedish journalists who had spent time in southern and northern Vietnam. The wisdom of his argument may not have mattered. The criticism could have been a result of King's race. Young believed so: "International relations in the 1960s were largely the province of an elite club of upper-class white males. I think they were as surprised to find a

Southern black preacher with strong and sophisticated opinions on international policy as by the opinions themselves."[40]

Despite the harsh criticism, King and Young continued to express their antiwar views throughout the summer of 1967. In July, Young addressed a ministers' conference organized by the National Council of Churches in Green Lake, Wisconsin. According to Young, the American intervention in Southeast Asia "denied our brothers in Vietnam the right to determine their own destiny." He considered this an unacceptable policy for Christians and suggested that all Americans faced a choice between "the cross and the flag." It was time to put loyalty to God ahead of loyalty to country. As ministers, it was their responsibility to oppose an immoral war. He realized that it might be difficult for ministers to start preaching against the policies of the U.S. government, recalling rebukes he had received after delivering an antiwar sermon at his old family church in New Orleans. He knew that the ministers listening to him would be under similar pressures to retain their conservative posture, but he urged them "to be willing to bear the cross to break out of it."[41]

During his speeches at Green Lake, Young explained that the SCLC was not interested in ending only the war in Vietnam. He and his colleagues hoped to end war in general. A key step was progress toward economic justice both in the Third World and in the ghettos of America. He characterized urban slums in the United States as domestic colonies, suffering from similar repression as India had as an English colony. The suffering of poor African Americans resembled the plight of poor people of color around the world. Alleviating poverty and economic inequity was the only way to achieve world peace. "For the people in Vietnam, for the people in South America, or for the people in India or the Congo," he asserted, "peace doesn't mean law and order or the status quo . . . peace for them means revolution or development. . . . Peace for people in the ghetto is development!"[42]

Young's vision for world peace through economic development was compelling and inspirational, but the reality of international affairs in 1967 rendered it a pipe dream. The number of U.S. troops in Vietnam surpassed four hundred thousand, intense fighting continued, and the Johnson administration refused to halt the bombing. Simultaneously, riots raged and fires burned in cities across America. Young and the SCLC contributed to a small victory by registering Cleveland voters, who elected Carl Stokes as the city's first black mayor that fall. Overall, though, the situation in late 1967 was gloomy, as Young admitted to some friends. "These are difficult times—to say the least. Each day gets a little more complicated than the last. . . . My only consolation is that things are so bad, they've got to get better."[43]

Even in the darkest days Young retained his characteristic optimism, and he and the other SCLC leaders quickly found a major project on which to focus their energies. The spark came from a conversation with Marian Wright (later, Edelman) in September. Wright, director of the NAACP's legal defense fund in Mississippi, brought four poor farmers with her to Atlanta. She proposed a fast in Washington to protest poverty. After hearing her plan, King and Young began discussing a much bigger project, which they soon dubbed the Poor People's Campaign. King promoted Young to SCLC executive vice president, and in that role he toured the country explaining their vision for a mass gathering of the impoverished in Washington. In December, Young explained that a central goal of the Poor People's Campaign was to persuade the Johnson administration to shift funds from the Vietnam War back into domestic programs. Young was deeply distressed. "A country that will appropriate about $500,000 for every enemy killed in Vietnam and $53 per year for every poor person—that country is going to hell," he warned.[44]

The situation in Southeast Asia would get much worse before it got better. The fighting intensified in early 1968, when Vietnamese forces launched the Tet Offensive. King and Young continued to denounce the war while simultaneously planning for the Poor People's Campaign. Jim Lawson asked King to speak in Memphis in support of striking garbage workers, and he did. On March 28, King participated in a demonstration that turned violent. In the aftermath he pledged to return and lead a nonviolent march. On April 3, he and his top assistants all returned to Memphis. That night in his final sermon, he proclaimed, "These are the years when the masses of people are rising up . . . in Johannesburg, South Africa; Nairobi, Kenya; Accra, Ghana; New York City; Atlanta, Georgia; Jackson, Mississippi; or Memphis, Tennessee, the cry is always the same: we want to be free."[45]

King had spelled out the connection between poor people of color around the world one last time. The next day he was assassinated. Late that night, Young and the rest of the SCLC staff agreed that they must carry on the struggle, and named Ralph Abernathy as King's successor. The following morning back in Atlanta, Young talked with the four King children about their father's death. As a family friend who had always had a way with children, Young was as qualified for this responsibility as anyone could be. Nonetheless, it was one of the most difficult conversations of his life.

Young and police, Resurrection City, Washington, DC, June 1968. *Courtesy of Library of Congress*

After the funeral, Young focused his energies on organizing the Poor People's Campaign, which took place in the summer of 1968. The demonstration dragged on without achieving any significant progress, eventually disintegrating into chaos. While in Washington, Young met with Secretary of State Dean Rusk. Young blasted U.S. policy toward southern Africa for supporting racist white regimes and urged an overhaul. Rusk listened politely, but no new initiatives toward South Africa or Rhodesia resulted.[46] Amid these disappointments, Young learned of the assassination of Robert Kennedy. In the wake of King's death, Young had held his emotions in check. In a state of shock, he had soldiered on with the fight for freedom. The murder of Kennedy unlocked all those pent-up emotions. Young later recalled: "After he died I sank into a depression so deep it was impossible for me to go on."[47] Like huge numbers of Americans, Young staggered through the second half of 1968, devastated by the seemingly endless violence that threatened to tear the country apart.

As the year wound down, Young was uncertain as to what to do next. His role in the SCLC was no longer clear, and he soon began to consider other options such as politics. With the death of King, an incredible chapter in Young's life came to a close. The effect of fighting with King on the front lines of the civil rights movement had been formative and far reaching: "In the profoundest of terms, my work with Martin gave my life a purpose and sustenance I could have hardly dreamed of when Jean and I left New York to return to the South in 1961. He left his mark on me, both in indelible memories and in the spiritual and practical lessons of our trials and triumphs."[48]

Among other things, Young's years with King greatly influenced his attitudes on international relations. Perhaps most important, working with King refined Young's understanding that the civil rights movement was an integral part of the larger global movement for freedom and justice. Although Young was by no means an influential player in the formulation of U.S. foreign relations during his tenure as King's assistant, his experiences between 1961 and 1968 shaped the worldview that he brought to Washington, DC, in the 1970s.

When Young first returned to the South in 1961, he already believed in the power of Gandhian nonviolence, and working with King reinforced that faith. Similarly, Young had previously noted the connections between the civil rights movement in the United States and other liberation struggles around the world. Participating in the compelling events in Alabama and Florida and seeing the inspiring results, however, showed Young how powerful those connections could be. Concerns about America's reputation overseas helped persuade Kennedy and Johnson to support groundbreaking civil rights legislation. At the same time, African-American activism contributed to Kennedy's decision to impose an arms embargo on South Africa. Other insights into foreign policy that Young gained during his years with the SCLC were not so positive. He realized how aggressive the FBI's campaign against King really was and concluded that racism was a strong factor in that attack. The FBI justified the persecution by claiming that the SCLC was being influenced by Communists, similar to the CIA's justification for plans to overthrow Third World leaders such Castro, Lumumba, and Mandela. Young learned much about the complexities of international relations during the 1960s, and that education prepared him well to become a civil rights ambassador in the 1970s. In Congress and at the United Nations, he would attempt to downplay the importance of anticommunism and increase the emphasis on fighting racism in the overall thrust of U.S. foreign relations.

Notes

1. Andrew Young, *An Easy Burden: The Civil Rights Movement and the Transformation of America* (New York: HarperCollins, 1996), 128.

2. Young, *An Easy Burden*, 138.

3. Thomas Noer, *Cold War and Black Liberation: The United States and White Rule in Africa, 1948–1968* (Columbia: University of Missouri Press, 1985), 72, 85.

4. Michael Krenn, *Black Diplomacy: African Americans and the State Department, 1945–1969* (Armonk, NY: M. E. Sharpe, 1999), 115–16.

5. Young, *An Easy Burden*, 203–4.

6. Howell Raines, *My Soul Is Rested: Movement Days in the Deep South Remembered* (New York: Bantam Books, 1978), 485–86.

7. Robert Massie, *Loosing the Bonds: The United States and South Africa in the Apartheid Years* (New York: Doubleday, 1997), 139–40.

8. Thomas Zeiler, *Dean Rusk: Defending the American Mission Abroad* (Wilmington, DE: Scholarly Resources, 2000), 90.

9. Nyerere to Kennedy, June 18, 1963, cited in Mary Dudziak, *Cold War Civil Rights: Race and the Image of American Democracy* (Princeton: Princeton University Press, 2000), 174.

10. Massie, *Loosing The Bonds*, 141–50.

11. Andrew Young, *A Way Out of No Way: The Spiritual Memoirs of Andrew Young* (Nashville: Thomas Nelson, 1994), 84.

12. Massie, *Loosing The Bonds*, 94.

13. Young, *An Easy Burden*, 282.

14. Ibid., 296; Taylor Branch, *Pillar of Fire: America in the King Years, 1963–65* (New York: Simon & Schuster, 1998), 333–35.

15. Young, *An Easy Burden*, 300.

16. Ibid., 306.

17. Andrew Young, "Sunday Morning Sermon," August 9, 1964, 8–11, folder 25, box 135, SCLC Papers, Martin Luther King Library, Atlanta, Georgia (hereafter MLK).

18. King's London speech is quoted in George Fredrickson, *Black Liberation: A Comparative History of Black Ideologies in the United States and South Africa* (New York: Oxford University Press, 1995), 274–75.

19. King's Nobel speech, quoted in Branch, *Pillar of Fire*, 542.

20. Margaret Tibbets, interview with author, December 22, 1993, Bethel, Maine.

21. DeLoach, quoted in Branch, *Pillar of Fire*, 558.

22. Young, *An Easy Burden*, 325.

23. Johnson's speech is cited and discussed in Thomas Borstelmann, *The Cold War and the Color Line: American Race Relations in the Global Arena* (Cambridge: Harvard University Press, 2001), 190.

24. Roy Wilkins, *Standing Fast: The Autobiography of Roy Wilkins* (New York: Viking Press, 1982), 309.

25. Jomo Kenyatta to Lyndon Johnson, April 8, 1965, "Kenya—Presidential" folder, box 30, National Security File—Special Head of State Correspondence, Lyndon Baines Johnson Library, Austin, Texas (hereafter LBJ).

26. Thomas Baker's interview of Andrew Young, June 18, 1970, 28–29, Accession Number 75–37, Oral History Collection, LBJ.

27. Young, *An Easy Burden*, 375.

28. Andrew Young, "An Experiment in Power," August 11, 1965, 12, folder 1, box 12, SCLC Papers, MLK.

29. Ibid., 8–9.

30. Joseph A. Fry, *Dixie Looks Abroad: The South and U.S. Foreign Relations, 1789–1973* (Baton Rouge: Louisiana State University Press, 2002), 239–43.

31. Ibid., 16.

32. Young, *An Easy Burden*, 387–88.

33. Andrew Young to Ira Sandperl, December 21, 1966, folder 14, box 38, SCLC Papers, MLK.

34. Andrew Young, "The Death of God and the Civil Rights Movement," Speech to the Hungry Club, Atlanta YMCA, February 1, 1967, notes in folder 27, box 49, SCLC Papers, MLK.

35. Andrew Young to Bill and Jean van den Heuvel, March 10, 1967, folder 19, box 38, Ibid.

36. Speech by Andrew Young in *Christianity and Crisis* vol. 31 (May 3, 1971): 81.

37. Planning and the main points of "Beyond Vietnam" are discussed in Young, *An Easy Burden*, 428–29; a detailed analysis of the speech and the resulting criticism are in David Garrow, *Bearing the Cross: Martin Luther King, Jr., and the Southern Christian Leadership Conference* (New York: Vintage Books, 1986), 553–55; Young's influence on King and Levison's criticism are considered in Adam Fairclough, *To Redeem the Soul of America: The Southern Christian Leadership Conference and Martin Luther King, Jr.* (Athens: University of Georgia Press, 1987), 340–41.

38. Andrew Young, ed., "Does Martin Luther King, Jr. Have the Right? The Qualifications? The Duty? To Speak Out on Peace," folder 19, box 142, King Papers, MLK.

39. Andrew Young to Eugene Patterson, May 3, 1967, Folder 2, Box 46, SCLC Papers, MLK, April 1967.

40. Young, *An Easy Burden*, 431.

41. Andrew Young, "Personal Pilgrimage," 12–13, folder 32, box 49; and idem, "Anatomy of a Slum," 8, folder 20, box 49, SCLC Papers, MLK, July 1967.

42. Young, "Anatomy of a Slum," 8–9.

43. Andrew Young to Marty and Ann Peretz, September 6, 1967, folder 10, box 39, SCLC Papers, MLK.

44. James McGraw, "An Interview with Andrew Young," *Christianity and Crisis* 27 (January 22, 1968), 329. The interview took place on December 21, 1967.

45. King quoted in Young, *An Easy Burden*, 462.

46. Dean Rusk's Memorandum for the President, "My Meeting with Dr. Ralph Abernathy and Representatives of the 'Poor People,' " May 3, 1968, "Oversized Attachments" folder, box 2, White House Central Files (WHCF), LBJ. Thanks to Chris Riggs for sharing this document with me.

47. Young, *An Easy Burden*, 486.

48. Ibid., 474.

3

Taking King's Vision to Congress

1969–1976

When the debate over Vietnam heated up in 1967, Andrew Young advocated a political approach. In 1968, he saw the Poor People's Campaign as a way to persuade politicians to refocus their energies on helping America's neediest inhabitants. In 1970, Young decided that the best way to continue his work for peace abroad and justice at home was to enter the national political fray himself. After losing that first election, he won a seat in the United States Congress in 1972. During his two terms in Congress, he applied the lessons he had learned in the 1950s and 1960s to influence U.S. foreign relations and to advocate peace and racial justice around the world. By 1976 he ranked as one of the leading congressional spokespersons for developing a new policy toward the Third World, particularly Africa. Young's accomplishments in Congress and his work in Jimmy Carter's campaign catapulted him to the post of U.S. ambassador to the United Nations in 1977, where he literally became America's "civil rights ambassador."

Rising to such lofty heights must have seemed unlikely, if not impossible, to Andrew Young in 1969. Serving as the vice president of the Southern Christian Leadership Conference (SCLC), he was still immersed in the struggle for civil rights. In late March over four hundred hospital workers in Charleston, South Carolina, went on strike when the hospital administration refused to recognize their union. The SCLC provided the workers with tactical advice and helped organize marches, mass meetings, and boycotts of downtown stores. The standoff dragged into the summer with no end in sight, until one day Young read an article about the head of the hospital, William McCord, who had grown up in South Africa, the child of Presbyterian missionaries. Young later recalled his response: "I said, damn, the guy can't be all bad, so I picked up the phone and called him and asked if I could come by and talk."[1] A series of meetings resulted, and Young's negotiating skills once again paid off. In late June the union was recognized and the strike ended. Charleston was Young's last major SCLC success.

In 1970, after a particularly contentious SCLC meeting, John Lewis told Young about his plan to persuade Julian Bond to run for the U.S. Congress in Georgia's Fifth District. They called Bond, who refused to run. Bond and Lewis then suggested that Young run instead. He agreed to think it over, but was off to meet with Harry Belafonte in New York to plan SCLC fundraisers. When Young told Belafonte about his conversation with Lewis and Bond, Belafonte immediately called his wife to begin organizing a fundraiser for Young's congressional campaign. Young objected that he had not discussed it with his family, but the campaign had begun, and the Belafontes soon held a fund-raising dinner at the Hotel Pierre on Fifth Avenue.

Young considered running for office to be a natural extension of the voter-registration work he had done throughout the 1960s. Since his childhood duty of greeting the patients in his father's dental office, he had always been comfortable meeting new people and campaigning came easily to him. Enthusiastic volunteers from all around the country came to Georgia to help and to promote the campaign slogan "Think Young." After capturing the Democratic nomination, Young faced a tough battle against the Republican incumbent, Fletcher Thompson. Thompson was white, as were 70 percent of the voters in the Fifth District. Race played a part in the outcome, as did the fact that voters were still optimistic about Republican President Richard Nixon. Young lost this first bid for office, but he and his wife Jean immediately agreed that he should try again in 1972.

In the interim, Young chaired Atlanta's Community Relations Commission, to which he had been appointed by Mayor Sam Massell. The group met regularly at City Hall to hear complaints about discrimination and other civic issues. The position provided Young with useful experience and valuable exposure for the next campaign, and by 1972 he was a much stronger candidate. Redis-

Andrew Young, congressional portrait, 1972. *Courtesy of Library of Congress*

tricting had increased the black vote to 38 percent and removed some conservative white neighborhoods, and Young supporters helped register twenty thousand new black voters. Young's team used the media wisely, counting on catchy radio jingles rather than expensive television time. Belafonte sang at a benefit that netted $5,000. Some leading whites rallied to Young's side. Former Atlanta mayor Ivan Allen endorsed Young and personally contributed $1,500 to the campaign. Young received valuable support from Jack Watson and Stuart Eisenstadt, who would later serve in Jimmy Carter's administration.

It rained on election day in 1972, prompting Young and his backers to work even harder to get blacks out to vote. He defeated Rodney Cook, a moderate Republican, by about eight thousand votes, receiving nearly every black vote and almost a quarter of the white votes. Young greeted many of his supporters early the next morning on their way to work to offer his thanks. He did not consider it his victory alone, but rather a triumph for the civil rights movement. He recalled, "It made me feel good just to imagine the satisfaction Martin would have felt about this election." Had King been alive, he probably would have agreed with John Lewis, who later described the significance of the 1972 election as follows: "I was ecstatic. Barbara Jordan of Texas also won a congressional seat that year, but Texas is not really the South, not the way Alabama, Mississippi and Georgia are. Andy's ascension was cause for us all to celebrate . . . the Deep South's first black U.S. congressman of the century."[2]

On January 3, 1973, Young took the oath of office as a member of the Ninety-third Congress. He was appointed to the House Banking and Currency Committee and joined its Subcommittee on International Trade. He viewed the appointment as an opportunity to connect Atlanta to the world. With Atlanta's future in mind, he attended a seminar in Japan on commercial development. He also became an active participant in the Congressional Black Caucus (CBC), which had been founded in 1971 to address special concerns of African Americans. One of Young's priorities in Congress was to carry on the work begun five years earlier in the Poor People's Campaign. During his first month in office, the CBC attacked the Nixon administration for neglecting the rural poor. Young argued that insufficient funding for housing, jobs, and education in rural areas forced people to migrate to cities and compounded urban problems. He also joined the CBC in its quest to establish a national holiday honoring King.

While Andy Young enjoyed the excitement of his first weeks in Congress, Jean was home in Atlanta going through the final weeks of pregnancy. On February 15, she gave birth to Andrew Jackson Young III, whom the family soon began calling "Bo." Jean had continued teaching until very close to delivery, and she returned to the classroom soon afterward. She stayed in Atlanta until the end of the school year, so Young flew back nearly every weekend to see her. He also wanted to maintain contacts with his constituency, and he enjoyed spending time with his newborn son. Jean later recalled that it was helpful for her occasionally to get some time away from Bo: "So Andrew would take Bo to Congress with him, and he'd sleep on a little rug under Andrew's desk."[3]

Although Young spent most of his time during his first year in Congress working on domestic issues, he did make some attempts to influence U.S. foreign policy, beginning with policy toward Southern Rhodesia. In 1965, Ian Smith, the leader of Southern Rhodesia, had unilaterally declared its independence from Great Britain. The United Nations imposed sanctions against Smith's rebel regime, and the Lyndon Johnson administration actively supported the sanctions. Most important, the United States stopped importing chrome from Southern Rhodesia. The sanctions against Southern Rhodesia were not a high priority for the Nixon administration. Due to the indifference of Nixon and the legislative skill of Senator Harry Byrd Jr. (I-Va.), the United States reversed its policy and renewed chrome imports in the fall of 1971.

With the Byrd Amendment, the United States joined Portugal and South Africa as the only nations openly violating the sanctions against Southern Rhodesia. Led by Representative Charles Diggs (D-Mich.), the CBC and a few liberal allies in Congress quickly mounted an effort to repeal the Byrd Amendment. The debate over chrome imports became a central foreign policy issue during the late 1970s. In May 1973, the issue attracted relatively little attention in the House of Representatives, but Young joined the small group that cosponsored a bill to halt the chrome imports and return the United States to compliance with the UN sanctions. An identical bill began moving steadily toward approval in the Senate, but the House did not address the issue until 1974.

Throughout the early 1970s, the most contentious foreign policy issue remained the war in Vietnam. In late June 1973, the House considered an amendment to an appropriations bill that would have funded the bombing of Cambodia until August 15. Young, carrying on his opposition to fighting in Southeast Asia, eloquently opposed the policy. He led a group of twenty-five freshmen legislators who employed tactics from the civil rights movement. Young recalled that they "went into the Speaker's office to demand that we have a vote on the cutoff of funds for the bombing of Cambodia. That amounted to a kind of demonstration, very much like a civil rights demonstration."[4] They succeeded in getting a vote.

In the ensuing floor debate, Young proclaimed that "this amendment is clearly a vote for 45 more dark days of destruction—45
days more of weakening of the American economy, 45 more days
of obliterating villages and killing and injuring civilians in Cambodia, 45 more days of bombardment that has cost as much as $4.5
million a day." Young then wondered how many schools, homes,
and health centers could be built with that much money instead.
He also contended that previous bombing had been unconstitutional and illegal. He concluded: "I can not vote to approve of
spending for another single day of this bombing in Southeast Asia,
this waste of resources and human life."[5] Young and like-minded
legislators eventually prevailed, and Congress prohibited all bombing of Cambodia after August 15.

   Young's first-term positions regarding U.S. policy toward
Southern Rhodesia and Cambodia reflected his goal of promoting
racial justice and peace around the world. This philosophy, which
he had refined during his days with King, also inspired his initiative regarding American relations with Portugal in 1973. Since the
early 1960s, Portuguese forces had battled rebels in Angola and
Mozambique, as Portugal desperately tried to retain its colonial
empire. Since 1946, the United States had supplied its Cold War
ally, Portugal, with over $570 million in military and economic as-
sistance, which Portugal employed in part against the guerrillas in
southern Africa. The commander of Portuguese forces in
Mozambique, after visiting American bases and meeting with General William Westmoreland, utilized many tactics that the U.S. military had been using in Vietnam. Bulldozers cleared trails, troops
herded peasants into strategic hamlets, and chemical bombs oblit-
erated the food supply. Like the Vietnamese, the people of
Mozambique were determined to cast off outside control. Led by
Samora Machel, who succeeded Young's old friend, Eduardo
Mondlane, following his assassination in 1969 by the Portuguese
secret police, the Mozambique Liberation Front (FRELIMO) was
gaining ground in the summer of 1973.

   On July 26, in his first real foreign policy initiative in Congress,
Young proposed an amendment to the foreign aid bill that would
prohibit Portugal from using U.S. funds to support its military operations in southern Africa. In his opinion, Portugal's attempts to
maintain colonial rule in Angola and Mozambique were simply
wrong. Over twenty years after the nationalist struggle for independence had begun sweeping over Asia and Africa, Portugal remained intransigent. Young concluded, "Instead of ceding to the

vast majority of the people of Mozambique, Angola, and Guinea-Bissau their legitimate rights to control of those African lands, the Portuguese colonialist government to this day pursues a policy of terror, massacre, torture, and violence."[6]

First and foremost, Young saw this as a moral issue, but he also grasped the concrete strategic aspects of the situation. He warned that U.S. support for the Portuguese operations could eventually draw American troops directly into the fighting, as support for the French in the 1950s had drawn Americans into Vietnam. When other legislators contended that his amendment could jeopardize American access to its air base in the Azores, which was leased from Portugal, he countered that Portugal needed us more than we needed them. In other words, Young believed that the United States could take a moral stance against Portugal's Africa policy without harming its own national security.

Young concluded his case by putting U.S. policy toward Portugal into the broader context of his international vision: "I consider it my duty to speak out against the repression of human rights, wherever it is found. . . . I urge the House today . . . to lead our country on a consistent and healthy new course against injustice in the world, to put the Portuguese government on notice that this is the year 1973 and the days of violent colonialist rule are over."[7] Young's amendment passed, 69 to 57. The following year a new government seized control of Portugal and began the process of ending the wars in Africa and recognizing the independence of Angola and Mozambique. Young's amendment probably had little effect on this chain of events, but it did serve to place U.S. policy symbolically in line with and reinforce developments in Portugal.

Young did not initiate any other foreign policy legislation in 1973, but he did weigh in on several important topics. He joined his colleagues in overriding Nixon's veto of the War Powers Act. With this act, Congress required the president to notify them promptly of any overseas commitments of U.S. troops and mandated that the president get specific approval from Congress for any intervention after sixty days. Young also opposed military aid to South Vietnam, appropriations for the B-1 bomber, antiballistic missiles, and nerve gas. Perhaps his most significant vote of 1973 was in favor of Gerald Ford as the new vice president, whom Nixon had named to replace Spiro Agnew, who resigned when an investigation determined that he had accepted bribes as governor of Maryland. Not only did Young vote for Ford, but he also gave a speech in his support. He believed that in the midst of Watergate and other scandals, it was not the time for partisanship, and that Ford was an honorable colleague. Young was the only black member of Congress to support Ford, and his courage in doing so earned him the respect of fellow CBC members Ronald Dellums (D–Ca.) and Shirley Chisholm (D–N.Y.). Young's support for Ford also earned Ford's gratitude and opened the door for the Georgia Democrat to have more influence with the White House than other congressional Democrats.

Congressional Black Caucus: (sitting) Augustus Hawkins, Cardiss Collins, Charles Rangel, Yvonne Burke, William Clay, Parren Mitchell; (standing) Ron Dellums, Robert Nix, John Conyers, Shirley Chisholm, Andrew Young, Stan Scott; Ralph Metcalfe, Walter Fauntroy, Barbara Jordan, Louis Stokes, Charles Diggs; White House, August 1974. *Courtesy of Gerald Ford Library*

Overall, Young's first year in Congress had been quite successful. His skills as a mediator, which had been central to his role in the civil rights movement, garnered admiration on Capitol Hill. He operated within the Black Caucus much as he had within the Southern Christian Leadership Conference. According to Chisholm, "In the Black Caucus, Andy will sit and listen, then in a very cool way will kind of get us all together." Furthermore, the faith in negotiating privately, that he had demonstrated again and again in the 1960s, also paid off in Congress. Representative Morris Udall (D–Ariz.) praised Young for dealing directly with his colleagues in private. As a semicelebrity associated with Martin Luther King, Young could have held press conferences to generate publicity for his causes. Instead, observed Udall, "he plays the inside game, works within Congress, and does it effectively."[8]

During his first year in Congress, Young also visited Jamaica and Panama. Those trips further convinced him of the need for the United States to continue providing financial assistance to less-developed regions of the world. Throughout 1974 he expressed this sentiment in the House, beginning with a January debate over funding for the International Development Agency (IDA). He refuted the argument that in providing foreign aid or loans the United States was neglecting its own people. First, maintaining positive relations with less-developed countries was necessary to ensure access to a wide range of important natural resources such as oil and strategic minerals. Helping nations in Africa or Central America would ultimately help American citizens. In exchange for allowing the United States to import natural resources, nations often requested IDA funds to build roads or provide electricity. Such improvements produced long-term economic benefits by making less-developed nations better able to participate in the world economy. Furthermore, he argued that the poor in the United States were much better off than the poor in less-developed countries: "We are talking about a distinction between relative poverty which we have in this Nation, where we have people with $1,000 to $3,000 a year income, and in aid to these developing nations we are talking about, aid to countries where the per capita income is less than $100 per year."[9]

While visiting Panama, Young had met with many students and government officials, all of whom requested more support from the United States primarily to develop their economy beyond the canal. He talked at length with the Administrator of Planning and Development in Panama, Nick Barletta. Barletta had studied under George Shultz at the University of Chicago and was making progress in many ways: developing a banking industry, supporting housing construction, and increasing food production. Young concluded that such good work deserved additional support. At the time the United States was paying Panama just under $2 million annually for use of the canal, and Young advocated a substantial increase in the annual payment to fund projects that would diversify Panama's economy.

While voicing additional support for foreign aid in 1974, Young contended that the proposed $375 million contribution to the IDA was "an investment in the peace of a new kind of world order."[10] As relations with the Soviet Union improved and the likelihood of armed conflict decreased, the danger to peace came less from Communist revolts and more from international instability caused by poverty. He pointed, in particular, to the example of India. Although it had recently become a nuclear power, India faced staggering challenges in agriculture, transportation, industry, power, and population control. For both strategic and economic reasons it was in the best interests of the United States to promote stability and development in India, and Young saw the IDA as a key vehicle for doing so.

Young's support for foreign aid reflected his long-held international philosophy that peace and racial justice should be the primary goals. This view came in great part from his Christian faith, which remained central to his life. In February he delivered the House's closing prayer, and his words underlined this connection. He asked God, "Help us to use the power and might with which Thou has blessed us . . . to feed the hungry, to educate the children, to heal the sick." Young's outlook on foreign affairs during his years in Congress also reflected his desire to carry on the work of his late friend, Martin Luther King. On the sixth anniversary of King's death, on April 4, 1974, Young proclaimed that King's "work for nonviolent social change and human justice will continue for generations, until his dream is completely fulfilled."[11]

A few days after the solemn observance of King's death, Young had a relaxing evening back in Atlanta. Still an active athlete and an avid sports fan, he attended the Atlanta Braves baseball game on April 9. Other celebrities in attendance included Sammy Davis Jr., Pearl Bailey, and Georgia Governor Jimmy Carter. They had all come to watch Hank Aaron, who started the evening tied with the legendary Babe Ruth with 714 career home runs. Aaron did not disappoint them. Just after 9 o'clock he hammered a fastball into the left-field bullpen and broke Ruth's record. It would have been an incredible accomplishment for any baseball player, but the fact that Aaron was black and had persevered through racist harassment and even death threats made it more remarkable. In praising Aaron on the floor of Congress the next day, Young emphasized the slugger's courage in the face of racism. He had not allowed "the abuse against him and his fellow black athletes to deter him from his historic purpose."[12] Since watching the newsreels of Jesse Owens's triumphs at Berlin as a youngster, Young had understood the way sports could help battle racism and promote understanding, a realization he retained long after his years in Congress.

Fighting for racial justice continued to play a key role in Young's foreign policy initiatives regarding southern Africa. As Portugal terminated its fighting in Angola and Mozambique in 1974, Young's attention turned increasingly to Southern Rhodesia and South Africa. First, he advocated ending the quota for imports of sugar from South Africa to demonstrate that the U.S. Congress did not support the apartheid policies of its government. He contended that any progress made against apartheid had resulted in part from the economic sanctions against South Africa initiated by English and American churches. Further sanctions, such as ending the sugar quota, would "encourage those forces working within South Africa to bring about change without violence." Much of Young's argument against the sugar quota for South Africa turned on morality, but he concluded with a practical point. Quotas had been initiated to assist struggling nations. With the incredible rise in the price of gold, South Africa was certainly not struggling. Appealing to his Republican colleagues concerned about balancing the budget and being fiscally conservative, Young concluded: "I ask what business do we have supporting a nation as rich as that with our taxpayers' money?"[13]

Young also blended realistic and moral arguments in his attempts to reinstate sanctions against Southern Rhodesian chrome. His CBC colleague, Charles Diggs, led the effort in the House to repeal the Byrd Amendment. Diggs's staff corresponded with over a thousand black groups throughout the United States to garner support for repeal, but victory would not be easy. The leader of the Ford Motor Company, Henry Ford II, explained that he needed large quantities of high-quality chrome to build catalytic converters in 1974. Environmental laws necessitated these new features, thereby increasing the automobile industry's consumption of chrome. Repealing the Byrd Amendment and thus stopping the import of Southern Rhodesian chrome could raise prices and hurt the auto industry. In spite of Ford's opposition, the House Committee on Foreign Affairs recommended repeal on June 27 by a vote of 25 to 9.

Winning a floor vote proved more difficult, as a poll in July of 166 representatives showed 104 opposed to repeal, 30 in favor, and 32 undecided. Before risking a general vote in the face of such discouraging evidence, Young appealed for more public support in a letter to constituents and House colleagues. He began his call for repeal by describing the institutionalized racism in Southern Rhodesia, where the white minority led by Ian Smith dominated the politics and economy. As with his argument in favor of ending South Africa's sugar quota, he saw sanctions against Southern Rhodesian chrome as a way for Congress to signal its disapproval of a morally objectionable system.

For those who viewed foreign policy as a more practical undertaking, he reminded them that Secretary of State Henry Kissinger favored repeal. He then elaborated on the long-term strategic benefits of reimposing sanctions against Southern Rhodesia. Most African nations desired such tough sanctions, and many of them possessed valuable resources that the United States needed. Nigeria, for example, supplied 25 percent of U.S. oil imports. Thus repealing the Byrd Amendment would improve U.S. relations with key black African states such as Nigeria. Young cautioned that the United States could not "afford to continue our defiance of African sensibilities," and emphasized that "now is the time to begin to build positive relationships on the Continent of Africa."[14]

Young had presented a powerful case in favor of repeal. A few weeks later Nixon resigned, ushering Gerald Ford into the Oval Office. Ford's press secretary soon announced that the president supported the repeal efforts. Perhaps more important, Henry Ford II reversed his earlier position and advocated an end to chrome imports from Southern Rhodesia. He acknowledged that the Ford Motor Company still needed large quantities of high-quality chrome, but decided foreign policy concerns should take precedence. Young and Diggs were quite pleased by Ford's pronouncement, and they emphasized it in their ongoing efforts. Still, support for retention of the Byrd Amendment remained formidable. Four times the repeal forces scheduled a vote, but, fearful of defeat, each time at the last minute they backed down. On December 19, 1974, they conceded and opted to start over from scratch the following year. The attempt initiated in the Senate early in 1973 to repeal the Byrd Amendment had failed.

Although President Ford officially favored repeal, he had not gotten involved in the debate in 1974. Many other issues took precedence. Perhaps his most controversial action was his decision to grant Nixon a full pardon, which drew criticism from every black member of Congress except Young. As much as he had disliked Nixon and his policies, he could not be vengeful. He saw Ford's pardon as an example of Christian forgiveness, and explained that "It's the preacher in me coming out."[15]

Young also endorsed Ford's treatment of those who had left the country to avoid being drafted to fight in Vietnam. Young believed that draft dodgers who returned to the United States should be granted amnesty, rather than serve jail time. He forwarded a report on amnesty from the American Civil Liberties Union to Ford in late August and expressed his personal support for such a measure. On September 16, Ford announced an amnesty program. He established the Presidential Clemency Board, which received applications for pardons from about 21,500 men. The board determined that 13,000 were worthy of consideration, and Ford issued immediate pardons to 42 percent of them.[16] Ford's action, popular among liberals, seemed to justify Young's willingness to give him a chance when Ford was chosen vice president and when he pardoned Nixon. Young's constituents evidently approved of his stance on most of these issues, and in November they reelected him with an impressive 72 percent of the vote.

Shortly after the elections, Young took advantage of an opportunity to pursue his interests in Africa. In December he visited South Africa for the first time. The trip was paid for by the United Church of Christ's Commission on Racial Justice, and thus it was not directly related to Young's duties as a congressman. However, it revealed much about the new approach to international relations that he had brought to Washington. The journey resulted from Young's close friendship with tennis superstar Arthur Ashe. The two played tennis together and, when Ashe won at Wimbledon, Young held a reception for him in Washington. Young later officiated at Ashe's wedding. Their mutual commitment to working for racial justice around the world was a key component of their friendship. Ashe had long opposed apartheid, and when he learned he was going to play in a tournament in South Africa, he asked Young to accompany him.

While in South Africa, Young decided to visit the black antiapartheid activist Robert Sobukwe. Sobukwe, leader of the Pan-African Congress, had been imprisoned from 1960 to 1969. In 1974, he was confined to the mining town of Kimberley and prohibited from public speaking or writing, an apartheid restriction known as being "banned." Young considered Sobukwe a South African equivalent of Martin Luther King, and the meeting strongly reinforced this opinion. Young asked Sobukwe how he could still be hopeful about a peaceful solution in South Africa after all he had endured at the hands of the apartheid regime. Sobukwe responded, "Well, it's because I know that we will prevail." He was inspired by the experience of African Americans, and added, "I read *Uncle Tom's Cabin*, and I decided that if you chaps could live through that and come to where you have now come, there's no question that we will be able to overcome in South Africa as well."[17]

Greatly impressed, Young asked how he could be of assistance in the struggle. Sobukwe replied that black South Africans had to fight their own battles. When Young insisted on helping somehow, Sobukwe asked him to facilitate an education in the United States for his two oldest children. Young offered to take them into his home in Atlanta to attend college there, and Sobukwe gladly accepted. His daughter Miliswa and son Dinilesizwe flew to Atlanta in June 1975 without a hitch, as Young had asked the U.S. consul general in Johannesburg to see personally that they got out of South Africa smoothly. They moved into the Youngs' house and stayed for two years. After starting their higher education at Atlanta Junior College, where Jean was teaching, Miliswa went on to study biology at Spelman, and Dini majored in engineering at Morehouse.[18]

Young's help and hospitality were kind acts, evidence of his (and Jean's) personal warmth and generosity. But these acts also revealed much about Young's potential as a completely new voice in U.S. foreign relations. As a result of the civil rights movement of the 1960s, African Americans began directly to influence foreign policy in the 1970s. Black policymakers who had been influenced by King acted in unprecedented ways, and Young personified this. Not only did he speak out against apartheid and racial injustice throughout the world, but he had actually opened his home to the children of one of South Africa's political prisoners. It is extremely difficult to imagine even the most liberal foreign policy figures in the 1960s, such as G. Mennen Williams or Robert Kennedy, hosting Sobukwe's children in their homes. This new reality spoke volumes for the different relationships that Young could forge with world leaders of color. He was truly on his way to becoming a civil rights ambassador.

Back in Washington in February 1975, Young was sworn in for his second term in the House. Having gained the respect of his colleagues, Young became the first black appointed to the powerful House Rules Committee. He remained involved in foreign policy issues, particularly those related to Africa. Early in the session he jumped into the debate over the nomination of Nathaniel Davis to be Assistant Secretary of State for African Affairs. He testified before the Senate Foreign Relations Committee and expressed his opposition to Davis. It was not an easy decision for Young, who acknowledged that Davis had had a long and distinguished career in the Foreign Service and had actually testified on Young's behalf in the past. Young pointed out that his opposition was not a criticism of Davis's character or ability, but solely of his former position as ambassador to Chile during the CIA's involvement in overthrowing Salvador Allende.

Young contended that Africans would distrust Davis because of his association with the notorious CIA operation in Chile. He outlined three specific cases where Davis's involvement with the removal of Allende could be a liability. First, he discussed the situation in Southern Rhodesia, where war had recently broken out in earnest. He cited the efforts of Bishop Abel Muzorewa to find a peaceful solution, and argued that Davis would not be able to contribute constructively to such delicate negotiations. Second, he pointed to Angola, which had recently achieved independence from Portugal and where three liberation movements were competing for power. A major fear in Angola was that Cabinda Province might attempt to secede with foreign support, reminiscent of the attempts by Katanga Province to secede from Zaire in the 1960s. Allegations of CIA involvement with the murder of Patrice Lumumba in that case cast a long shadow, so Davis's connection with the CIA in Chile could engender suspicion among leaders in Angola. Young's concern over Angola was ironic, to say the least, since unbeknownst to him the CIA had already begun to intervene in the struggle there.

Finally, Young argued that Davis's background could cause problems for U.S. relations with Nigeria. In January 1975, Nigeria had become the number-one foreign supplier of oil to the United States, refusing to participate in the Middle East's embargo. Therefore, continuing friendship with Nigeria was extremely important. Although it was unlikely, Young felt it was possible that naming Davis assistant secretary could alienate Nigeria and endanger America's access to oil. He concluded, "I would just hate to see the albatross of American policy, whether you agree with it or not, in Latin America brought to the African Continent in such a way that it jeopardized the future development of relationships between the United States and the States of Africa."[19] Young's concerns about an "albatross" being carried to Africa proved prescient, but Davis was not to blame. Although he was approved as assistant secretary, he did not keep the job for long. After the CIA's involvement in Angola escalated in July, Davis resigned. Kissinger persuaded him to remain in the State Department and appointed him ambassador to Switzerland.

In February 1975, Young also participated in the debate over establishing a national holiday in honor of Martin Luther King. While advocating this measure, he emphasized King's support for world peace. He inserted for the record King's most famous criticism of the Vietnam War, his 1967 speech at the Riverside Church.

Young believed that even eight years later, U.S. policy toward Vietnam was still flawed, as the Ford administration had requested millions of dollars of military aid for Southeast Asia. He concluded, "Dr. King's warnings about the American involvement in Indochina" remained "relevant."[20] King's vision of peace and racial justice around the world remained in the forefront of Young's thinking, even as he participated in the turmoil on Capitol Hill.

In Congress, Young also sought to create interest in African nations, similar to that King had demonstrated in the 1950s and 1960s. On March 6, 1975, Ghana celebrated the eighteenth anniversary of its independence from England. The ceremony in 1957, which King had attended, had been a watershed for anticolonialism.Young praised the people of Ghana for their efforts at development and their desire to build closer relations with the United States. He cited an optimistic report on Ghana's economy furnished by Ambassador Samuel Quarm, and in closing he asserted, "It is a pleasure to congratulate Ambassador Quarm and the people of Ghana for their nation's achievements and progress, and to extend best wishes for continued success and leadership in Africa and the world."[21] The fact that a member of the U.S. Congress took the time to recognize the eighteenth anniversary of a small African nation reflected the new voice that Young brought to Washington, and the very different direction he envisioned for U.S. foreign relations.

Although this new foreign policy view was significant, most of Young's work in Congress focused on his constituents in Georgia. In March, he attempted unsuccessfully to secure federal funding for low-income housing at the Edgewood Redevelopment Project in Atlanta. Also in March, Young joined with Mayor Maynard Jackson in an effort to elicit federal support for an expansion of Atlanta's Hartsfield Airport. This was primarily a domestic issue, as it would provide thousands of additional jobs for the people of Atlanta. Yet airport expansion was also an international matter, since it could bring more foreign tourism and trade to the South. Young certainly grasped that potential, and making Atlanta a more international city remained one of his main goals for the ensuing twenty-five years.

Even as he became increasingly involved in the economic aspects of international relations, Young remained an outspoken critic of military intervention. In May, the Cambodian navy seized an American cargo ship, the *Mayaguez*, and held its thirty-nine crew members hostage. Secretary of State Kissinger saw this as an opportunity to demonstrate American strength in the wake of the collapse of South Vietnam, which had occurred just two weeks before. President Ford agreed, and sent a force of 175 marines. The crew of the *Mayaguez* had been released minutes before the marines landed. The operation went forward anyway, and 41 U.S. military personnel perished. In hindsight it is difficult to see this as any sort of success, but at the time, Ford was praised for acting firmly and defending America's honor. During the three days after the incident, the White House received 1,436 telegrams approving the action and only 170 criticizing it. In Congress, Young was one of the few who spoke against this "senseless" intervention.[22]

In addition to denouncing the use of force, Young espoused limiting the sale of weapons to foreign countries. In July 1975, the House debated whether or not to provide arms to Turkey, which had recently invaded Cyprus. Kissinger emphasized that it was imperative for national security that the United States stand by Turkey, an ally and member of NATO. Young contended that supporting Turkey could actually harm national interests. He pointed to the example of Portugal, which had used American aid and weapons to suppress its African colonies for many years. When the former colonies of Mozambique and Angola gained their independence, the new governments distrusted the United States and resented its past support for Portugal. Young suggested that sending arms to Turkey could have similar consequences. He had briefly considered supporting the sales, but reading about a separate $385 million weapons deal with Jordan had changed his mind. He observed, "There is no way to make peace by giving guns to everybody."[23] In Young's view, foreign assistance should instead focus on providing food and education to the less-developed countries.

Young had participated in a number of foreign policy debates in the first half of 1975, but his most significant involvement came in still another battle over policy toward Southern Rhodesia. As in previous years, the vast majority of congressional activity related to Southern Rhodesia in 1975 dealt with the chrome issue. In January, Representative Donald Fraser (D–Minn.) had introduced a bill to repeal the Byrd Amendment. On March 18, the Subcommittee on International Organizations approved the bill, 4 to 1. In July, the Foreign Affairs Committee recommended the bill 17 to 8, but the Armed Services Committee opposed it 29 to 7. As this third attempt to repeal the Byrd Amendment staggered toward a floor vote, very few legislators gave it close attention, and President Ford remained silent. Had the president taken up the cause and pushed the argument that supporting sanctions would serve long-term U.S.

interests, the Byrd Amendment might have been overturned in 1975, but Ford never joined the battle. Instead, the responsibility for repealing the Byrd measure fell onto the shoulders of Fraser, Charles Diggs, and Andrew Young.

On September 25, Young introduced Fraser's bill, House Resolution 1287, and initiated the debate. He summed up the bill's purpose: to stop the importation of chrome from Southern Rhodesia. This would return the United States to compliance with UN sanctions, which only the United States and South Africa were violating, and provide "firm indication of our fundamental belief in the cause of international law and justice."[24]

Several lawmakers opposed Young, most notably Representative Charles Bennet (D–Fla.). A World War II veteran and published author who had not missed a roll-call vote in twenty-two years, Bennet noted that the combined vote of the committees that had considered the bill was 37 to 24 against it. He contended that imposing sanctions on Southern Rhodesia was immoral, because it was interfering in the internal affairs of another country. Moreover, repealing the Byrd Amendment would make Americans dependent on Soviet chrome, which in turn could threaten our national security. Congressman Floyd Spence (R–S.C.) added that passing Fraser's bill would decrease the supply of chrome and therefore increase the price. In turn, that would raise the cost of many crucial U.S. military armaments such as tanks, missiles, planes, and submarines.

Young countered that Congress would not determine the flow of chrome from Southern Rhodesia, since the new government of Mozambique was about to close off its borders with Southern Rhodesia. Furthermore, South Africa was negotiating with the black leaders of Zambia and Mozambique in hopes of avoiding a widespread race war across southern Africa. If South Africa joined Mozambique in honoring the UN sanctions, Southern Rhodesia would be isolated, and no chrome would be exported regardless of congressional actions.

Young added that much was to be gained by supporting the efforts of nations such as Mozambique, as its new leader, Samora Machel, was respected and influential throughout Africa. Although Machel and other leaders in Mozambique were distrustful of the United States, many of them had been educated by Christian missionaries, and some even had attended schools in America. Newly independent countries such as Mozambique would welcome American assistance and stronger ties of friendship. Helping them get on their feet would in turn improve U.S. relations with their allies, such as Nigeria, which possessed immense quantities of oil. In the long run, repealing the Byrd Amendment and rejoining the UN sanctions would benefit U.S. strategic and economic interests. Young warned, "I do not think we want to write off all of black Africa with its tremendous wealth and mineral resources and its moral right to freedom and dignity . . . for a little bit of chrome in Rhodesia which we do not need anyway. We have enough chrome in our junkyards to recycle for the next dozen years."[25]

Young's efforts in September 1975 again fell short, and the House defeated Fraser's bill 209 to 187. Had Young appealed directly to President Ford in the weeks leading up to the vote, he might have been able to get the president involved. White House staffer Jack Marsh had noted earlier in the month that "Andy Young is one of the President's favorites in Congress."[26] Even with presidential activism, however, it seems unlikely that Fraser's effort to repeal the Byrd Amendment would have succeeded in 1975. In November, White House aides determined that only four representatives were willing to consider switching their votes to support repeal. Ford thereafter advised Fraser and his allies to give up the fight for the time being. In the only significant area of direct U.S. relations with Southern Rhodesia in 1975, the Byrd Amendment survived, chrome imports continued, and the United States violated the UN sanctions for another year.

Undaunted, Young maintained his focus on African issues. In late November, he visited Zambia, Kenya, and Nigeria. Leaders of those countries talked enthusiastically of their growing economic power, both as suppliers of resources and as markets for American goods. Many developed nations such as Germany and Japan were working hard to get a slice of the economic pie in Africa. For example, both Germany and Japan had already joined the African Development Fund (ADF). Upon returning to Washington in early December, Young urged his colleagues in Congress to approve U.S. membership in that organization. He contended that the entrance fee of $25 million was a bargain, and that membership was necessary to compete with other nations. For example, a Michigan manufacturer was bidding against German and Japanese firms for a contract to supply $125 million in trucks to Nigeria. Another deal, in which Nigeria would purchase 200,000 pairs of combat boots from a Tennessee firm, was being discussed.

Young emphasized that joining the ADF would increase American contacts with economic decision-makers in countries such as

Nigeria, and put the United States on an equal footing with competitors such as Germany. Young insisted that fellow members of Congress not view the ADF as another form of international aid, but rather as an investment of American capital that would reap large profits in the long run. Although he had reservations about advocating the involvement of U.S. corporations in less-developed countries, he deemed "American multinational corporations . . . better than German and Japanese," even though it was "a very relative thing."[27]

Young's appraisal of the ADF and its potential benefits for U.S. companies helped win the day, and the House voted 249 to 166 in favor of American participation. The bill then went to the Senate for debate on March 30, 1976. Senators Hubert Humphrey (D–Minn.) and Edmund Muskie (D–Maine) strongly advocated American participation in the ADF; Senators Harry Byrd Jr. (I–Va.) and Jesse Helms (R–N.C.) were staunchly opposed. Helms decried African governments as corrupt and socialist. He initially proposed that the United States not support the fund at all, but then settled for an amendment prohibiting any ADF dollars from reaching Uganda and its notorious dictator, Idi Amin. The Senate approved the amended measure, and the United States joined the ADF.

Although the decision to support the ADF pleased Young, revelations regarding Angola certainly did not. In December 1975, the *New York Times* published a front-page report describing CIA involvement in the Angolan civil war. The CIA had first become involved in July 1974, and in December of that year, Ford and Kissinger had given their approval for the continuation of the covert operations. In January 1975, the CIA provided $300,000 to Holden Roberto's National Front for the Liberation of Angola (FNLA), America's primary ally. The CIA later extended small amounts of aid to Jonas Savimbi's National Union for the Total Independence of Angola (UNITA), which received major support from South Africa. Both of these groups were fighting Agostinho Neto's Popular Movement for the Liberation of Angola (MPLA).

In spite of CIA support for the opposition groups and intervention by Joseph Mobutu's troops from Zaire, Neto's MPLA seized the capital of Luanda in early July 1975. As a result, Kissinger decided to escalate U.S. aid, opting to spend nearly $50 million in Angola without consulting Congress. Also in July 1975, Neto requested aid from Cuba, and Fidel Castro initially provided $100,000. In August, Castro decided to augment this monetary support with about five hundred military advisers. The Cuban advisers arrived in Angola in October and helped repel an attack by Roberto's FNLA and their Zairean allies. To further complicate the situation, South Africa launched a full-scale invasion of Angola in mid-October, hoping to topple Neto's MPLA. The South African forces advanced rapidly, and clashed with MPLA soldiers and their Cuban advisers in a fierce battle at Catengue on November 2. Reports of the major South African presence at Catengue persuaded Castro to send a full complement of combat troops. A battalion of Elite Special Forces departed from Cuba on November 7 and entered the fray on November 10. The Cuban intervention quickly turned the tide, crushing Roberto's FNLA and thwarting the South African invasion.[28]

These developments alarmed Kissinger, and in late November he instructed the CIA to ask for $28 million from Congress for operations in Angola. The CIA made the request in a secret hearing, but the facts about U.S. involvement in Angola began to leak to the press. During the debate over American membership in the African Development Fund on December 9, Young provided this assessment: "Frankly, we have got another CIA-run war in Angola matched with equal brutality by the influx of the Soviet Union."[29] He contended that the harm done to America's reputation in Africa by CIA activities in Angola intensified the need for U.S. support for economic development in other African nations. He presciently predicted that even Angola would turn to the United States for technical assistance for drilling oil and mining uranium eventually, and the sooner we stopped inciting war, the sooner such development could begin.

A week later Young strongly denounced Kissinger's "dangerous" Angolan policy. During his November visit to Africa, Young had discussed the war in Angola with Zambian President Kenneth Kaunda and others involved in the struggle. They disapproved of the CIA intervention. Young agreed and asserted that it was "crucial that the Congress act now to cut off the flow of U.S. funding to various factions in Angola and that all U.S. military involvement in the way of armaments and supplies be immediately discontinued." He urged Congress to call for cessation of the military interventions by all other nations, such as Cuba and South Africa, and to support an African-brokered political settlement. Above all, he wanted Congress to stop the U.S. intervention in Angola: "To continue along the path of covert or overt intervention there will be a monstrous mistake."[30]

Many other members of Congress agreed with Young, and Senator Dick Clark (D–Iowa) proposed an amendment blocking all

covert aid to Angola. On December 19, the Senate passed his amendment, 54 to 22. On January 27, 1976, the House considered a similar
amendment to end covert aid to Angola, and Young again spoke
forcefully. He excoriated the CIA's activities in Angola as just another in a long line of ill-advised covert operations that included
those in Guatemala and Chile. Young predicted that Angola would
adopt some form of socialist government, but that Soviet influence
would not prevail because the Russians did not get along well with
people of color. The sooner Angola stopped being a military struggle
and became an economic and cultural struggle instead, the sooner
the United States would become a positive influence. He contended
that war was not the answer, observing that "the only thing we are
doing is putting more weapons in to kill more people."[31] The
amendment passed the House by a resounding 323 to 99, and covert U.S. involvement in Angola ended. The FNLA evaporated, and
the Cuban-backed MPLA took control. Young and the vast majority of Congress had thwarted Kissinger's policy toward Angola.

Young's stance on Angola reflected much more than his views
about that specific situation. He thereby manifested his longtime
opposition to military intervention as the main form of U.S. foreign relations, and thus his position represented a continuation of
his antiwar work with Martin Luther King during the 1960s. A key
part of his and King's argument against the U.S. intervention in
Vietnam had been that it diverted funds from social programs.
Throughout the spring of 1976, Young applied this same reasoning
to U.S. foreign policy. He favored spending $25 million to help vic-
tims of an earthquake in Guatemala. He suggested that human
rights should be a central concern in U.S. relations with the military regimes in Chile and Argentina, and he advocated a reduction
in military assistance to foreign countries in general. Young urged
President Ford to champion American participation in the International Fund for Agricultural Development and the World Food
Council. He backed appropriations for the United States Information Agency's educational and cultural exchange programs. When
assaying U.S. foreign relations, Congressman Young clearly preferred books and bread to artillery and ammunition.

While Young promoted these issues during the spring of 1976,
Kissinger intervened diplomatically in the escalating conflict in
Southern Rhodesia. Approximately seven hundred guerrillas rep-
resenting Robert Mugabe's Zimbabwe African National Union
(ZANU) had infiltrated Southern Rhodesia from Mozambique in
January and intensified the violence. In February, Samora Machel

closed Mozambique's border with Southern Rhodesia, tightening the economic noose significantly. When talks between Ian Smith and the other major nationalist leader, Joshua Nkomo, broke down in March, Smith asserted on British television that he did not "believe in majority rule ever in Rhodesia—not in a thousand years."[32]

Joshua Nkomo and Henry Kissinger, Lusaka, Zambia, April 1976. *Courtesy of Gerald Ford Library*

Soon after this discouraging remark, British Prime Minister James Callaghan delineated a plan for resolving the Southern Rhodesian crisis. If Smith would agree to four conditions, the British would oversee a constitutional convention to plan Southern Rhodesia's independence. The conditions were: the principle of majority rule; black suffrage within two years; no independence before majority rule; and timely negotiations. Not surprisingly, Smith rejected Callaghan's terms outright. Kissinger, however, praised them as a "most constructive approach" and pledged a major effort "to help all parties to return to the negotiating table."[33] Thereafter, Kissinger took the lead in the international mediation effort regarding Southern Rhodesia and adopted Callaghan's proposals as a framework. By mid-April he had decided to visit Zambia and articulate a new U.S. policy toward southern Africa.

As Kissinger departed for Africa on April 23, he announced that the new U.S. policy sought a transition from white rule in Southern Rhodesia to a majority-ruled Zimbabwe. He reached Zambia on April 26 and met with President Kenneth Kaunda that evening. After the two had talked for a while, Joshua Nkomo was ushered into the room to discuss Southern Rhodesia. Nkomo later recalled, "I spent about seven minutes with Kissinger . . . by the end I only knew that whatever he wanted, it was not what I wanted. He struck me as clever, of course, but unpleasant and untrustworthy."[34] Evidently, Kissinger did not intend to befriend Nkomo or deal with him as an equal in negotiations. He had no interest in hearing Nkomo's ideas about how to reach a settlement. Young's friendly style in later meetings with Nkomo would cast the negative impact of Kissinger's approach into bold relief.

Kissinger's public pronouncements the following day, nevertheless, were remarkably similar to Young's foreign policy vision. He opened his incredible address by espousing three broad, long-term goals for Africa—peace, economic development, and racial justice. He added that the United States supported African solutions for African problems, and he pointed to American history as an example of the possibility of achieving racial justice. He began a description of the new U.S. policy toward Southern Rhodesia by seconding Callaghan's plan—majority rule within two years, then independence. As for the United States, it would refrain from providing the Smith regime with any support whatsoever and would urge Smith to negotiate a majority-rule settlement rapidly. Moreover, Kissinger promised that the Ford administration would push Congress to repeal the Byrd Amendment.[35] His points resembled Young's views on Southern Rhodesia so closely that the speech sounded as if Young and his allies had written it.

Perhaps unaware of the contents of Kissinger's speech in Zambia or unwilling to believe his ears if he had heard it, Young sought confirmation from the Ford administration about their policy toward Southern Rhodesia. On May 19 he sent a letter containing ten specific questions to National Security Council staffer Jeanne Davis. Among his key concerns were whether or not the Ford administration would support an internal settlement between Smith and tribal leaders that omitted the nationalist forces, and whether there was any possibility of sending U.S. troops to support Smith if the Cubans intervened on the side of the guerrillas. Davis assured him that the Ford administration did not favor an internal settlement and was not considering the use of troops. She also asserted the administration's intent to call for repeal of the Byrd Amendment and to press for a peaceful solution in Southern Rhodesia that met the guidelines for majority rule laid out by Prime Minister Callaghan.[36]

Young must have been pleased by this response, as it outlined a policy nearly identical to the one that he had been advocating and that he would later help implement. In any case, for the rest of 1976, Young and his allies in Congress refrained from initiatives regarding Southern Rhodesia, postponing their next assault on the Byrd Amendment until after the fall elections. The White House also remained inactive, content to leave southern African diplomacy to Kissinger and his subordinates at the State Department. Kissinger, in fact, was making considerable progress with his plans to use South Africa to force Smith to accept a settlement. In late June he met with South African Prime Minister John Vorster in the Bavarian mountains of West Germany and discussed Southern Rhodesia at length. Most important, Vorster agreed to pull the plug on Smith to foster a settlement that would lead to majority rule.

For Kissinger, this was just another example of balance-of-power diplomacy. He viewed working with Vorster on Southern Rhodesia as essentially no different from working with Communist China to promote détente with the Soviet Union and peace in Vietnam. For blacks in Africa and in the United States, however, his working with the leader of apartheid South Africa was generally unacceptable. Recent events in Soweto, the impoverished black township outside Johannesburg, had rendered working with Vorster even less acceptable. On June 16, some fifteen thousand school children in Soweto had staged a peaceful demonstration against apartheid education policies, only to be met by bullets from the security forces that killed 58 of them. News of the massacre prompted rioting across South Africa, and police crackdowns left at least 575 dead and 2,389 wounded.

In a late August statement to Congress, Young denounced the Vorster regime and its security forces for this atrocious conduct. He stated, "South Africa should be made to face the reality that the interests of the United States are not coterminous nor reconcilable with those of the present Vorster government." He urged U.S. bankers and businesspersons to cease their dealings with such an oppressive state, whose white leaders obviously feared change. On the other hand, Young saw the protests as a clear sign that the blacks of South Africa wanted to end apartheid, and he believed it was time that Americans took a firm stand in support of them. Young concluded his statement by criticizing Kissinger for working with Vorster and for practicing "a bankrupt personal diplomacy."[37]

In an early September letter, Young appealed to his constituents with the same message. He reported, "In view of the terrible violation of life in South Africa . . . I feel that we must demonstrate our concern about the people of South Africa." He then pointed out that Kissinger was carrying on secret negotiations with Vorster. The congressman urged his constituents to write Kissinger and protest the apartheid government's brutality: "Please let him know that you oppose that racist regime in its repression toward its majority population and that you are for majority rule and social justice in South Africa." He then outlined in considerable detail the extreme hardship of life in Soweto, where at least four hundred thousand people lived without real homes. He concluded, "We must begin to play a more aggressive role in helping to fashion a responsible U.S. commitment to African aspirations and self-liberation."[38]

Later that month, Young took action along those lines. During the annual Congressional Black Caucus weekend, he and Charles Diggs convened about thirty black leaders for a discussion of Kissinger's approach to Southern Rhodesia. During the discussions, two Diggs staffers, Herschelle Challenor and Randall Robinson, emerged as key players in U.S. relations with Africa. When the group decided to form a lobbying organization for progressive policies toward Africa, they asked Robinson to chair the working group. The new entity was incorporated in July 1977 and named TransAfrica; it made a crucial contribution to enacting tough sanctions against South Africa in the 1980s. Helping to found TransAfrica was certainly one of Young's most important contributions during his four years in Congress.

In spite of the criticism from Young and other black leaders in the United States and Africa about his working with the South African government, Kissinger continued the same approach to negotiating a settlement in Southern Rhodesia. In mid-September he returned to southern Africa and met with Kaunda in Zambia and then Vorster in South Africa. On September 19, he confronted Ian Smith. After lecturing Smith and his cohorts on their grim predicament, Kissinger unveiled a five-point plan that required majority rule within two years. Smith accepted the plan, but only under the condition that Kissinger get black approval for a crucial amendment. The minister of defense and the minister of law and order had to be white for the duration of the interim government. Kissinger approved the amendment, and Smith flew back to Salisbury to announce the plan.

While Smith made the historic announcement that he had agreed to a plan that would eventually bring majority rule to Southern Rhodesia, Kissinger met with Kaunda and Nkomo in Zambia.

When they learned of the amendment that would keep the military and police under white control during the transition period, both were visibly dismayed. Nkomo in particular objected to Kissinger's methods and later recalled that the secretary of state's "southern Africa proposals were not really concerned with African problems at all, but with super-power politics."[39] There was the rub. Kissinger had not cleared the plan with Nkomo or other black leaders before offering it to Smith.

To make matters worse, Kissinger then informed Vorster that the black leaders had accepted the plan, which simply was not true. In hopes of achieving another dramatic diplomatic triumph, Kissinger had operated in an arrogant and disingenuous fashion. His tactics probably undermined any hope of a settlement in 1976, although there were many other obstacles in its path. In any case, a conference to discuss his plan opened in Geneva on October 28. Nkomo and Mugabe entered the discussions viewing the Kissinger plan as only the most basic starting point, while Smith claimed that the agreement was a done deal. Over the next seven weeks, the two sides never bridged the gap between their positions. The conference disbanded on December 14 with no resolution in sight.

By then, Kissinger was a lame duck and was removed from future negotiations regarding Southern Rhodesia when Jimmy Carter defeated Ford in the November presidential election. Kissinger's legacy was still significant. On the positive side of the ledger, he had set a precedent of top-level U.S. involvement in the Southern Rhodesian conflict and had forced Smith publicly to accept eventual majority rule. On the negative side, his unwillingness to listen to the concerns of black Africans and his occasional dishonesty sowed seeds of distrust of American officials. The task of regaining black Africans' confidence fell primarily to Andrew Young, whom President-elect Carter had chosen as U.S. ambassador to the United Nations. Young's background and style made him ideally suited to mend the fences Kissinger had broken. Although he agreed with Kissinger's strategy of placing a high priority on Africa and advocating racial justice, he dealt with people in an entirely different way. Instead of lecturing arrogantly, he listened patiently. Instead of bending the truth when it hindered his goals, he was honest to a fault.

As he was about to leave Congress and take a key position in the Carter administration, Young was well prepared to bring a new voice to U.S. foreign policy. He still believed strongly in the ideals of Martin Luther King that sought racial justice around the globe, and he still possessed the mediation skills he had honed as King's assistant. Moreover, during his four years in Congress he had demonstrated strong convictions about foreign relations. He had favored economic development while consistently opposing military intervention and covert CIA activity. He had championed progressive policies toward southern Africa by opposing aid to Portugal, blocking CIA funds to Angola, fighting for repeal of the Byrd Amendment, and helping to found TransAfrica. To a great extent, he had succeeded in bringing King's worldview onto the floor of Congress. During his tenure as UN ambassador, he attempted, with mixed results, to infuse that same vision into the foreign policy of the Carter administration.

Notes

1. Andrew Young interview with author, Atlanta, Georgia, March 2, 1994.
2. Andrew Young, *An Easy Burden: The Civil Rights Movement and the Transformation of America* (New York: HarperCollins, 1996), 520; John Lewis, *Walking with the Wind: A Memoir of the Movement* (New York: Simon & Schuster, 1998), 414–15.
3. Jean Young, quoted in James Haskins, *Andrew Young: A Man with a Mission* (New York: Lothrop, Lee, and Shepard, 1979), 114–15.
4. Paul Sherry, "A Sense of Place: A Conversation with Andrew Young," *Journal of Current Social Issues* 13 (Winter 1976): 45.
5. June 30, 1973, *Congressional Record*, 93d Cong., 1st sess., 22635.
6. July 26, 1973, ibid., 26192.
7. Ibid.
8. Chisholm and Udall, quoted in Carl Gardner, *Andrew Young: A Biography* (New York: Drake, 1978), 184.
9. January 23, 1974, *Congressional Record*, 93d Cong., 2d sess., 478.
10. July 2, 1974, ibid., 22013.
11. February 28, 1974, ibid., 4639; April 4, 1974, ibid., 9862.
12. April 9, 1974, ibid., 10407.
13. June 5, 1974, ibid., 17856.
14. Andrew Young to Dear Friend, July 19, 1974, Folder "Byrd Amend.—Gen.," Box 110, Charles Diggs Papers, Moorland–Spingarn Library, Howard University, Washington, DC.
15. Quoted, in Haskins, *Andrew Young*, 118.
16. Robert Schulzinger, *A Time for War: The United States and Vietnam, 1941–1975* (New York: Oxford University Press, 1997), 317–18.
17. Sobukwe, quoted in Haskins, *Andrew Young*, 125.
18. Benjamin Pogrund, *Sobukwe and Apartheid* (New Brunswick, NJ: Rutgers University Press, 1991), 325–26.
19. March 10, 1975, *Congressional Record*, 94th Cong., 1st sess., 5825.
20. February 19, 1975, ibid., 3626.
21. March 10, 1975, ibid., 5946.

22. May 14, 1975, ibid., 14426. Statistics regarding telegrams are cited in Robert Schulzinger, *Henry Kissinger: Doctor of Diplomacy* (New York: Columbia University Press, 1989), 204.

23. July 24, 1975, *Congressional Record*, 94th Cong., 1st sess., 24525.

24. September 25, 1975, ibid., 30184.

25. Ibid., 30196.

26. Jack Marsh, memo to Russ Rourke, September 4, 1975, folder "Andrew Young," box 107, John Marsh Files, Gerald R. Ford Library, Ann Arbor, MI (hereafter GF).

27. December 9, 1975, *Congressional Record*, 94th Cong., 1st sess., 39397.

28. Piero Gleijeses, *Conflicting Missions: Havana, Washington, and Africa, 1959–1976* (Chapel Hill: University of North Carolina Press, 2002), 250–72.

29. Ibid.

30. December 16, 1975, *Congressional Record*, 94th Cong., 1st sess., 41096–7.

31. January 27, 1976, ibid., 2d sess., 1041–3.

32. Smith, quoted in George Houser, *No One Can Stop the Rain: Glimpses of Africa's Liberation Struggle* (New York: Pilgrim Press, 1989), 329.

33. Excerpts from Kissinger's March 22 speech in Dallas in "Kissinger on U.S. Intentions on Rhodesia and Cuba," March 23, 1976, in folder "Rhodesia," box 124, Ron Nessen Papers, GF.

34. Joshua Nkomo, *Nkomo: The Story of My Life* (London: Methuen, 1984), 171.

35. Henry Kissinger, "Address at a Luncheon in the Secretary's Honor," State House, Lusaka, Zambia, April 27, 1976, folder "Kissinger's Trip to Africa," box 16, Michael Raoul-Duval Papers, GF.

36. Andrew Young to Jeanne Davis, May 19, 1976, and Davis to Young, June 22, 1976, folder "CO 124: Rhodesia (2) 6/1/76—1/20/77," box 43, White House Central File—Subject, GF.

37. August 31, 1976, *Congressional Record*, 94th Cong., 2d sess., 28706–7.

38. Andrew Young to "Dear Friend," September 2, 1976, folder "International Relations," box "Andrew Young Personality File," Atlanta History Center, Atlanta, Georgia.

39. Joshua Nkomo, *Nkomo*, 11.

4

Helping Carter with Human Rights and Africa

1976–1978

As Jimmy Carter's most influential black supporter, Andrew Young played a key role in the Georgia governor's election to the presidency in 1976. Soon after his victory, Carter asked Young to become the U.S. ambassador to the United Nations. Young accepted, primarily to help Carter emphasize human rights as a key element of foreign policy and to improve relations with the new African nations. During his first year at the UN, Young succeeded remarkably well on both fronts, particularly in regard to Africa. From the beginning of the Carter administration, the primary African issue was the conflict in Southern Rhodesia. Young worked closely with Carter and Secretary of State Cyrus Vance to develop the U.S. policy, which ultimately facilitated the transition to the new nation of Zimbabwe.

Young also helped design the Carter administration's strategy toward Namibia, which was seeking independence from South Africa. This policy was not successful in the short run, but it was a step in the right direction. Regarding South Africa itself, Young openly criticized the apartheid regime, called for sanctions, and led a move at the UN that resulted in the imposition of an arms embargo on that nation. Perhaps most important, Young engineered a drastic improvement in U.S. relations with Nigeria. Much of his success resulted from the strong personal ties he built with African leaders, culminating at the Malta Conference in January 1978, when he befriended Zimbabwean nationalists Joshua Nkomo and

Robert Mugabe. Young's civil rights background and informal style of diplomacy contributed to many foreign policy successes in the first year of Carter's presidency.

In 1974, Georgia Governor Jimmy Carter began sending out feelers for his presidential candidacy. Andrew Young, then a congressman from Atlanta, initially withheld support and was skeptical about the chances of a white southerner's becoming president. Gradually, Carter won him over. He first impressed Young with his sincere interest in African issues, requesting on several occasions that Young provide him with information on Namibia, South Africa, and Southern Rhodesia. In 1975, when Carter officially announced his plans to run, at the Hyatt Regency in downtown Atlanta, he asked Young to introduce him. Young complied, and at this point was warming to the governor. He feared that the Democratic nomination might come down to a contest between Carter and George Wallace, and he clearly preferred Carter.

Back in Congress in 1976, Young frequently was asked by his colleagues why he supported Carter. Many of them seemed to like the Georgia governor and wanted to back him, but some feared racist skeletons might tumble out of his closet at any minute. Assurances about Carter's stance on racial issues coming from Young, a respected veteran of the civil rights movement, alleviated their concerns. It had taken Young a long while to decide what he thought about Carter's relationship with African Americans. The turning point came at a meeting between Carter and the Congressional Black Caucus (CBC). The CBC met with all the Democratic candidates and asked them a series of questions, including a query about the number of blacks on their staffs. Most had just one or two black staffers, and one liberal Northerner had none. When the CBC asked Carter, he was unsure of the number. It turned out there were twenty-seven black staffers working for him, all involved in fundraising, media relations, community organizing, and other key aspects. From that point on, Young had no doubt about Carter's intentions to serve African Americans fairly.

Young accompanied fellow members of Congress on visits to forty-one states during the 1976 campaign, and steadily grew more optimistic about Carter's chances. He sensed that the American people, reeling in the aftermath of Vietnam and Watergate, desired an outsider candidate like Carter and responded to his themes of decency and honesty. The final showdown in Carter's quest for the Democratic nomination came in Pennsylvania, where traditional liberals and labor leaders backed Hubert Humphrey, the former vice president. Young called some close friends in Philadelphia, including the Reverend William Gray, and asked them to assemble ministers and labor activists to rally support for Carter. Young journeyed to the gathering at Bright Hope Church expecting to find perhaps thirty people, but instead he was greeted by more than four hundred. After the session with Young, they spread the pro-Carter message across Pennsylvania, which contributed to Carter's crucial primary victory there.[1]

At the Democratic convention in July at Madison Square Garden in New York City, Young took center stage to give a seconding speech for Carter's nomination. By that time, Young himself had drawn significant attention from reporters, and one characterized him as "the most important black man in America." In spite of such heady talk, Young remained calm and down-to-earth. During a press conference before his convention speech, while Candice Bergen snapped photos for *Time* magazine, he relaxed with his wife Jean and son Bo. Many writers speculated whether Young would receive a cabinet post if Carter won in November, but he did not seem interested and instead envisioned helping Carter in Congress. He understood that he could "exercise leadership in the House without having the big limousine or the leadership title."[2] Choosing between Congress and the cabinet was not an easy decision.

Young would have no choice to make if he and Carter did not win in November; so after the convention, it was back on the campaign trail. The hard work came to fruition when Carter narrowly defeated Gerald Ford, with black votes turning the tide in key areas of the South and urban Northeast. Overall, 94 percent of African-American voters backed Carter, and they were particularly important in Carter's winning Ohio, Pennsylvania, Louisiana, Mississippi, and the Carolinas. In Louisiana, only 41 percent of whites supported the Georgia governor, compared to more than 90 percent of black voters. The civil rights movement, in particular the Voting Rights Act of 1965, made a measurable impact on a presidential election for the first time. Nowhere was this more true than in Mississippi. In the early 1960s, virtually no African Americans in Mississippi had dared to vote, but in 1976 they won the state for Carter. Young summed up the significance of the Mississippi vote: "When I heard that Mississippi had gone our way, I knew that the hands that picked cotton finally picked the president."[3] Young won his own race for reelection to the House, garnering two-thirds of the vote, and seemed to be faced with the difficult choice between Congress and the cabinet.

A week later, responding to rumors that he was on Carter's short list for secretary of state, Young reiterated that he would like to stay in Congress. He believed that Carter, who had no real background in international relations, should choose a secretary of state with foreign policy experience and establishment credentials. Carter evidently concurred and opted for Cyrus R. Vance, a well-known New York City lawyer, who had been assistant secretary of defense during the Johnson administration and participated in the Vietnam peace talks. Vance joined a group of foreign relations advisers that already featured Columbia University scholar Zbigniew Brzezinski. Carter knew Brzezinski from participating in the Trilateral Commission, a New York group committed to increasing trade with Europe and Asia, and had selected him as national security adviser. An immigrant from Poland and a realist along the lines of Henry Kissinger, Brzezinski considered confronting the Soviet Union as the top priority for U.S. foreign relations. The reputations of the first two members of Carter's foreign policy team suggested that there would be no radical departure from past administrations.

In early December, Young traveled with a congressional delegation to a conference on U.S. relations with Africa in Lesotho, a tiny independent nation within South Africa. The group was led by Representative Charles Diggs (D–Mich.) and included Randall Robinson, leader of the fledgling black lobby organization, TransAfrica. Young briefly left the conference to visit his imprisoned friend Robert Sobukwe. After Young returned to Lesotho, an Atlanta radio commentator called and asked him to discuss the rumor that he had been offered the ambassadorship to the United Nations. He responded honestly that he had received no such offer and still intended to return for his third term in Congress—and yet the call stimulated his curiosity about a possible offer to work at the United Nations.

Shortly after Young flew back to Atlanta, Carter invited him to the governor's mansion to discuss the Lesotho Conference. After Young summarized the situation in southern Africa, Carter asked him to join his cabinet as the U.S. permanent representative to the UN. Young initially responded that his congressional colleague Barbara Jordan (D–Tex.) would be a better choice. Carter agreed (somewhat tongue-in-cheek) that she might be a better orator and more intelligent, but contended that Young's close personal connection to Martin Luther King during the civil rights movement made him uniquely qualified for what the president wanted his UN ambassador to accomplish. Carter told Young that the fact that he had been "associated with Martin Luther King would help people take human rights seriously from the United States."[4] He added that he wanted an emphasis on human rights in his foreign policy that represented a direct extension of King's civil rights philosophy, and that Young was the perfect person for the job.

Carter presented a convincing argument. Moreover, he was no longer just Governor Carter requesting a favor, he was the President of the United States asking Young to serve his country. Young liked the idea of working at the UN, where one of his lifelong heroes, Ralph Bunche, had done great things and won the Nobel Peace Prize. On the other hand, he realized that the UN ambassadorship was a difficult job and that U.S. permanent representatives usually did not last long. Friends such as Jesse Jackson advised him against taking the post, arguing that he could do more good in Congress. Finally, accepting the assignment would require his wife to give up her teaching job in Atlanta and move to New York with their two youngest children. He explained this to Carter, who understood and agreed to speak with Jean. When he talked with her, he emphasized her husband's unique qualifications to give credibility to a focus on human rights in foreign relations. Jean and Andrew then discussed it, acknowledging that going to the UN was not the convenient or secure option. In spite of their reservations, they decided to accept the position. They were excited about the chance to help advance human rights and both saw it as part of God's plan for them.[5]

After a holiday break, Young ventured to Washington to go through the official process. On January 25, 1977, the Senate Foreign Relations Committee held his confirmation hearing, during which he made it clear that he intended to listen carefully to the problems of other nations. On January 26, the Senate approved Young's nomination, 89 to 3, with Jesse Helms (R–N.C.) among the opposition. It was no surprise, as Helms had been an outspoken critic of the civil rights movement during his days as a television commentator in North Carolina and disagreed with Young's views on southern Africa. On Saturday, January 30, Carter met with Young, Vance, and Brzezinski in the Oval Office to discuss foreign policy. They focused on how to integrate the UN with the State Department and the National Security Council and what Young's role in the policy-making process would be. Carter made clear once again his strong support for the UN and Young.[6]

Fittingly, at the White House on Saturday night, Thurgood Marshall, former civil rights lawyer and the first black Supreme

76 *Andrew Young*

Court justice, swore in Young as UN ambassador to a rousing ovation. Carter joked about the crowd's enthusiasm for Young: "I can
see that I have made the wrong choice. Andy is the first Cabinet-
level officer who has gotten more applause than the president."[7]
Such humor reflected the strong bond between Carter and Young,
which would be a key asset as he took up the reins at the UN. His
popularity, evidenced by the cheering onlookers, was another
strength. Although he had no formal diplomatic training or experience, he did possess several other important qualifications. He
had traveled to over thirty countries, primarily in Africa, and had
friends in many governments there. He was intelligent, friendly,
well-spoken, and a good listener. Furthermore, he represented an
exciting departure from traditional U.S. diplomats in several aspects: he was the youngest UN ambassador in U.S. history (at forty-
four), the first minister, and the first African American.[8]

Andrew Young, Zbigniew Brzezinski, Cyrus Vance, and Jimmy Carter, Oval Office, January 1977. *Courtesy of Jimmy Carter Library*

Young brought many positive attributes to his new job, but he
never hesitated to speak his mind. That could be problematic for a
U.S. diplomat, as became evident in the week of his confirmation.
During a national television interview on the CBS program *Who's
Who*, Dan Rather asked Young if the presence of Cuban troops in

Angola assured a protracted guerrilla war. Young responded, "No, it's not assured. In fact, there's a sense in which the Cubans bring a certain stability and order." He then clarified his position, explaining that the only truly justifiable reason for the Cuban involvement in Angola was to counter the South African troops. Instead of an example of Fidel Castro's expanding communism, Young believed the Angolan move should be viewed as Castro's taking a stand against racism. He shared the view of Castro and many people of color around the world that racism was a much more serious threat to their well-being than communism.[9]

Taken as a whole his remarks made sense, but the media and political opponents pounced on the initial phrase regarding Cuban troops. Cartoons in the newspapers depicted a cigar-smoking Castro in Angola, armed to the teeth, below Young's words about "stability and order." The interview and resulting cartoons generated a substantial flow of mail to members of Congress from concerned conservative constituents. Representative David Evans (R–Ind.) received so many letters that he requested a transcript of Young's full remarks from White House staffers. Responding to constituents who criticized Young's remarks and accused him of being a Marxist, Senator Harry Byrd Jr. (I–Va.) expressed his concern about Young, whom he characterized as an "extremist."[10] Senator Byrd's criticism of Young was no surprise considering his past support for segregation and his 1971 amendment that undermined the sanctions against Southern Rhodesia.

In the early days of the Carter administration, however, Young's champions far outnumbered his critics. On January 31, 1977, when he presented his credentials at the UN, several hundred well-wishers applauded enthusiastically. A few days later he departed for Africa, as Carter wanted to waste no time in capitalizing on Young's popularity and connections there. The president directed that he "go to Africa and get some sense of what the African leadership expected."[11] Young did just that, visiting fifteen countries and meeting with seventeen African heads of state.

Young spent several days in Nigeria. On February 8 he witnessed the African Festival of Arts and Culture in Lagos, sitting in the stands with such dignitaries as the Sultan of Sokoto, leader of Nigeria's Muslim community. On February 10, Young talked with General Olusegun Obasanjo, Nigeria's head of state, for several hours, convincing him that the United States supported majority rule throughout southern Africa. Obasanjo then praised Young and told the media of the productive nature of their conversation. The contrast between Young and Henry Kissinger, who had been banned from Nigeria the previous year, could not have been more pronounced. Young's visit initiated a remarkable improvement in relations between the United States and Nigeria, which ranks as one of his most important accomplishments as UN ambassador.

The Nigeria stop also generated controversy. During the Festival of Arts and Culture, a horse draped with ceremonial tribal fabric passed in front of Young. Evidently the cloth resembled the American flag and the horse looked like a donkey as the scene appeared on the evening television news in the United States. An irate state senator from Florida, Richard Renick, demanded an explanation from the White House. He contended that Young had sat silently in the stands while a jackass draped in the U.S. flag paraded before him. Renick concluded that "Ambassador Young was too tied up with his 'roots' and not too concerned with correcting this biting insult . . . he owes our country a public apology." A White House staffer responded to Renick's erroneous accusations, explaining that the U.S. flag was not involved and therefore no apology from Young was necessary.[12]

Back in Washington on February 14, Young reported his findings to the cabinet. Carter thanked him for doing an "extraordinarily good job in Africa."[13] Indeed, Young had learned exactly what key African leaders such as Julius Nyerere of Tanzania wanted from the U.S. government. Nyerere and others emphasized the importance of the Carter administration's repealing the Byrd Amendment, thereby putting the United States back in compliance with the sanctions against Southern Rhodesia. Nyerere's suggestion was surely music to Young's ears, and a strong move to repeal the Byrd Amendment was already under way. He himself had introduced the bill to repeal it on January 11 while still a member of Congress.

While Young was in Nigeria, Secretary of State Vance testified before a Senate subcommittee and described sanctions against Southern Rhodesia as a crucial step toward reaching a settlement. On February 24, Young called repeal of the Byrd Amendment a "kind of referendum on American racism" and a signal that the United States did not support Ian Smith. In mid-March, Congress voted in favor of repeal. Upon signing the bill on March 18, Carter proclaimed: "This legislation . . . puts us on the side of what is right and proper. It puts us in a strategic position to help with the resolution of the Rhodesian question."[14] Along with his success in Nigeria, helping to reinstate tough sanctions against Southern Rhodesia represented one of Young's major successes during Carter's presidency.

Over his first few months in office Young accomplished several significant breakthroughs in U.S. relations with Africa. His connections there, and his credibility from his days with Martin Luther King, paid off quickly. Young's success also could be attributed to his style, which differed in many ways from those of his predecessors. Much of his activity occurred in his apartment at the Waldorf-Astoria Hotel in New York, where he frequently hosted late-night gatherings of friends and Third World diplomats. He and Jean often cooked meals of soul food and personally served their guests, who, on any given evening, could include Jesse Jackson, the Cuban vice president, or African leaders such as Abel Muzorewa. Although these sessions usually lasted late into the night, Young rose early in the mornings and pushed himself relentlessly. He typically maintained this "superhuman" pace for six weeks or so, and then disappeared for a few days to rest.[15]

Young not only used his informal approach during unofficial gatherings at the Waldorf, but he also practiced it in public. He preferred to ride in the front of his government limousine, next to his chauffeur, rather than in the usual back seat. He worked closely with a small group of staffers whom he had selected, including his deputy ambassador, Donald McHenry, his secretary at the State Department, Anne Holloway, and his personal aide, Stoney Cooks. Cooks, an old friend from the 1960s, was the key member of Young's entourage, and he essentially did the sorts of things that Young had accomplished for King—circumventing bureaucracy and gaining results. Young's approach shocked traditionalists at the UN, particularly European ambassadors, but it scored points with other diplomats. For example, Young canceled one of his initial meetings at the UN with African representatives that had been planned as a formal session around a table and, instead, held impromptu hallway chats, which featured plenty of high fives.[16]

Young's African diplomacy also benefitted from his general agreement over policy with key players at the State Department, beginning at the top with Vance. Young and Vance shared the basic view that racism was a more serious problem than communism, and this view shaped their strategy on policy and appointments. They worked together in choosing subordinates such as Assistant Secretary of State for Africa Richard Moose and Assistant Secretary of State for International Organizations Charles Maynes. This good working relationship between Young and the State Department greatly facilitated his work at the UN, and the ideas and hard work of Moose and Maynes contributed considerably to the Carter administration's improving relations with Africa.

In addition to his official duties during his first months as ambassador, Young still found some time to be a minister and counselor for friends such as Arthur Ashe, the African-American tennis star who won at Wimbledon in 1975. He and Ashe had been pals for several years, and it had been Ashe who first took Young to South Africa. On February 19, Andrew and Jean hosted Arthur and his fiancée Jeanne Moutoussamy for dinner in New York, and the Youngs advised the couple on the challenges of marriage. They described it as a sacred institution that should not be taken lightly and they emphasized the importance of forgiveness. Ashe never forgot that advice and warmly recounted it in his autobiography years later. He believed it typical of Young, whom he characterized as "a reconciler rather than a divider of persons."[17] Young presided at Ashe's wedding the next day, and they remained friends until Ashe died in 1993.

Evenings like the one with the Ashes were rare, however, and the ambassador devoted the vast majority of his time in the winter and spring of 1977 to Africa. In addition to his primary focus on Nigeria and Southern Rhodesia, Young also labored for independence and peace in Namibia. Twice the size of California but with only one million inhabitants, Namibia passed from German control to South African control after World War I. In 1966 the UN General Assembly approved Namibian independence, but South Africa refused to withdraw. In 1976 the UN Security Council adopted Resolution 385 calling for free elections throughout an independent Namibia, but again South Africa balked. During his first few months in office, Young got a feel for the Namibian situation by having early breakfasts with several African delegates to the UN. They explained to him that talks with the Pretoria regime were necessary but would have to be convened by a third party.

Young discussed Namibia with Carter and Vance, who realized that Namibia carried much more international significance than such a sparsely populated region normally would. For example, getting the South Africans out might possibly induce Cuban withdrawal from Angola. With support from Carter and Vance, Young formed a working group known as the Gang of Five, consisting of the United States, Great Britain, Canada, France, and West Germany.

In April 1977, the Gang of Five began calling on South Africa to comply with Resolution 385 and allow free elections in Namibia. For nearly a year, the Gang of Five acted as intermediaries between Pretoria and the South West African People's Organization (SWAPO), which was the primary guerrilla force in Namibia. After Young got the ball rolling, most of the negotiations were handled by Donald McHenry, who drafted a plan based on Resolution 385. Sam Nujoma, the leader of SWAPO, whom Young had known for ten years, agreed to McHenry's plan early in 1978, but South Africa refused to sign.[18] Namibia would not gain independence until 1990, but Young and McHenry had made a solid effort.

After forming the Gang of Five, Young's next major African initiative came in mid-May when he attended a UN conference on majority rule in Maputo, Mozambique. Just getting there took some doing, since the Ford administration had decided during the planning stages of the conference that the United States would not send delegates. Young insisted otherwise. When the State Department hesitated to provide him with transportation to Maputo, Young contacted Carter directly and got a plane. He joined representatives from more than ninety nations at the opening session on May 19. He denounced colonialism and minority rule and explained that he was there to begin implementing a new U.S. approach to southern Africa and to demonstrate his "personal commitment to human rights."[19] He argued that all parties fighting minority rule should work together, whether guerrillas or nonviolent nuns.

Young pressed this point of cooperation in talks with key African leaders such as Samora Machel, president of Mozambique. Machel agreed with Young's view and welcomed any help that Americans wanted to provide southern Africa. That was the general consensus at Maputo. In their talks with Young, southern African leaders expressed optimism about the Carter administration's potential to facilitate peace in their region. In summing up his findings at Maputo for the president, Young concluded that "the Africans continued to endorse armed struggle but agreed to support our efforts for peaceful settlement as a second legitimate form of struggle."[20] During the conference, the ambassador first manifested his willingness to meet with anyone he thought could help solve a problem, regardless of the official American policy toward them. In one instance, he talked publicly with delegates from the Polisario Front, a rebel group fighting to end Morocco's rule over the Spanish Saharan region. He thus violated instructions from the State

Department, which feared alienating Morocco's King Hassan II. Although Young escaped reproof for this, his disdain for diplomatic protocol eventually contributed to his demise at the UN.

From Maputo the ambassador flew to Johannesburg for a series of lively discussions about how best to end apartheid. Since taking office, Young had condemned apartheid, but cautioned against too radical an approach. He opposed divestment by U.S. businesses or comprehensive economic sanctions, and at a cabinet meeting in mid-March, he warned Carter that the United States should be careful not to "drive South Africa into a corner." Young envisioned white and black South Africans working together to end apartheid, as he had negotiated with whites in the South to end racial discrimination during the 1960s. Young realized that most people did not believe such cooperation could ever occur in South Africa, but on April 19 he reasserted his faith in multiracial rule, even in Pretoria. "The impossible dreams make life worthwhile and I wouldn't trade them for any amount of realism, caution, or protocol in the world." He left no doubt about his loathing for apartheid, however, and a few days later he characterized the Pretoria regime as illegitimate. "I hate anything to do with that government," he declared.[21]

When Young arrived in Johannesburg on May 21, the customs officers directed the plane to a remote part of the airport to minimize publicity. It was a futile effort. Young waved to the customs police, then enthusiastically shook hands with the black limousine drivers, double-clutching in the Black Power style. Soon after his arrival, he addressed two hundred business leaders, emphasizing that it was in their best interests financially to end apartheid. He contended that they could play a key role in finding a solution, just as business leaders had in Birmingham in 1963. He praised the potential of capitalism to end apartheid peacefully. If the economy included more blacks, there would be less likelihood of armed rebellion. Until such opportunity opened up for blacks, they could utilize boycotts to put pressure on the system. Again, Young compared the battle against apartheid in South Africa to the civil rights movement in the South in the United States, a comparison that angered the Pretoria government.[22]

The next day the ambassador spoke to a racially diverse group of about seventy liberals. His inspirational account of his own experiences in the 1960s drew a standing ovation. Mangosuthu Buthelezi, a powerful chief, embraced Young and praised his peaceful approach. The crowd sang the black national anthem, "God Bless

Africa," and cheered Young again as he departed. During his next stop at the U.S. Information Service office, he admitted that it would be hypocritical of Americans to condemn black South Africans for using violence, considering the extremely violent revolution the United States had fought against Great Britain. Young did realize that the problem in South Africa was complex and would not be solved quickly by a few boycotts. His tendency to compare apartheid to Jim Crow segregation, however, convinced white South Africans that he was naive. At the same time some black South Africans denounced Young as a front man for American capitalism. Steve Biko declined a chance to meet with Young, in part because he thought the ambassador should visit Nelson Mandela instead, but also because he disliked Young's procapitalist philosophy. In Biko's opinion the ambassador had "no program except the furtherance of the American system."[23]

Biko characterized the ambassador correctly in the sense that Young was certainly not a Communist and definitely preferred the American to the Soviet system. However, this not only reflected his faith in capitalism, but also manifested his confidence that the United States had a better record on race relations. He contended that he and Carter, because they had been dealing with civil rights issues for years, could appreciate the racial challenges confronting southern Africa better than the Soviet diplomats. In late May he criticized the Russians as "the worst racists in the world."[24] Moscow was not Young's only target on this issue; the ambassador also blasted Britain and Sweden for their poor records on race relations.

In spite of his occasional condemnation of Soviet racism, Young developed a very positive relationship with his Soviet counterparts at the United Nations. He accomplished some of his best diplomacy on the tennis court, where he and Jean frequently played with Soviet Ambassador Oleg Troyanovsky and his wife Tanya. In order to mitigate Cold War hostility, Jean teamed with the Soviet ambassador against Tanya Troyanovsky and Andrew. Furthermore, the partners usually split sets and left it as a tie. These tennis matches represented another example of Young's informal style and allowed him to work very well with Troyanovsky. They could discuss upcoming resolutions in a relaxed environment and agree to acceptable compromises. Contests on the court avoided stalemates in the Security Council, and as a result, the Soviets did not veto a single American proposal during Young's tenure.

The Soviets appreciated Young's cooperative approach, but never believed that he could be converted into a Communist agent.

Viktor Lesiovsky, a KGB agent who worked at the United Nations, often consulted with Young. As he did with Ambassador Troyanovsky, Young shared information with Lesiovsky in order to avoid confrontations at the Security Council. Lesiovsky did not view Young as pro-Communist, however, and informed his KGB superiors that the ambassador's overall opinion of the Soviet Union was "negative."[25] In other words, the KGB had considered recruiting Young but concluded that it was impossible. Political opponents had long accused Young of being a Marxist, but the KGB knew better.

Nonetheless, the Conservative Caucus, a national right-wing political group, launched a campaign to remove the ambassador from office in June 1977 because of his alleged support for communism. Meldrim Thomson, governor of New Hampshire and chair of the Conservative Caucus, spearheaded the movement. He recounted Young's words about Cuban troops bringing stability to Angola and his statement that racism was a bigger threat to the United States than communism. Young's gravest crime, in Thomson's opinion, was his friendship with Robert Sobukwe and the hosting of Sobukwe's children in his Atlanta home. Thomson argued that Sobukwe incited violent revolution in South Africa, and, by extension, so did Young. He described the ambassador as someone who "aids and supports Communist butchers and terrorists." He urged fellow conservatives to demand that Young be fired. Together with Thomson's outrageous cover letter, caucus members received an Anti-Young Action Kit that featured a postcard to send on to President Carter, a brochure with some of Young's controversial comments, and a bumper sticker that read "Andrew Young Must Go!"[26]

Young ignored these attacks from the far right and continued to work primarily on African issues, and on Southern Rhodesia in particular. Carter not only supported the ambassador's efforts, but also practiced some very controversial diplomacy himself. On August 4, Tanzanian President Julius Nyerere arrived in Washington, the first African head of state to visit during the Carter administration. Nyerere represented a coalition of the black-ruled nations adjoining Southern Rhodesia, known as the Frontline, which also included Zambia and Mozambique. In two days of meetings, Nyerere talked with Carter about Southern Rhodesia. Nyerere advocated removing the Ian Smith regime, dismantling the security force, and replacing it with an army "based on the liberation forces."[27] To Nyerere's astonishment and British consternation, Carter agreed with the plan.

In so doing, Carter seemingly undermined the consultations that the British negotiators had been conducting since May. Conceding Nyerere's point that the new army of Zimbabwe should be "based on the liberation forces" so altered the equation that Ian Smith would surely reject it. Nonetheless, an agreement between presidents could not simply be ignored, and any further talks would have to try to iron out the wrinkles Carter had caused. In a rare role reversal, it was Young who needed to explain the president's controversial words and actions when he met with British diplomats. At the same time, Carter's diplomacy demonstrated his willingness to listen to the views of black African leaders such as Nyerere, which set him apart from his predecessors in the Oval Office and also signified his commitment to the thrust of Young's African diplomacy.

Julius Nyerere, Andrew Young, and Jimmy Carter, Washington, DC, August 1977. *Courtesy of Jimmy Carter Library*

Nyerere was grateful. After the talks with Carter, he visited Atlanta and spoke at a dinner on August 9 hosted by Mayor Maynard Jackson. He urged the audience to support the Carter administration's policies toward southern Africa. The next day a reporter asked Nyerere if the appointment of a black UN ambassador had improved relations with Africa. Nyerere responded that simply appointing an African American would not necessarily have made any difference. That Young and the other Carter administration officials were dedicated to ending minority rule in southern Africa was the key innovation. Naming a token black man as UN ambassador would not have helped anything, but Young's background and ongoing actions made a positive impact. Nyerere declared, "For President Carter to appoint not just a black man, but a black man who believes in human rights, is more than a symbol."[28]

Young, meanwhile, was in the middle of a sojourn to the Caribbean region, another area with which the Carter administration intended to foster better relations. Rosalynn Carter had been to Latin America earlier in the summer, and the president of Costa Rica had asked her if Young could visit. The First Lady passed on the request to her husband, who found his UN ambassador very willing. Young was happy to follow in the footsteps of Rosalynn Carter, with whom he had a warm and mutually respectful relationship, and he praised her for the "renewed hope" that she had spread through the southern hemisphere.[29] On August 5, the ambassador kicked off his tour of ten Caribbean nations in Jamaica, a locale that he had visited many times.

At Young's suggestion, Jamaican President Michael Manley did not greet him at the airport. This diplomatic maneuver deferred to the fact that Manley had alienated the Ford administration by backing the Cuban intervention in Angola and by introducing some socialist reforms into the Jamaican economy. Young did, however, spend most of his two days in Jamaica with the president. He had known Manley for many years and did not consider him to be a Communist, any more than Martin Luther King had been a Communist. Young informed his friend that the Carter administration planned to increase aid to the island nation from $10 million per year to over $50 million per year. Manley responded with a pledge to pursue a "Third Way" between capitalism and communism.[30] Young's good chemistry with Manley facilitated an improvement in U.S.–Jamaican relations, and his Caribbean trip was off to a great start.

In Mexico, Young endorsed a proposal to legalize millions of Mexicans who were then illegal aliens in the United States. In Costa Rica, he supported its government's call for a UN investigation of Idi Amin's human rights abuses in Uganda. In Guyana, which had offended the Ford administration by nationalizing U.S. property, he championed an increase in aid as good for regional stability. In Suriname, he espoused better relations between the United States and Cuba, but in Trinidad he sharply criticized Castro's human rights record and said that he did not mind "raising a little hell."[31] Frequently the ambassador was asked about U.S. policy toward southern Africa, and in particular why the Carter administration would not supply weapons to the guerrillas. He replied that it was easy to support violence when you were far away from it, but that it was far better to seek a negotiated settlement. One of the key guerrilla leaders, Joshua Nkomo of the Zimbabwe African People's Union, talked with Young in Guyana and requested material assistance. The ambassador explained that the Carter administration was not going to chose among the various liberation forces in Southern Rhodesia, but instead sought peace talks with all of them.

For the most part the trip was a very enjoyable experience for Young, and he relaxed in the evenings by playing tennis with his assistant, Stoney Cooks. In Venezuela, the ambassador was flattered to learn that one of the couples working at the American Embassy had named their new son after him. His relations with the Caribbean leaders were generally warm and friendly, with the notable exception of Haiti's Jean-Claude Duvalier. Young sternly admonished the dictator that his denial of human rights to Haitian citizens jeopardized American aid and raised the possibility of an investigation of his regime by the Organization of American States. He gave Duvalier a list of twenty political prisoners whom the dictator had arrested without due process. Duvalier was so uncooperative that Young opted to criticize him in public, and he made a point of never smiling in Duvalier's company to avoid any photos being taken that could suggest U.S. approval of his regime.

In addition to accentuating the Carter administration's emphasis on human rights, Young's trip facilitated two key specific aspects of the new American policy regarding Latin America. First, at each stop he enthusiastically endorsed the proposed Panama Canal Treaty, which would return control of the canal to Panama after 1999. When he returned to Washington, he called several senators to lobby for their support of the treaty, which Carter signed in September. Congress eventually approved two Panama treaties in March and April 1978. Second, Young's trip led to the creation of the Caribbean Group for Cooperation in Economic Development, overseen by the World Bank. By 1980 the efforts of this group quadrupled aid to the Caribbean to more than $1 billion per year.

The American media showered great praise on Young for his work in Latin America. A *Washington Post* editorial characterized him as "the ideal person to articulate a message that transfers the ideas forged in the U.S. civil rights struggle to international relations."[32]

During his whirlwind tour of the Caribbean, he succeeded in advancing several of Martin Luther King's fundamental principles: human rights, nonviolence, self-determination, and economic development. In doing so, Young contributed considerably to the Carter administration's goal of transforming foreign relations from the traditional Cold War east–west orientation to a new north–south focus.

Soon after concluding his Caribbean tour, Young embarked on another trip to Africa, primarily to seek a solution to the conflict in Southern Rhodesia. He first stopped in Nigeria and addressed an antiapartheid conference on August 25. He lauded the Nigerian government for its role in leading the fight against the South African system. He explained that he personally favored a nonviolent solution, but that he would not condemn those who opted to use force in their struggle for freedom. In private discussions with General Olusegun Obasanjo, the Nigerian head of state, Young sought input regarding the Anglo-American Plan for a settlement in Southern Rhodesia. David Owen, the British Foreign Minister, joined them to discuss the proposals. Young and Owen then flew to Zambia to present their recommendations to Joshua Nkomo and Robert Mugabe, the leaders of the two main guerrilla forces fighting for a majority-ruled Zimbabwe.

Owen laid out the main points of a blueprint he intended to announce on September 1. The key modification in the plan was a stipulation for "one man—one vote," which certainly made it more attractive to the black leaders than the Kissinger Plan of the previous year. However, the new proposal did not specify that the security force in a postindependence Zimbabwe would be "based on the liberation forces." Some of the Africans reacted harshly to this, disappointed that Owen had reverted to what they considered an unacceptable position.[33] From Zambia, where he and Owen were criticized for not being progressive enough in support of racial equality, Young went on to Pretoria, where the white rulers considered him far too progressive. He met Prime Minister John Vorster for the first time, and the two said very little but politely shook hands. When Young called Carter from South Africa, his phone was tapped by the security forces. The ambassador, who had had much experience with FBI eavesdropping in the 1960s, said nothing of importance to the president and made light of the South Africans' spying.[34]

On the eve of announcing the Anglo-American Plan, Young expressed little hope that Smith would agree to it. If negotiations ceased, he feared an "internal settlement" engineered by Smith that would bypass Mugabe and Nkomo.[35] Young's concerns were well founded, as Smith was indeed arranging such a deal. He called for an election in hopes of rallying white support. If Smith could once again get a strong mandate, he would gradually pursue an agreement with black leaders, such as Abel Muzorewa, who were not leading guerrilla forces. Election results rolled in on the morning of September 1, and Smith's Rhodesian Front Party triumphed, gaining 85 percent of the vote. Before Young and Owen arrived in Salisbury, Smith declared that he would pursue an internal settlement.

After Owen presented the Anglo-American Plan in tiresome detail, Smith launched into a diatribe about broken British promises. Young listened patiently to Owen's lecture and Smith's litany of complaints and finally interjected that "there was no point in crying over spilt milk." Smith smiled for the first time that day, and afterward praised Young as someone with "a sense of humour and a streak of humanity."[36] Despite Young's ability to ease the tension, Smith expressed no interest in the proposal. Young and Owen's hectic week of diplomacy drew to a close. None of the principals in the Southern Rhodesian conflict completely accepted the package, but none had entirely rejected it, either.

Back in New York in September, Young welcomed two new members of the United Nations, Djibouti and Vietnam, with remarks before the General Assembly. Young, of course, had long been concerned about U.S. policy toward Vietnam. He reminded the audience of his personal views on the subject and some of his past actions. Most notably, he mentioned participating in an antiwar demonstration in 1967 outside the UN with Martin Luther King and voting to cut off funds for the war during his first term in Congress in 1973. He pointed out that Coretta Scott King, an antiwar activist in her own right, was among the current American delegation to the UN General Assembly. He concluded, "It is my sincere hope that Vietnam's entry into this body is one more step in the worldwide struggle for peace, justice, and prosperity."[37] Once again, the ambassador applied King's ideals to his work at the UN and manifested a new approach to U.S. foreign relations. It is difficult to imagine any key diplomat in the Ford or Nixon administration giving such an address.

In the fall of 1977, circumstances in South Africa went from bad to worse. The Carter administration had opted against trying to impose economic sanctions on the Pretoria regime, but activist groups such as newly incorporated TransAfrica lobbied for economic measures against apartheid. Their cries grew louder as rioting and repression escalated in South Africa, sparked by the September 12 death of Steve Biko, the popular thirty-year-old black leader of the Black Consciousness Movement. Biko died in custody after police beat him with a hose and slammed his head against a wall. Police Minister James Kruger denied that his officers caused the death, thereby intensifying the international demand for justice.

As Young attended a UN memorial service for Biko on September 23, outrage over the tragedy was widespread. In the streets of New York, demonstrators marched behind a banner that read: "Avenge the Murder of Stephen Biko." In Congress, forty representatives and two senators founded an ad hoc group to monitor events in South Africa. At the United Nations in October, forty-nine African nations requested that the Security Council consider imposing tough comprehensive sanctions against South Africa. Young announced on October 24 that he personally favored such measures, but added, "The president and the secretary of state will have to decide what sanctions are appropriate."[38] The UN initially considered three resolutions: the first would have banned foreign investment, the second would have ended nuclear cooperation, and the third would have stopped internal arms production in South Africa. Following Carter's instructions, Young joined the representatives from Great Britain and France in vetoing all three.

The UN then considered an Indian proposal to ban arms sales to South Africa. On October 31, Young discussed the situation before the Security Council. He contended that people within South Africa ultimately must take the lead in resolving their own crisis and expressed his faith that they eventually would do so. He cited the late Steve Biko, among others, as an example of the type of South African with the potential to create a multiracial society: "The ideas of men like these will prevail, for though they may be silenced, the power of these ideals have been implanted in the hearts of men and women by their Creator."[39] He explained that the U.S. government had decided it was necessary to stop the flow of weapons to Pretoria in order to mitigate escalating tension that threatened international peace. On November 4, he voted in favor of a mandatory arms embargo that prohibited sales to Pretoria of weapons, ammunition, military vehicles, paramilitary police supplies, or spare parts. The measure passed, and it was the first time the UN had imposed mandatory sanctions against a member state.

A few days later Young addressed the Council on Foreign Relations in Chicago and afterward attended a fundraiser at the home of nationally syndicated columnist Eppie Lederer, better known as Ann Landers. The ambassador's speech drew an overflow crowd, and his enthusiastic presentation brought a very lively ovation. According to Landers, "Andy was magnificent in both places. His expertise, command of the language, low-key warm human approach is dynamite." Young evidently explained the Carter administration's foreign policy goals very clearly and convincingly. Landers observed, "Everyone who left that auditorium went away feeling better about this country and its president."[40] In spite of his controversial remarks during his first year in office, the ambassador remained extremely popular among liberals and a strong advocate for Carter's foreign relations.

The crisis in Southern Rhodesia remained a high priority. Diplomats from the United States and England sought an all-parties conference to negotiate a settlement based on the Anglo-American Plan, but the situation was not encouraging. Nkomo and Mugabe believed they stood to gain more by continuing the guerrilla war. On November 23, Smith's security forces launched the largest attack of the war into Mozambique. Three days of fighting left more than one thousand people dead, including about one hundred children. Mass graves of women were later discovered. The guerrillas were more determined than ever to fight, and Smith was gradually progressing toward an internal settlement with Muzorewa. At the end of 1977, it seemed that the Anglo-American Plan stood no chance.

Nonetheless, Assistant Secretary of State for Africa Richard Moose deemed the circumstances ripe for a meeting with the guerrilla leaders. The looming threat of an internal deal that did not include them forced Nkomo and Mugabe, who had formed a loose alliance known as the Patriotic Front (PF), to take the Anglo-American Plan more seriously. If the British and Americans could make some progress with them, then Owen could possibly obtain South African support and broker a settlement. It was agreed that talks with Nkomo and Mugabe should be arranged, so Owen asked them to meet with him and Young. On January 19, 1978, the PF leaders accepted Owen's invitation to meet later in the month on the island of Malta.

Young approached the sessions optimistically, largely because of his training as a minister. While many American officials viewed the liberation forces in southern Africa as Communist movements, the ambassador saw them "as a natural progression from Christian missionary education."[41] The PF leadership had all been educated in missionary schools, and part of their worldview revolved around

a Christian message of overcoming oppression. Nkomo was a Presbyterian, and Mugabe a Catholic. In fact, the first person who recommended that Young meet with Mugabe was a retired monsignor
who praised Mugabe as the best student he had had in over fifty
years of teaching. From Young's perspective, then, the struggle for
a majority-ruled Zimbabwe resembled the civil rights movement
in the southern United States. Martin Luther King had led a Christian movement there, and he had also been persecuted as commu-
nistic. In addition to serving as a connection with the PF leaders,
religion even provided a link to Ian Smith, who was a Presbyterian
Elder.[42] The Reverend Andrew Young, not surprisingly, recognized
the potential for Christianity to help bridge the gaps between Smith
and the PF. ·

As the final logistics for the Malta meeting were being arranged,
Young insisted that he stay in the Dragonara Hotel with the PF to
allow for "in depth discussions." The conference opened on the
morning of January 30, with Owen reiterating the Anglo-American
Plan. In the first two days of formal sessions, the PF demanded a
"dominant role" during the transition period between the cease-
fire and the elections. The sessions, which were the first occasion
at which Owen and Young had talked with Nkomo and Mugabe at
length, afforded both sides a good opportunity to explain their
ideas. Reporting on the first two days, British radio announced that
the PF had agreed to a policing role for the UN. This premature
report angered Nkomo. Young succeeded in calming him down,
and Nkomo "clearly felt himself in the presence of a friend in Andy
Young."[43]

Indeed, much of the progress at Malta resulted from Young's
informal personal interactions with the PF. During the initial cof-
fee break, General Josiah Tongogara, a large and imposing figure
in his military fatigues, accosted the ambassador, declaring, "I need
to talk to you." Young, caught off guard and slightly intimidated
by the big man, followed him to a corner. The Zimbabwean inquired, "What happened to the Oakland Raiders?"[44] He had earned
a Ph.D. at the University of California at Berkeley and wondered
how the Raiders' season wound up. This exchange reinforced
Young's generally positive view of the PF delegation, which included several individuals with degrees from American and British universities. He established a relationship of mutual respect with
many of them while swimming in the hotel pool or jogging with
them. He drank beer with Nkomo and drank orange soda with tee-
totaler Mugabe during a late-night conversation.

Remarkably, Young was able to orchestrate talks over lunch beween the PF and British Field Marshal Richard Carver, who was scheduled to become resident commissioner during the transition to Zimbabwe, if a settlement were reached. Carver had served in World War II and later commanded the force that crushed the Mau Mau rebellion in Kenya in the 1950s. During a low point at the start of the Malta Conference, a PF aide accused Young of bringing along the Mau Mau crusher to quell the Zimbabwe liberation movement. After Young gained the trust of the PF, however, its leaders were willing to talk over military details—even with Carver. Informal talks facilitated two of the key areas of progress at Malta. Partly because of the atmosphere Young created, the PF agreed to active roles in the transition for the resident commissioner and a UN force. Overall, however, the substantive results of the conference were negligible.

Still, it would be wrong to judge the Malta Conference too harshly, since no settlement could have been reached without Smith. Furthermore, because the Americans and the British were entirely unwilling to become directly involved in the war or to extend sanctions against South Africa, the PF could not be expected to make significant concessions while the fighting continued. Young realized that Soviet promises of weapons for the PF also limited the leverage of the United States and Great Britain. Despite the lack of a major substantive breakthrough at Malta, the PF wanted to continue talks with Owen and the Americans. Young concluded that Malta was only a "minimal success," but that it had kept "a negotiated settlement alive."[45] Ambassador Steve Low lauded the unprecedented opportunity for detailed discussion with Nkomo and Mugabe. By keeping the negotiating process going, the Malta Conference resuscitated a middle course between war and Smith's internal settlement with the non-PF black leaders.

Young's activities at Malta brought his first year as UN ambassador to a generally successful close. Due mainly to his informal style and civil rights background, he contributed to several positive developments in the Carter administration's foreign policy. Most significantly, he fostered better relations with Nigeria and played a key role in American efforts to facilitate a settlement in Southern Rhodesia. His visit to the Caribbean was also noteworthy, as it improved U.S. relations with Latin America. Young's emphasis on seeking racial justice rather than fighting communism resonated well throughout the Third World, and his religious perspective provided a helpful link to a wide range of leaders. At the same time, his approach shocked traditional diplomats. His willingness to speak his mind and to meet with anyone he thought necessary to the peace process, furthermore, were problematic tendencies during his first year at the UN and subsequently would cause him greater difficulty.

Notes

1. Andrew Young, *A Way Out of No Way: The Spiritual Memoirs of Andrew Young* (Nashville: Thomas Nelson, 1994), 114–22.

2. Hal Gulliver, "Big Day for National Political Figure," *Atlanta Constitution*, July 19, 1976, A4.

3. John Dumbrell, *The Carter Presidency: A Re-Evaluation*, 2d ed. (Manchester, England: Manchester University Press, 1995), 88–89.

4. Andrew Young, interview with the author, March 2, 1994, Atlanta, Georgia.

5. Young, *A Way Out of No Way*, 122–25.

6. Memoranda, Jimmy Carter to Zbigniew Brzezinski, January 26 and 28, 1977, folder "IT 86-27 1/20/77–6/30/77," box IT10, White House Central File (hereafter WHCF), Jimmy Carter Library, Atlanta, Georgia (hereafter JCL).

7. Bartlett C. Jones, *Flawed Triumphs: Andy Young at the United Nations* (Lanham, MD: University Press of America, 1996), 24–25.

8. Seymour Finger, *American Ambassadors at the UN: People, Politics, and Bureaucracy in Making Foreign Policy* (New York: Holmes and Meier, 1988), 260–62.

9. Transcript of Dan Rather's interview of Young, January 25, 1977, 14–16, folder "IT 86-27 1/20/77–6/30/77," box IT10, WHCF, JCL.

10. Michael Hornblow, acting staff secretary of the National Security Council, to Congressman David Evans, March 11, 1977, ibid.; Harry Byrd to Stephen Hartwell, March 17, 1977, folder "1977 Mar 1–17 For Rel Rhod," box 284, Collection 10320a, Manuscripts Department, University of Virginia Library, Charlottesville (hereafter UVA).

11. Andrew Young, interview with the author, March 2, 1994, Atlanta, Georgia.

12. Richard Renick to Jimmy Carter, mailgram, February 11, 1977, and response from staffer Valerio Giannini to Renick, March 9, 1977, folder "IT 86-27 1/20/77–6/30/77," box IT10, WHCF, JCL.

13. Carter, quoted in Jones, *Flawed Triumphs*, 58.

14. Young and Carter, quoted in Andrew DeRoche, "Standing Firm for Principles: Jimmy Carter and Zimbabwe," *Diplomatic History* 23 (Fall 1999): 667.

15. Finger, *American Ambassadors*, 270.

16. Jones, *Flawed Triumphs*, 33–35.

17. Arthur Ashe and Arnold Rampersad, *Days of Grace* (New York: Alfred Knopf, 1993), 51, 56, 156, and 298.

18. Finger, *American Ambassadors*, 280–83.

19. Jones, *Flawed Triumphs*, 20–21, 76.

20. Young's confidential report to Carter, "My Trip to Africa," June 3, 1977, Mandatory Review document number 91–078, received by the author from the Jimmy Carter Library.

21. Young's comments to the cabinet and on hating the Pretoria government are quoted in Jones, *Flawed Triumphs*, 80; Young's impossible-dream comment, quoted in Robert Massie, *Loosing the Bonds: The United States and South Africa in the Apartheid Years* (New York: Doubleday, 1997), 410.

22. Massie, *Loosing the Bonds*, 412–13.

23. Jones, *Flawed Triumphs*, 82–83; Biko, quoted in Massie, *Loosing the Bonds*, 421.

24. Jones, *Flawed Triumphs*, 111.

25. Christopher Andrew, *The Sword and the Shield: The Mitokhin Archive and the Secret History of the KGB* (New York: Basic Books, 1999), 290.

26. Copies of Thomson's letter and the other materials attached to a memo from Tom Offenburger, Young's press secretary, to Jack Watson and others, July 27, 1977, folder "IT 86-27 7/1/77–12/31/77," box IT10, WHCF, JCL.

27. Julius Nyerere, *Crusade for Liberation* (Dar es Salaam: Oxford University Press, 1978), 8.

28. Ibid., 59–60.

29. Young to Rosalynn Carter, June 10, 1977, Name File–"Andrew Young," JCL.

30. Jones, *Flawed Triumphs*, 95.

31. Ibid., 96.

32. *Washington Post*, August 18, 1977.

33. The meeting of August 27 described in Stephen Low to the State Department, confidential telegram, August 27, 1977, was obtained by the author from the State Department via the Freedom of Information Act (hereafter FIA), request number 8802626.

34. Memo, Peter Bourne to President Carter, "Message from Andy Young," September 1, 1977, folder "9/1/77 [1]," box 47, Staff Secretary Files, JCL.

35. Message from Young to Obasanjo, in telegram from U.S. Embassy in Nairobi to U.S. Embassy in Dar es Salaam, August 31, 1977, FIA 8802626.

36. Ian Smith, *The Great Betrayal: The Memoirs of Africa's Most Controversial Leader* (London: Blake, 1997), 233.

37. Statement by Young in the General Assembly, September 20, 1977, in Lee Clement, ed., *Andrew Young at the United Nations* (Salisbury, MD: Documentary Publications, 1978), 76–77.

38. Young quoted in the *Washington Post*, October 25, 1977, A1.

39. Statement by Young in the Security Council, October 31, 1977, in Lee Clement, *Andrew Young*, 96.

40. Ann Landers (Eppie Lederer) to Jimmy Carter, November 9, 1977, folder "IT 86-27 7/1/77–12/31/77," box IT10, WHCF, JCL.

41. Young, interview with author, March 2, 1994, Atlanta, Georgia.

42. Young, phone interview with author, May 7, 2001; Young, *A Way Out of No Way*, 130–31.

43. Telegram from the State Department to the U.S. Embassy in Valletta, Malta, January 25, 1978; telegrams from Valletta to State, January 26, 30, and 31, 1978; quotation about Young and Nkomo in Ambassador Steve Low's report on Malta, from Lusaka to State, February 4, 1978, FIA 8802607.

44. "The Survival of Andy Young," *Washington Post*, August 8, 1979, E1 and E3.

45. Telegram from Young in New York to State and to the White House for Brzezinski, February 4, 1978, FIA 8802607.

5

Triumphs and Tribulations

1978–1980

During his second and third years at the United Nations, Andrew Young continued to focus on human rights issues, particularly in less-developed regions of the world. He remained a central figure in U.S. relations with southern Africa, most notably participating in further discussions regarding Southern Rhodesia. Continuing to listen to the desires of black African leaders, he firmly opposed a 1978 agreement because he felt it would not bring peace. This specific stance drew severe criticism from conservatives in Congress. More generally, Young's tendency to express his personal views on controversial subjects frequently got him into hot water. Whether criticizing the legal system of the United States or defending the rights of Aborigines in Australia, he spoke his mind. Ultimately it was his willingness to meet with whoever he believed could help solve a problem, regardless of official U.S. policy, that ended his tenure as UN ambassador. When his meeting with a representative of the Palestine Liberation Organization became public knowledge in August 1979, Young agreed to resign from his UN post. Nevertheless, he contributed constructively to relations with Africa until the end of Carter's presidency.

In February 1978, relations with Southern Rhodesia were at the top of the ambassador's agenda. He and others who had participated at the recent Malta Conference argued vigorously for ongoing actions to maintain the momentum. He suggested encouraging Frontline leaders Julius Nyerere of Tanzania and Kenneth Kaunda of Zambia to pressure Robert Mugabe and Joshua Nkomo to remain committed to the Anglo-American Plan, proposed the previous September. Young simultaneously spoke against the internal settlement that Ian Smith and Abel Muzorewa were attempting to hammer out in Salisbury.

While Young and others in the Carter administration opposed this internal settlement, support for it mounted in Congress. A group of twenty-four representatives led by Edward Derwinski (R–Ill.) praised the Smith–Muzorewa negotiations and requested that Carter terminate the Anglo-American initiative. The debate intensified suddenly on February 15, when Smith and Muzorewa signed a preliminary pact, stipulating principles for an internal settlement. On the following day, Young vehemently decried the deal as unacceptable and unlikely to yield peace. The pact failed to address the rights for which approximately forty thousand guerrillas were fighting. He contended that excluding Mugabe and Nkomo's Patriotic Front forces would probably result in a situation like Angola's, with blacks fighting blacks in a bloody civil war. Key U.S. diplomats stationed in Africa, such as Ambassador to Zambia Steve Low, concurred with Young's assessment. Senators Robert Dole (R–Kan.) and Orrin Hatch (R–Utah), however, applauded the tentative agreement and attacked Young's view as "irresponsible and inflammatory." They requested that Carter give Smith's plan a chance and let the people of Southern Rhodesia solve their own problems. They especially emphasized that "Ambassador Young should keep out of these negotiations."[1]

On March 3, Dole and other members of Congress critical of Young and supportive of the preliminary settlement welcomed the news that Smith and Muzorewa had signed an agreement. The package, known as the Salisbury Plan, called for elections after a one-year transition, during which whites would retain control of the police and military. Smith's army would enforce martial law during the elections. Of the hundred seats in parliament, twenty-eight would be reserved for whites, and black guerrilla soldiers could not vote unless they renounced their armed struggle. Nkomo and Mugabe rejected the plan outright. Dole and other congressional conservatives urged the president to recognize the Salisbury Plan, but Carter did not believe it could end the war and thus withheld his support. The Carter administration continued seeking an agreement that included the Patriotic Front (PF) forces of Nkomo and Mugabe.

In mid-March, at the UN Security Council, African delegates submitted a resolution condemning the Salisbury Plan as illegal. Young followed his instructions from Secretary of State Cyrus Vance and abstained on the vote, which passed 10 to 0. In defense of the abstention, which Mugabe and others denounced, Young pointed to past American actions and emphasized that the Carter administration still supported the Anglo-American Plan. He credited Muzorewa with wanting independence for Zimbabwe and equality for Zimbabweans as much as the PF did. But, since Muzorewa's deal with Smith would not allow all parties to participate in the elections, it would prolong the violence. Young advocated an all-parties conference to revisit the Anglo-American proposals, and proclaimed the ultimate goal of U.S. policy as "a just and lasting settlement for a Zimbabwe whose people would at last know the blessings of independence, freedom, and peace."[2] Considering Young's propensity for speaking from the heart, his handling of the African resolution was quite moderate. Young and Nyerere pondered what to do next. The Tanzanian leader indicated that the PF was prepared to reach an agreement with the Americans and British, so planning for a high-level conference began.

Before that meeting convened, Carter paid the first visit to sub-Saharan Africa by a U.S. president, stopping in Liberia and Nigeria. The remarkable trip to Nigeria reflected the groundwork done by Young during the past year. During Carter's five days in Lagos, Nigeria, President Olusegun Obasanjo proposed selling 50 percent of Nigeria's oil to the United States and sending ten thousand students to American universities. The two leaders discussed the Southern Rhodesian situation in depth. Obasanjo urged the president to continue opposing the internal settlement, and Carter agreed. In a public speech, Carter cited Martin Luther King, stating that Nigeria would soon be able to exclaim, "Free at last. Great God Almighty, we are free at last."[3] Carter's visit represented the high point of U.S. relations with Nigeria and was a proud moment for Young, whose attention soon turned back to Southern Rhodesia.

Young, Secretary of State Cyrus Vance, and British Foreign Secretary David Owen flew to Africa in April to arrange a peace conference. The trio met in Dar es Salaam, Tanzania, with Nkomo and Mugabe. To the chagrin of the Anglo-American team, Nkomo and Mugabe insisted that they must control the executive council during the proposed transition from cease-fire to elections. Although some progress was made on other details, the disagreement over control of the executive council precluded any comprehensive arrangement in Tanzania. The PF would make no further concessions until Smith could be brought to the table. In a subsequent meeting, the Anglo-American diplomats explained to Smith and Muzorewa that they could not support the internal settlement and that they wanted to facilitate a solution acceptable to everyone at a roundtable. Smith and Muzorewa agreed to consider attending but would not commit to it. Thus, the unprecedented collection of U.S. and British diplomats who toured southern Africa in April failed to arrange an all-parties conference.

In a sense, though, there had been some progress toward a settlement since Young had succeeded in impressing Ian Smith further with his sincerity. Smith praised Young for listening carefully to the presentations by Muzorewa and other black members of his government. He also lauded Young's observation that the PF leaders were in part motivated by their desire for personal power. He noted that during another point in the conversation when Young was making a "forthright contribution," Vance diplomatically silenced the ambassador and took over. When the talks concluded, Smith privately told Young, "You're far too honest to make a success of this game of politics."[4] As he had done so often when serving as Martin Luther King's mediator in the 1960s, Young had gained the trust of a key white leader. Smith's fondness for Young helped to mitigate his strong dislike for Owen and to keep the possibility of a final settlement alive.

The centrality of religion provided another similarity between Young's approach to Southern Rhodesia and his earlier work in the civil rights movement. He considered it very significant that most of the black leaders had been educated in Christian missionary schools. Joshua Nkomo was a Presbyterian Elder, and Robert Mugabe was a devout Catholic. Young related to these men as fellow Christians. Whereas some American officials such as Bob Dole looked at the liberation movement as a Marxist phenomenon, Young "viewed it as a natural progression from Christian missionary education."[5] The fact that Martin Luther King had also been persecuted as a Communist by his opponents only served to underscore the connection Young felt with guerrilla leaders such as Nkomo. Christianity also facilitated his interactions with other principals in the conflict: Ian Smith was a Presbyterian Elder and Abel Muzorewa was a Methodist bishop.

Young gained much of his information about the situation on the ground in Southern Rhodesia from two Catholic organizations. The Salisbury-based Commission for Peace and Justice and the London-based Catholic Institute for International Relations both had started investigating the conduct of Smith's security forces in 1972. They paid particular attention to conditions in the protected villages where peasants were being isolated to cut off support for the guerrillas. As conditions in the villages deteriorated, the religious groups provided clothes, food, and medical supplies. They also reported on the villages' conditions. In 1977 the Commission for Peace and Justice published a study documenting the hardships in the camps and the widespread use of torture by Smith's troops. Sister Janice McLaughlin, a Catholic nun who helped to write the report, explained the commission's intention: "We prepared the papers because we felt that when Andrew Young and David Owen met with the government they would only hear one side."[6] After the internal settlement in March 1978, these groups continued to provide reports. Their critical assessments of the Smith–Muzorewa policies strengthened Young's hand in his efforts to prevent U.S. approval of the settlement.

Young needed all the help he could get, as Carter's policy of withholding recognition of the internal settlement faced powerful challenges in Washington. Senator Jesse Helms (R–N.C.) emerged as the administration's most formidable opponent. He had opposed integration as an editorialist and city politician throughout the 1960s. Often he had contended that the civil rights movement was controlled by Communists, and his most severe attacks were aimed at Martin Luther King. He had supported the Byrd Amendment in 1971 while still a television commentator in North Carolina. So it was not surprising that Helms should criticize Carter's policy for three reasons: one, it was championed by Young, King's former assistant; two, it seemed to favor Nkomo and Mugabe, who were portrayed as Marxists; and three, it reinstated sanctions.

On June 28 the Senate narrowly defeated a Helms amendment that would have lifted sanctions against Southern Rhodesia and promoted the internal settlement. Helms tried again in July, but once again he failed, partly due to the lobbying of Young and others. Congress passed a compromise amendment that lifted sanctions after December 31, but only if Carter determined that two conditions had been met: a peace conference held among all the principals and elections open to all groups. Young and other Carter officials succeeded in the summer of 1978 by blocking Helms and defending two key points: an all-parties conference and elections that included the Patriotic Front.

During the debates over Southern Rhodesia policy, Helms had attempted to paint a simplistic picture of Communist aggression in Africa. Young had countered with a much more sophisticated depiction based on his extensive travel on the continent and his close contact with African representatives at the United Nations. He argued that it was certainly not a clear-cut case of monolithic Soviet and Cuban domination. He pointed out that many French areas of Africa, such as Cameroon and Senegal, staunchly disapproved of both Soviet and Cuban interventions. He believed that Tanzania and Nigeria wanted to be leaders of a nonaligned Africa and did not want the Cubans or Soviets to have excessive influence. He knew many Angolans who hoped to avoid dependence on the Soviets and, instead, desired building stronger ties to American companies such as Gulf Oil. In Mozambique, the leaders had rejected a Soviet initiative to build a naval base and they were very appreciative of American food supplies received in the wake of a tragic flood. Although Young readily admitted that the Cubans were heavily involved in the war between Somalia and Ethiopia, he denied that they had gained anything of strategic value.[7] Young's grasp of African affairs impressed several members of the Senate Foreign Relations Committee and helped to keep the Carter administration's policies on track, heading into the summer of 1978.

In a July 10 interview with the French paper *Le Matin*, the ambassador again offered a very detailed and impressive analysis of African affairs. He discussed an incredible range of conflicts, from the ubiquitous Southern Rhodesian war to the relatively obscure French intervention in Chad. Overall, he was optimistic about the Carter administration's foreign policy. When discussing the Soviet Union and its treatment of dissident Jews, however, he commented, "We still have hundreds of people that I would categorize as political prisoners in our prisons."[8] He was referring mainly to the arrests of civil rights activists like himself in the 1960s and the jailings of people for protesting the Vietnam War. He added that most of these demonstrators attained freedom quickly and that the legal system of the United States was preferable to those of other countries. Nonetheless, his one sentence about "political prisoners" in the midst of a lengthy and overwhelmingly pro-American interview sparked intense controversy in Washington.

In response to these remarks, Representative Larry McDonald (R–Ga.) called for Young's impeachment on July 13, but the motion was defeated 293 to 82. Representative Dan Quayle (R–Ind.) requested that the White House provide documentation on the "political prisoners" in the United States. If no proof existed, he suggested that the ambassador resign in order to "spare the nation further embarrassment."[9] He contended that Young's comment jeopardized ongoing arms-limitation talks with the Soviets and could endanger Russian dissidents then on trial. Though Quayle certainly overstated the potentially negative impact of Young's words, the congressman had a point. The "political prisoners" remark angered Secretary of State Vance and embarrassed the Carter administration when it was trying to encourage reform in the Soviets' treatment of dissidents. During a July 20 news conference, Carter expressed his disappointment about Young's "unfortunate statement."[10]

Nevertheless, many people agreed with the ambassador's view. Between August 7 and August 18, the White House received sixty letters or cards commenting on Young's "political prisoners" statement, and fifty of them were supportive. One of Young's strongest advocates during this controversy, not surprisingly, was his mother, Daisy Young. In early September she wrote to President Carter: "He is a dedicated Christian man. No one can challenge his truthfulness or his character. Andrew has always championed the poor and exploited, and I am sure that he wants to bring human rights to the world." She concluded by thanking Carter for standing by her son, "when many would have liked to have seen him destroyed."[11] Young's mother was certainly correct about her son's having enemies in Washington, and one of them was Senator Harry Byrd Jr. (I–Va.). Byrd believed that Young had persuaded Carter not to meet with Ian Smith during his October visit to the United States. The Virginia senator favored U.S. recognition of the internal settlement in Southern Rhodesia and contended that, because of Young, "the President has made the pro-terrorist position the policy of our government."[12]

Byrd saw the PF as the terrorists, but subsequent events in October and November raised serious doubts about that interpretation. Smith's forces bombed two refugee camps in Zambia, both of which supplied education and medicine and were funded in part by the United States. After realizing that one of the camps was inhabited almost entirely by girls and young women, the soldiers staged a cover-up. They then bombed Nkomo's house in Lusaka and began sending poisoned clothes to the refugee camps. These brutal tactics, in conjunction with Smith's ongoing plans for an election based on the internal settlement, made it clear that he had no intention of attending an all-parties conference. In response, the PF forces escalated their attacks. In late 1978, therefore, the Anglo-American peace initiative for Southern Rhodesia had bogged down and was in serious danger of complete abandonment.

Young defended the Anglo-American plan and U.S. policy toward southern Africa at a conference in Khartoum, Sudan, in early

December. Many Africans challenged Young and accused the United States of being racist in its dealings with southern Africa. They pointed to Smith's recent visit to America as evidence. One PF representative confronted Young and wondered what the United States had ever done to help the liberation forces. Young remained calm, as he did throughout the conference, and spoke to the Zimbabwean in good humor. He apologized for not calling him "Doctor," a title he had earned at a U.S. university. Young added that the higher degrees from American colleges held by more than thirty PF leaders could surely be viewed as a contribution to the liberation struggle.

In such lively exchanges, Young's strengths were evident. Although Africans argued with him about U.S. policy, they clearly felt very comfortable around him, calling him "Andy" and acknowledging that he was among the greatest advocates in America for African rights. Although they liked him personally, many Africans considered him to be a right-winger politically and an apologist for a fundamentally conservative American policy. Being branded a right-wing conservative in Khartoum on the basis of the same positions for which many in Washington called him a radical leftist did not dismay Young, and he clearly articulated the American strategy. He still believed that settlements could be negotiated in Southern Rhodesia and Namibia and that ultimately these pacts would help bring a peaceful end to apartheid in South Africa.

Young maintained his optimism about the work he was doing in Africa and joked with Hal Gulliver of the *Atlanta Constitution* that his greatest concern was how he would get back to Atlanta after his UN job ended. Stephen Rosenfeld of the *Washington Post* summarized Young's performance at Khartoum as "terrific." Gilbert Cranberg, editor of the *Des Moines Register*, also witnessed Young in action in the Sudan and concluded, "America needs to be sophisticated enough to overlook Young's occasional verbal gaffes and to recognize him for the major asset he is for the United States in this part of the world."[13]

Indeed, during his second year at the UN, Young had continued to foster better relations between the United States and Africa. Carter's visit to Nigeria was probably the highlight, but Young had also helped to keep the negotiations for a peaceful settlement in Southern Rhodesia alive. His ability to work with white leaders and his religious focus, both legacies of his work in the civil rights movement, were key contributions. Furthermore, in testimonies and interviews, he demonstrated his impressive understanding of the political and military landscape of Africa, and in his speeches, he clearly expressed the overall strategy behind U.S. policies. When discussing international relations, Young occasionally interjected views that did not coincide with official American policy. These statements, such as his remark about "political prisoners" in the United States, could easily be taken out of context and used to denigrate him and embarrass the president. Although Carter admittedly was displeased with some of Young's comments in 1978, in his year-end holiday card, the president reaffirmed his faith in the ambassador who he felt had been "extremely valuable to our nation & to the world."[14]

The first major challenge for the ambassador in 1979 involved Southeast Asia. In January, Vietnamese forces invaded Cambodia in an attempt to dislodge the Khmer Rouge regime of Pol Pot. A flurry of diplomatic activity ensued at the UN, where Cambodia was represented by Norodom Sihanouk, the country's former king. Sihanouk disapproved of the Vietnamese invasion of his homeland, but also was increasingly critical of the brutal Khmer Rouge government. On January 15, Sihanouk secretly informed security at the Waldorf-Astoria Hotel that he was being held as a prisoner by the Khmer Rouge guards. Upon hearing of Sihanouk's precarious plight, American agents liberated him from the Khmer Rouge and brought him to meet with Young. They worked out a plan whereby Sihanouk initially was checked into a hospital as a cover and then was transported to China where he went into exile.

A few weeks later China invaded Vietnam, and Young urged the UN representatives from smaller Asian states to take the lead in protesting the attack. On this issue, as with the Vietnamese invasion of Cambodia and the escalating crisis of Vietnamese refugees, Young basically felt the United States should not take a central role and, instead, should work behind the scenes for peaceful solutions. He believed that the American military operations in Southeast Asia in the 1960s and early 1970s were a main cause of the instability, and hence it would be best in 1979 for the U.S. government to refrain from taking initiatives in that war-torn region. He eventually called for the Security Council to act, and advocated a cease-fire and withdrawal of all forces from Vietnam and Cambodia.[15]

Early 1979 found Young again enduring criticism for controversial remarks to the press. On January 17 the *New York Times* reported the ambassador's comments on the Palestine Liberation Organization (PLO). He contended that the PLO members should be viewed realistically as leaders of the Palestinian people and a "tremendous influence" in the Arab world. Upon reading the *Times* story, Representative Peter Peyser (D–N.Y.) immediately rebuked Young in a very stern letter. Peyser was "deeply disturbed" by Young's "inference that the United States should reexamine its relationship with the PLO." After recalling the deep admiration he had always felt for Young while they were congressional colleagues, he added, "I cannot imagine what has happened to you that would make it possible to even suggest support for the Palestine Liberation Organization. I frankly don't give a damn if, as you say, the PLO's representatives in the United Nations are 'very skilled politicians and very intelligent, decent human beings.' " Peyser concluded by asking Young to rethink what he had said and to avoid giving the PLO the impression that the United States approved of its terrorist attacks on Israeli civilians.[16]

Young's response to another crisis in the Middle East caused additional controversy in February. In mid-January the Shah of Iran had fled the country and been replaced by an interim government led by Shahpur Bakhtiar. On February 1, the Ayatollah Ruhollah Khomeini returned from exile, and ten days later his supporters overthrew the Bakhtiar government. In the midst of the turmoil, Young remarked, "Khomeini will be somewhat of a saint when we get over the panic." He also predicted the downfall of the Bakhtiar regime. Carter quickly rebuked Young at a press conference, pointing out that the U.S. government was not in the canonization business and that American officials should not speculate on the future of foreign governments as if they were at a football game. On February 10, the ambassador met with Khomeini's representatives in New York, seeking assurances that the new government would respect human rights, particularly those of Iranian Jews. Two days later, upon hearing of the uprising by Khomeini's followers, Young credited the Iranian revolution to the thousands of students who had learned of democracy in the United States. "The idea that all people are somebody," the most powerful force in the world, had again triumphed.[17]

Although in early 1979 Young participated in diplomacy regarding Southeast Asia and the Middle East, his most significant contribution to the Carter administration's foreign policy remained his work in Africa. In February he updated the Senate Foreign Relations Committee on some of the key African issues. He summarized the ongoing efforts to persuade South Africa to support UN-monitored elections in Namibia. He reaffirmed the administration's faith that a settlement in Southern Rhodesia based on the Anglo-American Plan remained the best option, and that it was crucial to continue diplomatic efforts: "To those who say that our diplomatic initiatives have failed, I remind them that the military solution has failed as well. Certainly, diplomatic initiatives deserve as much time and patience as military solutions." He closed with an eloquent plea for increased economic assistance to Africa, arguing that African markets and resources could help stimulate economic prosperity in the United States.[18]

Although Young advocated continued negotiations over Southern Rhodesia, he acknowledged that circumstances looked bleak for a settlement that would include the Patriotic Front and thus end the fighting, which raged throughout February, with Nkomo's forces downing a passenger jet for the second time in six months. Smith also scheduled elections based on the internal agreement for mid-April, further complicating the situation. Under the Case–Javits Amendment from 1978, Carter would be forced to lift sanctions if the Southern Rhodesian government agreed to attend a conference and held free and fair elections. Therefore, it would be necessary to determine whether the April elections were free and fair. Carter decided not to send a team of observers, however, because it would lend legitimacy to Smith's internal settlement.

The two candidates were Muzorewa and Ndabaningi Sithole, and everyone except Sithole expected Muzorewa to win easily. The security forces visited rural villages and encouraged the peasants to vote. The Patriotic Front denounced the election as a sham and pledged to carry on the war. Nkomo excoriated the United States and Great Britain for their ambivalence over the elections and accused them of "collaborating and conniving at Smith's gimmick and gamble."[19] Despite the PF opposition, over 60 percent of eligible blacks voted between April 17 and 20. They selected candidates from Muzorewa's party for 51 of the 72 black seats in parliament, and thereby designated him the first black prime minister of Southern Rhodesia.

On April 25, the *MacNeil–Lehrer Report* examined the results of the elections. Young appeared in defense of the administration's policy. He compared the elections to the pre-1965 elections in the Southern United States, when blacks were influenced and intimidated. He argued that recognizing Muzorewa would only guarantee continued fighting and could bring about greater Soviet involvement. He pointed out that if the United States lifted sanctions, it would lose credibility with the PF and Frontline leaders

and also surrender any remaining leverage for bringing Muzorewa
and Smith to an all-parties conference. Carter stated his position to
the press on April 27. He characterized the elections as a "step in
the right direction."[20] Under the provisions of the Case–Javits
Amendment, he was required to wait until Muzorewa was officially
installed as prime minister to determine whether the elections had
been free and fair. Muzorewa's inauguration was scheduled for
May 31, and until then Carter made no final decision.

Young underwent hip surgery in late April, but it did not slow
him down. While he was still in his hospital bed, he met with Dan
Rather to brief him on the situation in southern Africa. Rather, who
was leading an investigative trip for CBS News, in turn heaped
praise on the "magnificent" ambassador and his staff at the UN in
a letter to the president. "They were efficient, intelligent, and working harder than plowhorses," he informed Carter. Rather added
that the information he got from Young and his staff proved accurate and helpful on the ground in Zambia.[21] Shortly after leaving
the hospital, the ambassador hobbled on crutches onto a plane and
flew with his wife Jean to Papua New Guinea. Young, the highest-
ranking U.S. official ever to visit New Guinea, met with Prime Minister Michael Samore. The visit, although primarily symbolic,
represented a positive step in American relations with the Pacific
nation.

On May 3 the Youngs landed in Canberra, capital city of Australia, where they were welcomed by Foreign Minister Andrew
Peacock. On the following day, Ambassador Young met with Prime
Minister Malcolm Fraser and discussed southern Africa, Vietnam,
and economic issues. He then attended a seminar on the UN in
Sydney and visited Melbourne. Back in Canberra on May 8, in
speaking to the National Press Club, he touched on the sensitive
issue of Aborigine rights. He suggested that they press their claims
in the courts of Australia, rather than appeal to the UN. On May 9,
in Perth he sat down for two hours with fifteen representatives of
western Australia's Aborigines. He agreed that their case was a legitimate and serious one, and he pledged to seek aid for them from
the Australian government. The Australian media praised Young
for his sympathy with the indigenous peoples and concluded that
his advice would be helpful to their cause.[22]

While in Canberra, Jean and Andrew had stayed with U.S.
Ambassador Philip Alston and his wife Elkin, pillars of Atlanta
business and social circles. Ambassador Alston described for Carter
the tremendous impact of Young's visit: "You have few, if any, more

effective Ambassadors than Andrew Young. I doubt the country has a greater patriot. This afternoon he completely fascinated 500 students at Australian National University—standing room only. We have not looked so good in Australia in the past two years. I am very proud to be identified with him and what he had to say."[23] After the successful stop in Australia, the Youngs spent a few days in the Philippines before returning to the United States. During the sojourn Down Under, the ambassador had impressed students, reporters, Aborigines, and high-ranking officials. He enthusiastically espoused the Carter administration's human rights policy. Although his foray into the Pacific took up a very small percentage of Young's tenure at the UN, it did much to improve America's image there.

When Young returned to the United States in mid-May, a critical juncture in American policy toward Southern Rhodesia was fast approaching. Muzorewa's inauguration was just two weeks away, and the debate over whether or not to lift sanctions intensified. Carter's decision took on added significance because a Conservative government led by Margaret Thatcher had recently assumed control of British policy. Thatcher was inclined to support Muzorewa and Smith, but she realized that the most important goal was to stop the fighting. With that in mind she opted to move cautiously and sent Foreign Secretary Peter Carrington to consult with the Carter administration. On May 21, Carrington discussed Southern Rhodesia with Secretary of State Vance. Carrington explained that Thatcher was seriously considering recognition of the Muzorewa government, but that she did not want to damage British relations with the United States and black African nations such as Nigeria.

In late May and early June, Carter received messages from African-American leaders encouraging him to maintain sanctions against the Muzorewa government. Jesse Jackson, Coretta Scott King, and Atlanta Mayor Maynard Jackson all opposed lifting sanctions. Another plea to maintain the sanctions, circulated by TransAfrica, was signed by 185 prominent African Americans. In Congress, the Black Caucus came out strongly against recognition of Muzorewa. White House aide Louis Martin, a black himself, emphasized to Carter the importance of these leaders' views on Southern Rhodesia. Although the input of black leaders certainly influenced the president's thinking, arguably the key player in the drama was Representative Stephen Solarz (D–N.Y.), who went to great lengths to dissuade Carter from recognizing Muzorewa. On

June 7, Carter announced that he did not consider the elections free and fair and that the United States would keep sanctions in place until an all-parties settlement was achieved.

Members of Congress such as Jesse Helms and Harry Byrd immediately launched counterattacks, proposing amendments that would override Carter's decision. Young joined the administration's successful lobbying effort against these maneuvers. In July, Muzorewa arrived in Washington to ask Carter for support. Appearing on *Good Morning America*, he blamed Carter's decision on Young and contended that sanctions actually exacerbated the war by encouraging the PF. Nevertheless on July 11, at Camp David, Carter firmly rejected Muzorewa's request for recognition. By holding firm in the face of Muzorewa's pleading and pressure from Congress, Carter demonstrated his resolve to the British. The U.S. policy influenced Foreign Minister Carrington's thinking as he weighed British options in July, and so the sanctions remained in place. In August, he and Thatcher began organizing an all-parties conference at Lancaster House in London, which started in September and would ultimately lead to a settlement.

Carter's decision to maintain sanctions against Southern Rhodesia in the summer of 1979 was one of the high points of Young's service at the UN. The president demonstrated a steadfast commitment to the policy that the ambassador had done so much to craft and implement. Young had accepted the job in part because it would allow him to carry the ideals of Martin Luther King onto the international stage, particularly regarding southern Africa. In this instance he had succeeded, and therefore the Carter administration contributed to the process that soon resulted in the independent, majority-ruled nation of Zimbabwe. Any satisfaction Young may have felt about this triumph in the summer of 1979 proved short-lived, since helping to keep the sanctions in place was his last major accomplishment as UN ambassador.

In late July, Young learned that the UN Committee on Palestinian Rights had requested that its latest report not be issued until August, when he would be presiding over the Security Council. Young examined the report before it was made public and was pleasantly surprised to find that it essentially recognized the right of Israel to exist. On the other hand, the report also called for the creation of a Palestinian state. The ambassador realized that he would be instructed to veto any such resolution. In late July 1979, the Carter administration faced increasing economic problems and was focusing its diplomatic energy on an arms-limitation treaty with the Soviets. Furthermore, Young did not want to quash an Arab move toward recognizing Israel. Thus, he determined that the best course of action was to postpone consideration of the report.

In order to arrange a postponement, Young hosted a lunch for the UN ambassadors from Egypt, Syria, Lebanon, Jordan, and Kuwait. They discussed the situation in depth. The Arab diplomats agreed that postponement would be best, but insisted on getting the Palestine Liberation Organization (PLO) to agree. They requested that Young meet personally with the PLO representative to the UN, Zehdi Terzi, a Columbia University professor. Young realized that such a meeting would be controversial, because the United States had promised Israel it would not deal with the PLO until that group had recognized Israel officially. Yet he decided that as president of the Security Council he was obligated to meet with all parties in any dispute that body was considering. He later contended that "it would have been irresponsible to avoid going forward with this process."[24]

During the early evening of Saturday, July 26, Young and his son Bo walked over to the apartment of the Kuwaiti ambassador, Abdullah Bishara. There he talked with Zehdi Terzi, the PLO representative, about the report on Palestine. While his son played on the floor, Young told Terzi that it would be best to postpone consideration of the report because the Carter administration was overwhelmed with other issues and could not give it the attention it deserved. Terzi agreed to make an effort to get the PLO's leader, Yasir Arafat, to accept a delay. With that, the meeting came to an end, but Young's problems were only beginning. On July 31 the Security Council officially decided to postpone any discussion of the report, and Young assumed the presidency of the Security Council on the following day.

On August 10, 1979, a *Newsweek* correspondent in Israel received a tip that Young had met with Terzi, and on August 11 a reporter queried the State Department for details. Assistant Secretary for International Organizations Bill Maynes contacted Young in New Orleans and inquired about the rumored rendezvous. Young responded that it was an accidental encounter and that nothing official had been discussed, and Maynes relayed this version to *Newsweek* and Israel. On August 13, Young provided a more accurate account to Israel's UN Ambassador Yehuda Blum, admitting that he and Terzi had discussed postponing the report on Palestine. Blum informed the Israeli government, which decided to file a formal protest. Word of Israel's intention quickly reached the State

Department, and Cyrus Vance called Young early on the morning of August 14. After hearing Young's explanation, Vance summoned him to Washington and told Carter that he felt Young should resign.[25]

Later on August 14, the ambassador notified his staff at the UN that he was going to submit a letter of resignation, and they left him alone to draft it. Young opened his letter by thanking Carter for his support and praising his commitment to the UN, which "made it possible to advance the cause of peace, human rights and economic development." Young acknowledged that while he had always acted in what he thought were the best interests of the country, he had "created serious difficulties for the administration on several occasions." He thought that the Carter administration had the potential for additional important foreign policy achievements, particularly in the Middle East. "It is therefore extremely embarrassing that my actions, however well-intentioned, may have hampered the peace process," he admitted. To avoid additional "complications," he was offering to step down.[26]

On August 15, Young met with Vance, who definitely believed resignation was the best alternative. Young then met with Carter and submitted his letter. As the president explained, in a lengthy handwritten response, he accepted Young's resignation "with deep regret." Carter lauded Young in general for his good work in a difficult position, then offered specific praise: "You have proven that we are sensitive to the demands for world peace and racial justice, and have earned for us the friendship, trust and respect of many nations which had previously considered the United States to be suspect." Carter added that Young should be proud of his accomplishments at the UN and assured him, "You have my best wishes and personal thanks."[27]

Deciding whether or not Young should leave the administration surely had been a difficult decision for Carter. He still shared Young's faith in the UN and desire to fight racism and improve relations with Africa, and he was genuinely happy about much that Young had done along those lines. Politically, he remembered clearly how crucial the southern black vote had been in 1976 and realized that Young's resignation would hurt him in 1980. Personally, he liked Young and knew he would miss his friend during the challenging days ahead. On the other hand, the pressure for Young's resignation was compelling. He had initially misled the State Department about the nature of his meeting with Terzi, falling short of the complete honesty that Carter so cherished. He had angered the government of Israel at a time when Carter had hoped to keep the peace process moving forward. Again, politically, Carter recognized that Young's continued presence in the cabinet would cost him Jewish votes in 1980. Not surprisingly, Republican candidates such as Bob Dole and George H. W. Bush demanded Young's resignation. More important, so did Senate Majority Leader Robert Byrd (D–W.Va.), which probably weighed heavily on Carter's mind when he decided that Young must go.

The August 15 announcement of Young's departure from the UN sent shock waves throughout the African-American community. The Black Leadership Forum, which included Coretta King and Vernon Jordan, responded the next day with a detailed statement. They expressed their regret that Carter had accepted Young's resignation. They praised his work on behalf of human rights and his success in improving relations with the Third World. "Andy Young has served honorably and we believe his accomplishments will be long remembered," they summed up. In addition to their positive assessments of Young's work, they raised two concerns. First, they questioned why the American ambassador to Austria, Milton Wolf, was not being punished for his meeting with the PLO. Second, they voiced their hope that the incident would not "incite or exacerbate tension between the black and Jewish communities."[28]

Both of their concerns had merit. Ambassador Wolf, in fact, had met on three occasions with a PLO official named Isa Sartawi. Although the State Department characterized the meetings as chance encounters that had not been authorized or encouraged by the Carter administration, Wolf's meetings arguably manifested a gradual move toward recognition of the PLO. In a provocative column in the *Washington Post*, Joseph Kraft spelled out this view. He contended that Wolf's meetings reflected the administration's desire to ease the PLO into the negotiating process. He reminded his readers that President Carter had likened the PLO to the African-American civil rights movement during a dinner in July, and that Vance had supported the Austrian government's May initiative to invite Yasir Arafat to a state function. According to Kraft, Young's talks with Terzi were just one more component of the Carter administration's general policy of "being nice to the PLO." He concluded that it was not Young who should be criticized, but Carter and Vance.[29]

Kraft had elaborated on the Black Leadership Forum's concern that Young was being punished while others were not. The forum's other worry, that tensions with the Jewish community would increase, was immediately addressed by the American Jewish Congress. They concurred with the black leaders who had advocated dialogue between the two communities in the wake of Young's resignation. They wanted to set the record straight and make it clear that it was not because of Jewish influence over Carter that the ambassador had left the UN. They emphasized that Young had violated the pledge not to meet with the PLO and then misled the State Department. Indeed, "The American Jewish Congress and other Jewish organizations deliberately refrained from calling for Ambassador Young's resignation." They pledged to cooperate with black leadership in efforts to organize discussions about the controversial situation.[30]

The eloquent statement from the American Jewish Congress did not mollify black disappointment over Young's resignation. On August 24 about two hundred African-American leaders, including Jesse Jackson and representatives from the SCLC and NAACP, gathered in New York. They decried the "double standard" by which Young had been judged. They advocated a meeting between Terzi and the head of the SCLC. They blasted Israel for its ties to South Africa. They admitted that Jews had been important allies for blacks in the past, but charged them with abandoning blacks on key issues such as affirmative action. They concluded that "Jews must show more sensitivity . . . before taking positions contrary to the best interests of the black community."[31] These black leaders clearly felt betrayed by the Jewish community, and Young's resignation brought those feelings into the open. Although Young himself insisted that Jewish influence had nothing to do with his departure from the administration and called for dialogue, the reaction of some black leaders clearly showed that additional damage had been done to black–Jewish relations.

Later assessments of the significance of Young's resignation varied widely. In his 1982 memoirs, Carter briefly discussed the uproar surrounding the incident. He contended that Young had not violated policy by meeting with Terzi, but that he should have been completely honest with the State Department about it from the beginning. "A mountain was made of a molehill," concluded Carter.[32] In his fine 1986 overview of Carter's foreign policy, Gaddis Smith depicted Young's departure as a firing and argued that because of it the administration "suffered."[33] In his 1995 study of the Carter presidency, John Dumbrell characterized the event as "more firing than resignation." He faulted Young both for participating in a meeting that violated policy and for not initially informing Vance or Carter about it. However, he praised Young's overall contribution to U.S. foreign policy and concluded that Young's resignation "was unfortunate, both from the Administration's viewpoint, and from that of developing U.S. race relations."[34] Bartlett Jones, in his 1996 biography of Young, contended that the resignation seriously harmed the Carter administration both at home and abroad. According to Jones, "Support from American blacks and Jews was eroded; black Africa, Israel and the Arabs were alienated."[35]

Losing Young certainly hurt the Carter administration in many aspects, but it would be wrong to exaggerate how much difference he could have made in foreign policy had he remained in office until the end of Carter's term. The seizure of the U.S. Embassy and American hostages in Iran in November, coupled with the Soviet invasion of Afghanistan in December, dominated all other international issues. It is unlikely that Young would have been called on to play a central role in those crises. Carter's foreign policy team sustained another blow in April 1980, when Vance resigned in protest of a failed attempt to rescue the hostages in Iran. The voters delivered the knockout punch to Carter's approach to foreign relations by overwhelmingly electing Ronald Reagan in November 1980, and it is inconceivable that Young could have altered that outcome had he still been at the UN. On the positive side of the ledger, it can be argued that, in many respects, relations with Africa continued throughout the remainder of Carter's presidency as if Young were still in office.

Carter hosted the Young family at the White House on September 4, 1979, for an overnight visit, and on the following day Andrew and Jean left for Africa as the leaders of a trade delegation. The president considered the fostering of economic links to be an important function of the trip, but he realized that it was at least as valuable diplomatically. Most significantly in that regard, the Youngs visited Julius Nyerere in Tanzania and delivered a message from Carter. "Andy's visit with you at this time is especially important because he can reaffirm to you personally my determination that the fundamental tenets of U.S. policy in Africa will continue on the course we initiated over two years ago," promised the president.[36] He assured Nyerere that the United States would keep working for peace, human rights, and economic development in Africa. Specifically, he pledged ongoing American support for the efforts to negotiate a settlement of the confict in Southern Rhodesia. No one was better qualified to deliver such a message to Nyerere than Young.

While the Youngs were in Africa, the long-awaited all-parties conference on Southern Rhodesia began at Lancaster House in London on September 10. Although none was particularly enthusiastic about being there, all the principals—Mugabe, Nkomo, Muzorewa, and Smith—attended. As the sessions chaired by the British slowly got under way, conferees on Capitol Hill simultaneously began haggling over one final piece of relevant legislation. The Senate version of the Defense Authorization Bill contained a proposal by Harry Byrd that mandated an immediate end to sanctions. The Carter administration faced a tough fight and focused its efforts on the chair of the Armed Services Committee, Senator John Stennis (D–Miss.). Carter himself turned the tide when he met with Stennis on September 24 and threatened to veto the Defense Authorization Bill if it lifted sanctions. Once again, Carter took a stronger stand on Southern Rhodesia than any of his predecessors had. As a result, Stennis prevailed on his colleagues, and the final version of the Defense Bill left sanctions in place. Carter thus proved that he truly intended to continue the policy toward Southern Rhodesia that Young had helped formulate.

The decision on when to lift sanctions would be left with the president and would depend on progress at the Lancaster Conference. The United States did not officially participate at Lancaster, where British Foreign Secretary Peter Carrington was clearly in charge. Carrington laid down the law from the outset and firmly controlled the agenda. He decided to tackle one issue at a time and began with the constitution. After forging an agreement that reserved twenty of one hundred seats for whites, he turned to the issue of elections. Eventually all sides agreed that the British would supervise them. In early November, Carrington brought up the final major issue—the ground rules for the cease-fire. Mugabe resisted the proposal that all Patriotic Front guerrillas be rounded up and observed during the period leading up to the elections, and the conference dragged on into December. In order to pressure Mugabe into signing, the British requested that Carter lift sanctions, and he complied on December 16. More important was Mozambique President Samora Machel's leaning heavily on Mugabe, who finally initialed the settlement on December 17. The White House declared, "The world can celebrate a triumph of reason

Robert Mugabe, Jimmy Carter, Rosalynn Carter, Donald McHenry, Andrew Young, White House, August 27, 1980. *Courtesy of Jimmy Carter Library*

Robert Mugabe and Jimmy Carter, White House, August 27, 1980. *Courtesy of Jimmy Carter Library*

and an extraordinary diplomatic success. A long, destructive and tragic conflict is ending."[37]

The cease-fire went into effect on December 28, and violence markedly diminished. Mugabe returned to his homeland on January 27, 1980, and elections took place one month later. Mugabe's party won fifty-seven seats in parliament, Nkomo's twenty, and Muzorewa's three. Mugabe therefore became the first prime minister of the new nation of Zimbabwe, which celebrated its Independence Day on April 17. Young chaired the American delegation to the festivities, which featured Bob Marley and the Wailers playing "Zimbabwe" and Prince Charles officially handing power to Mugabe. It was an emotionally gratifying moment for Young, who had worked hard to facilitate peace, racial justice, and independence in the southern African nation. Carter lauded Young for his "able representation" at the ceremonies.[38]

Mugabe visited the United States in August and was warmly received, first at the UN and then in Washington. On August 27, 1980, Carter presided over a reception for Mugabe at the White House. He pointed to the parallels between the U.S. and Zimbabwean struggles against racial injustice and he maintained that his administration had placed a much higher priority on Africa than its predecessors. Citing Martin Luther King's principle that "injustice anywhere is a threat to justice everywhere," he praised Young, who was in attendance, for his long-standing efforts for human rights. He recalled that Young had "never let me forget" the struggle in Zimbabwe and attributed much of the impetus for U.S. policy to his former UN ambassador. Young's dedication had helped the Carter administration maintain sanctions and stand on the side of justice. "The peaceful transition of Zimbabwe to popular majority rule is the strongest affirmation of our own human rights policy," concluded Carter.[39]

The reception for Mugabe in August 1980 allowed Young to take pride in his contribution to one of the most successful components of Carter's foreign policy. The peaceful transition from Southern Rhodesia to Zimbabwe was a major focus of his work between 1978 and 1980, and it succeeded. During his second and third years as UN ambassador, and even after resigning, Young further developed positive relations between the United States and Africa. He also spread Carter's human rights message and improved the image of the United States in the Pacific region, most notably in Australia. Throughout Carter's presidency, Young succeeded to a great extent in bringing Martin Luther King's vision onto the international stage. When Ronald Reagan soundly defeated Carter in November 1980, it was clear that American foreign policy would revert to a traditional Cold War stance. Obviously there was no place in the new administration for Andrew Young, and his focus returned to his adopted home city of Atlanta.

Notes

1. Dole and Hatch to Carter, February 22, 1978, folder "CO 129:1/1/78–6/30/78," box CO50, White House Central File—Subject (hereafter WHCF–S), Jimmy Carter Library, Atlanta, Georgia (hereafter JCL).

2. Statement by Young, March 14, 1978, untitled folder, box 81, Charles Diggs Papers, Moorland–Spingarn Library, Howard University, Washington, DC (hereafter CD), 10.

3. Carter quoted in Robert Shepard, *Nigeria, Africa, and the United States: From Kennedy to Reagan* (Bloomington: Indiana University Press, 1991), 110.

4. Ian Smith, *The Great Betrayal: The Memoirs of Africa's Most Controversial Leader* (London: Blake, 1997), 252.

5. Young, interview with the author, March 2, 1994, Atlanta, Georgia.

6. McLaughlin, quoted in Ron Kraybill, "Transition from Rhodesia to Zimbabwe: The Role of Religious Actors,"in Douglas Johnston and Cynthia Sampson, eds., *Religion: The Missing Dimension of Statecraft* (New York: Oxford University Press, 1994), 215.

7. Young's testimony in "U.S. Policy Toward Africa," Hearing before the Subcommittee on African Affairs of the Committee on Foreign Relations, United States Senate, 95th Cong., 2d sess., May 12, 1978.

8. Young's interview in *Le Matin* (Paris), printed in the *Congressional Record*, July 24, 1978, copy in folder "IT 86-27 1/1/78–7/31/78," box IT10, WHCF–International Organizations, JCL.

9. Dan Quayle to Jimmy Carter, July 13, 1978, Name File–Andrew Young, JCL.

10. Carter quoted in Bartlett C. Jones, *Flawed Triumphs: Andy Young at the United Nations* (Lanham, MD: University Press of America, 1996), 121.

11. Statistics regarding correspondence about Young's statement in memos from Barbara Renter to Young, August 11 and August 18, 1978; Daisy Young to President Carter, September 6, 1978, folder "IT 86-27 8/1/78–1/20/81," box IT10, WHCF–Subject, JCL.

12. Byrd to Lee Brubaker, October 13, 1978, folder "1978 Oct–Dec For Rel Rhod," box 284, Harry F. Byrd Jr. Papers, University of Virginia Library, Charlottesville (hereafter HB).

13. Hal Gulliver, "Young: Conservative? Radical?" *Atlanta Constitution*, December 4, 1978; Stephen Rosenfeld, "Andrew Young at Work in Africa," *Washington Post*, December 8, 1978; Gilbert Cranberg, "Andrew Young Earning Respect as 'Defender of African Rights,' " *Des Moines Register*, December 6, 1978.

14. Handwritten note at the bottom of card from Carter to Young, December 22, 1978, Name File–Andrew Young, JCL.

15. Southeast Asian issues are discussed in Jones, *Flawed Triumphs*, 103–4.

16. Peyser to Young, January 17, 1979, folder "IT 86-27 8/1/78–1/20/81," box IT10, WHCF–Subject, JCL.

17. Discussion of Iran and the Young quotations appear in Jones, *Flawed Triumphs*, 100–101.

18. Young to Senator Edmund Muskie, February 5, 1979, folder "Foreign Relations–Rhodesia, #9," box 2972, Edmund Muskie Collection, Muskie Archives, Bates College, Lewiston, Maine.

19. Nkomo, quoted in Andrew DeRoche, *Black, White, and Chrome: The United States and Zimbabwe, 1953–1998* (Trenton, NJ: Africa World Press, 2001), 274.

20. Carter, quoted in ibid., 275.

21. Rather to Carter, April 23, 1979, folder "IT 86-27 8/1/78–1/20/81," box IT10, WHCF–Subject, JCL.

22. Young's trip is summarized in Jones, *Flawed Triumphs*, 104–6.

23. Philip Alston to Carter, May 4, 1979, folder "IT 86-27 8/1/78–1/20/81," box IT10, WHCF–Subject, JCL.

24. Andrew Young, *A Way Out of No Way: The Spiritual Memoirs of Andrew Young* (Nashville: Thomas Nelson, 1994), 137.

25. The events from July 26 to August 14 are detailed in Jones, *Flawed Triumphs*, 130–31.

26. Young to Carter, August 14, 1979, folder "Andrew Young," box 109, Staff Offices–Louis Martin, JCL.

27. Carter to Young, August 15, 1979, Andrew Young–Name File, JCL.

28. "Statement of Black Leadership Forum," August 16, 1979, folder "IT 86-27 8/1/78–1/20/81," box IT10, WHCF–Subject, JCL.

29. Joseph Kraft, "Andrew Young's Transgression," *Washington Post*, August 16, 1979.

30. American Jewish Congress, "The American Jewish Congress Responds to SCLC in Its Call For New Black–Jewish Dialogue Following Resignation of Ambassador Young," August 16, 1979, folder "IT 86-27 8/1/78–1/20/81," box IT10, WHCF–Subject, JCL.

31. Discussion of the meeting and the statement are quoted in Jonathan Kaufman, *Broken Alliance: The Turbulent Times between Blacks and Jews in America* (New York: Simon & Schuster, 1995), 246.

32. Jimmy Carter, *Keeping Faith: Memoirs of a President* (New York: Bantam Books, 1982), 491.

33. Gaddis Smith, *Morality, Reason and Power: American Diplomacy in the Carter Years* (New York: Hill & Wang, 1986), 168.

34. John Dumbrell, *The Carter Presidency: A Re-Evaluation*, 2d ed. (Manchester, England: Manchester University Press, 1995), 103–4.

35. Jones, *Flawed Triumphs*, 151.

36. Letter from Carter to Nyerere included in telegram from Vance to the U.S. embassy in Tanzania, September 5, 1979, Name File–Andrew Young, JCL.

37. Press release, quoted in DeRoche, *Black, White, and Chrome*, 285.

38. Carter to Young, April 30, 1980, Name File–Andrew Young, JCL.

39. Remarks by Carter at White House, August 27, 1980, *Public Papers of the Presidents: Jimmy Carter* (Washington, DC: United States Government Printing Office, 1982), 1580–82.

6

Atlanta's Globetrotting Mayor

1981–1989

From 1981 to 1989, Andrew Young influenced U.S. foreign relations to an unprecedented degree for a mayor. He traveled the globe ceaselessly, promoting trade and attracting investment for Atlanta with enthusiasm and charisma. He consistently criticized the Reagan administration's foreign policy. Instead of confronting communism, he sought to build bridges to the Soviet Union, China, Nicaragua, and Angola. Young contributed significantly to the antiapartheid movement that imposed sanctions on South Africa and helped to keep Martin Luther King's vision alive, both at home and abroad. He informed people around the world that Atlanta was a human rights capital and that the city's prosperity reflected its progressive race relations. Capitalizing on his people skills, his reputation as a civil rights leader, and his connections at the United Nations, Young capped off his mayoral tenure by securing a shot at the 1996 summer Olympics for Atlanta. Journalists observed that Young was more like a secretary of state than a mayor and that Atlanta was a city with its own foreign policy. His globe-trotting transformed Atlanta into an international city and redefined the potential role of mayors in foreign relations.

After attending the celebration at the White House of the independence of Zimbabwe in August 1980, during which he was praised for his role in one of the Carter administration's few foreign policy successes, Young returned to Atlanta. He was developing a nonprofit company called Young Ideas and was in high demand as a speaker. He was recognized and respected around the city, but he was unsure of what he would do next. Maynard

Jackson, the first black mayor of Atlanta, whose tenure was nearly over, hoped Young would be his successor. Jackson knew that the white establishment wanted a white mayor, and hence it would take a remarkable black candidate to win the post. He set up several dinners to rally support and convince Young that he should run, and the turning point came during a meeting at the Omni Hotel. After Jackson summarized the political and economic landscape of Atlanta, Susie Labond rose to speak. As president of the Public Housing Tenants Association, Labond stated her case: "Andy, when you came to Atlanta you wasn't nobody. We took you in and made you somebody. We sent you to Congress, you been Ambassador to the U.N., but now we need you to be mayor."[1]

The combination of Jackson's pressure and Labond's plea persuaded Young to run. To raise money for the campaign he called on such friends in New York as Harry Belafonte. By late summer 1981, they had raised hundreds of thousands of dollars in contributions from wealthy liberals of all races. Back in Atlanta, it was a different story. The white leadership almost unanimously backed Sidney Marcus, a white state legislator. Among the few influential whites favoring Young was Republican furniture magnate Charles Loudermilk. When Loudermilk sought support from banker Robert Strickland, the latter replied, characteristically, "Over my dead body. This is our last chance of having a white mayor."[2]

In addition to staunch white opposition, Young also faced a worthy black challenger in Reginald Eaves. A former police chief who had resigned amid controversy, Eaves ran a racially charged campaign. Young, on the other hand, advocated interracial cooperation as designed to make Atlanta a center for international trade, particularly trade with Africa. This vision impressed a few leading whites, including Ivan Allen III, whose wife later recalled that "Ivan thought Andy hung the moon."[3] Allen's father had been mayor during the 1960s and had backed Young's run for Congress in 1972. Father and son both believed Young would make a great mayor, but their support was behind the scenes and they did little to persuade other wealthy whites to jump on the bandwagon.

Young finished first in the general election with 41 percent of the vote, just ahead of Marcus, who garnered 39 percent. Since neither had received a majority, Atlanta law stipulated a runoff. As expected, most blacks voted for Young and most whites voted for Marcus. Because two-thirds of Atlanta's population was African American, Young won easily, receiving 55 percent of the vote.

Although blacks put Young in office, he still deemed the assistance of the white business community crucial to his success as mayor. The day after his election he met with several leading white citizens to form an alliance. "I didn't get elected with your help," Young told them, "but I can't govern without you."[4]

The forty-nine-year-old Young prepared to take control of Atlanta's government with his typical optimism, and in many ways his new position benefited his entire family. After three years in New York, his wife welcomed the return to Atlanta where they could raise their eight-year-old son Bo in more familiar surroundings. Their eldest daughter, Andrea, practiced law in Atlanta, and their youngest daughter, Paula, was a student at Duke University. During her husband's tenure at the UN, Jean had chaired the American Commission for the International Year of the Child. As Atlanta's First Lady, she intended to continue working on children's issues and also to focus on women's concerns and international relations. Embarked on his new career in city politics, her husband needed her as much as ever.

On January 4, 1982, Andrew Young took the oath of office as Atlanta's fifty-fifth mayor before a crowd of about eight thousand people in the Omni Coliseum. Dignitaries in attendance included many of Young's comrades from the civil rights movement such as Jesse Jackson, Marion Barry, mayor of Washington, DC, and Walter Fauntroy, Washington, DC, representative to Congress. Fittingly, the new mayor opened his inaugural address by praising Atlanta's leadership in the civil rights struggles of the 1960s. In the 1970s, he continued, Atlanta played a key role in the political revolution that put African Americans into office across the country. He then called on Atlanta to point the way again for the nation in the 1980s, when the challenge was primarily economic.

Young espoused a close relationship between City Hall and the business community in order to attract investment from outside the city. He hoped to create "a new consciousness of Atlanta as a regional center for international finance and export trade." Part of the city's appeal, he argued, was its reputation for progressive race relations. He contended that the delegations attending his inaugural were there not only to see him, but also because they considered Atlanta "a beacon light of people living and working together." For Atlanta to become a truly international city, he concluded, minority rights must remain a hallmark. The city attracted new residents from every continent, and "all must be well represented and must be consulted and respected as a part of our total Atlanta family."[5] Just as his own work in the civil rights movement had led him to the international stage at the UN, Young believed that Atlanta's positive race relations were a key to the city's becoming a force in the global economy.

As a personification of Atlanta's progressive race relations, Young could do much to generate international interest in the city. During his first year in City Hall, he worked hard to attract foreign investment. In at least one instance, his influence was decisive: his introductions led a Nigerian official to contract for $1 million worth of satellite equipment with an Atlanta company. In December 1982, he cosponsored the International Conference on Central America and the Caribbean Basin, which attracted several foreign leaders, including former Jamaican prime minister Michael Manley to Atlanta. When asked why he had come, Manley smiled, pointed at Young, and said, "He brings me here."[6] During his first year in office, Young had visited Suriname, Tunisia, Algeria, Italy, Britain, and Nigeria, always plugging his city.

In late March 1983, the mayor again went on the road to sell his city, this time to Manhattan as part of a delegation of politicians and business people from across Georgia. Speaking to editors at *Business Week*, Young praised Atlanta's potential as an international trade center. He contended that New York was so big that out-of-towners could easily get lost, but that if potential clients came to his city looking for business, he would help them find it. Later the Georgians hosted a lunch for thirty business people at the Waldorf-Astoria, where Young had lived as UN ambassador. The return visit invoked good memories. Entering the lobby, he recalled, "I taught my son to ride a bike in that alley over there."[7] His star power shone brightly in his old stomping grounds, and his value as a salesman for Atlanta could not have been clearer. His frequent travel did spark complaints, however, and some of his constituents believed he should pay more attention to the daily concerns of his city. During an early April sermon, Young responded to these criticisms. He stated that there were so few potholes in Atlanta that he could fix them himself. About eighty people called the next day, requesting that the mayor fill potholes; and so later that week Young spent three hours in a hard hat and work gloves repairing streets.

Although he enjoyed his road work, international affairs still remained high on Young's agenda. In addition to promoting foreign investment in his city, the mayor emerged in 1983 as an outspoken critic of the Reagan administration's foreign relations. During Human Rights Week in April, he condemned Reagan's

policy in El Salvador, where the United States supported the government in its fight against insurgents. He condemned the policy for "attempting to solve a human rights problem by military means," and concluded that this approach would do more harm than good.[8]

Young continued his efforts to make Atlanta an international city, and he could point to many positive gains as his second year in office drew to a close. Hartsfield International Airport ranked among the busiest passenger airports in the world and featured nonstop flights to eight foreign countries. Representatives of some thirty-seven foreign governments resided in Atlanta, and the metro area featured more than four hundred foreign-owned companies and nineteen foreign banks. The Atlanta Council of International Organizations included some fifty groups that made life easier for foreign visitors in the city. The Southern Center for International Studies promoted awareness of world affairs, thus making Atlanta more comfortable for foreigners and boosting business. The City Council formed an international relations committee with the same goals in mind. Clearly, Young was only part of a broad effort to put Atlanta in a prominent position on the world map.

Despite the progress in transforming Atlanta into an international city, not everyone approved. As Young's frequent travel invited criticism, so, too, did some of his foreign guests. In mid-September 1983, he welcomed Robert Mugabe, the president of Zimbabwe, to Atlanta. Charles Wood, a member of the Rotary Club, characterized Mugabe as a Stalinist and blamed him for massacres in Zimbabwe. Young responded to Wood and justified his hospitality: "I don't defend the human rights practices of Zimbabwe. I just think Robert Mugabe is the best hope we have. . . . I don't want to see us isolate them and lead them to the Russians."[9] Surprisingly, support for Mugabe was one foreign policy view that Young shared with Ronald Reagan. Before his stop in Atlanta, the Zimbabwean leader had met with Reagan at the White House. Reagan had praised Zimbabwe "as an inspiration in its part of the world."[10] The Reagan administration acted on this assertion by requesting $75 million in aid for Zimbabwe. Congress approved only $40 million, but that was still a large grant for a small nation in southern Africa. Ongoing positive American relations with Zimbabwe surely pleased Young, who had done so much to bring peace and majority rule there while UN ambassador.

On January 1, 1984, the *Atlanta Journal and Constitution* ran a feature story on the mayor's frequent trips. Businessman Dillard Munford told a reporter he believed Young should be focusing on his job instead of "gallivanting around the country." The mayor defended his travels on several levels. First, he pointed out that he always stayed in contact with City Hall by telephone. Second, he argued that he worked such long days when he was in Atlanta that he was putting in requisite time on city affairs, anyway. Most important, he contended that his excursions were a key part of his job. Whenever he went on the road he expended considerable energy drumming up business for Atlanta. His main concern about traveling, in fact, was that he had not been doing enough. He intended to make even more expeditions during 1984. "I want to know what it is the city needs that will get it ready for the next century. I think the way I'm going about it, I'm much more likely to stumble upon that, than sitting at a desk pushing paper," he explained.[11]

During the first three months of 1984, Young succeeded in his goal of increasing his travel. He enjoyed the globe-trotting aspect of his job considerably and could joke about it, as he did in a speech to the Atlanta Chamber of Commerce: "All I have to do, really, is go around the world bragging about what we are doing—what you are doing, because I probably am not here long enough to do anything."[12] By the end of March he had been to five foreign countries and ten American cities, spending nearly half his weekdays outside Atlanta. He delivered speeches in the Bahamas and the Virgin Islands. He visited Tunisia twice, first to plan and then to attend a conference on world trade. During a six-day journey in South Korea, Young stopped in Atlanta's sister city of Taegu. He also met with South Korea's president and persuaded him to send a Korean trade delegation to Atlanta.

In addition to international trade, in 1984, Young put significant energy into national politics. In early March the mayor appeared on *Meet the Press* to discuss the presidential election, especially the candidacy of Jesse Jackson, Young's friend from the civil rights days. This was a tricky subject for the mayor, because he had spoken out against the groundswell for a black candidate during the previous spring. He had stuck to his guns, insisting that blacks should not back a candidate just because he was black. Instead, they should support Walter Mondale because he had the best chance of defeating Reagan. It was a courageous stand for integrationist principles—and also for practical politics. By the time of his appearance on national television, however, Jackson's popularity had caused the mayor to temporize. When questioned about the chances of Jackson's winning the Democratic nomination, Young responded, "I don't want to be the one that pours cold water on the possibility."[13] Young's struggles with the Jackson candidacy were just beginning.

Back in Atlanta later in the month, Young played host to François Mitterrand, the president of France. Approximately seventy-five foreign reporters covered Mitterrand's visit, and the mayor greeted them all. They asked Young a wide range of questions regarding international relations. He offered his insights on the Third World and took the opportunity to criticize Reagan's policies in Central America. Young's performance seemed more like that of a secretary of state than of a mayor. He acknowledged once again that his focus on world affairs was controversial: "They joke that we are a city that tries to have its own foreign policy."[14] He was not far off the mark. Although Young was not involved in the formal diplomacy of foreign policy, in the strictest sense of the word, as mayor of Atlanta he continued to influence American foreign relations.

Andrew Young with François Mitterrand (*right*), Paris, 1988. *Courtesy of Louise Suggs*

In late May, Young joined a group of about twenty Atlantans on a trip to Sweden seeking investments. He talked with the president of Scandinavian Airlines about adding flights to Atlanta and he delivered several speeches, including one about the new role that cities were playing in the growth of the American economy. Young's ability to attract attention at the highest level of government was his greatest contribution to the trip. Two prime minsters, Olof Palme of Sweden and Kalevi Sorsa of Finland, hosted a luncheon for the group in Stockholm. It was remarkable testimony to

Young's reputation that two heads of state welcomed a group of politicians and business people from a midsized American city.

In the summer of 1984, Young focused much of his energy on the presidential race. Jackson's campaign continued to gather momentum, astounding all observers. He amassed startling percentages of the primary votes in major states: 26 percent in New York, 24 percent in New Jersey, and 19 percent in California. When Jackson arrived at the Democratic National Convention in San Francisco in July, he brought 3.5 million votes—representing 21 percent of all Democratic votes in the primaries and caucuses. His performance translated into 384 delegates, or third place behind Mondale and Senator Gary Hart (D–Colo.), but was very significant nonetheless. With such a measure of credibility, Jackson believed he deserved some say in shaping the Democratic platform.

One of Jackson's proposed platform planks espoused eradication of primary runoffs, a Southern tradition that he considered racist because it tended to eliminate minority candidates. In front of millions of television viewers, Young opposed Jackson's proposal. He contended that runoffs were not racist and that he and many other minority candidates had benefited from the system. Jackson supporters in the crowd hissed and jeered, and Young could barely finish his remarks. He left the stage shocked and hurt and found his wife crying in the wings. The next day, Coretta King scolded a group of Jacksonians, who promptly heckled her to the point of tears. Jackson took the podium and asked his unruly backers to recall "the roads I've walked with Andy, and the leadership of Mrs. King, her home bombed, her husband assassinated." The crowd came to order and everyone on stage linked arms and sang "We Shall Overcome."[15]

It was a noble gesture, and the Jackson–Young friendship survived their political differences. Young certainly agreed with Jackson on a number of issues, such as their outrage over the South African system of apartheid. In late August 1984, the eyes of the world turned toward South Africa to view its first elections under a new constitution. That document allowed some participation by Indians and mixed race "coloreds," but continued to deny blacks any political rights. Trouble began on September 3, when protests erupted in the townships. The security forces shot at crowds, detained thousands, and clamped down on the press. In the United States, news broadcasts showed South African police attacking unarmed demonstrators. The brutality prompted Senator Paul Tsongas (D–Mass.) to question the Reagan administration's policy of "constructive engagement" and to call for sanctions against South Africa.

Young would eventually join Tsongas and others in the push for sanctions, but in the fall of 1984 he was busy campaigning for Mondale. The most interesting thing about Mondale's campaign was his choice of a female running mate, Congresswoman Geraldine Ferraro of New York. Even this historic first could not save Mondale, who admitted he would raise taxes and tried to focus on such serious issues as the economy. The people preferred Reagan, who preached patriotism and family values. Reagan won in a landslide, capturing every state except Minnesota, Mondale's home state.

Young was distressed at the prospect of four more years of Reagan's hard-line Cold War foreign policy. In particular, a continuation of the Reagan policy toward South Africa displeased many activists, most notably Randall Robinson. An African-American graduate of Harvard Law School, Robinson headed TransAfrica, the group Young had helped found to lobby for African concerns. On November 21, 1984, Robinson and some compatriots sat down in the South African Embassy in Washington and announced that they would not leave until the government in Pretoria released all political prisoners. Arrested promptly, they spent the night in jail, and the story of the sit-in appeared on the network news.

TransAfrica's use of the sit-in tactics associated with Martin Luther King sparked considerable interest. To coordinate demonstrations at the South African Embassy and at other locations around the country, Robinson organized the Free South Africa Movement, hoping to see comprehensive sanctions imposed. Long hours by Robinson and his staff got the campaign off the ground. Entertainers such as Tony Randall joined the picketers. High-profile arrests of members of Congress and leaders of such organizations as the Southern Christian Leadership Conference kept the issue in the news. Protesters marched daily in Washington, and by early December similar actions were occurring in New York and Boston.

In spring 1985, Young joined the antiapartheid struggle and continued criticizing Reagan's foreign policy generally. On March 18, he met with leaders of several groups planning a Washington demonstration to support stopping the arms race, imposing sanctions against South Africa, and ending U.S. military intervention in Central America. He hoped that the protests would remind the American people of the choice the nation could make in its foreign policies between "death and destruction," on the one hand, and "life and development," on the other. A few days later he led an antiapartheid rally in Atlanta's Central City Park. "We are still concerned and are still opposed to the system of apartheid," Young stated.[16] He added that Atlanta was doing its part by refusing to invest in any companies that did business in South Africa.

In April, Young traveled to Paris as part of a large trade mission sponsored by the Atlanta Chamber of Commerce. After a few days of selling his city to the French, he visited his daughter Paula in Uganda, where she was teaching English and participating in the Habitat for Humanity program there. At her request, he brought one thousand pine tree saplings, which she intended to plant to help control soil erosion. The mayor met General Basilio Okello, leader of the Ugandan Army. Young introduced the general to his daughter and asked him to look out for her. A few weeks later, the mayor addressed the Atlanta Chapter of the French–American Chamber of Commerce, which had been established in January. Serge Bellanger, president of the French–American Chamber, also attended the luncheon and praised Young. He proclaimed, "We are proud of having a chamber of commerce in Atlanta because your mayor is a very, very good friend in our country."[17]

Meanwhile, the crisis in South Africa escalated. In February 1985, blacks outside Capetown erected barricades to resist their removal to "homelands," the rural locations in which they were required to live under apartheid. After security forces and some 3,000 blacks exchanged rubber bullets and stones, a real battle erupted that left 250 civilians wounded and 18 dead. On March 21, about 4,000 people gathered near Port Elizabeth to celebrate the International Day of the Elimination of Racial Discrimination. Without provocation, police opened fire and killed 19 participants. They then placed sticks in the hands of the dead to disguise the massacre and instructed firemen to hose away the blood. News of the brutality prompted members of the U.S. Congress to take action, and a strong push for sanctions ensued. In March, Representative Ronald Dellums (D–Ca.) introduced a resolution to block new U.S. investment in South Africa, prohibit American bank loans to South Africa, ban sales of Krugerrands in the United States, and stop American computer sales to South Africa. The Congressional Black Caucus, of which Dellums was a key member, had grown to twenty members and wielded increasing clout.

In April and May, the Senate Foreign Relations Committee held extensive hearings regarding possible sanctions against South Africa. Young testified on May 22. Senator Nancy Kassebaum (R–Kans.) asked the mayor if he thought the sanctions against Southern

Rhodesia in the 1970s had been effective. He believed they had been. First, they targeted particular items such as chrome. Second, they were part of a larger effort to resolve the conflict, which also included military and diplomatic activities. Unfocused sanctions on their own, he asserted, would not have achieved results in Southern Rhodesia, nor would they end apartheid. They could, however, become a key piece in a bigger puzzle. Young argued that the U.S. government needed to make a forceful statement against apartheid and that the legislation under consideration would do just that.

Young next provided insight into how sanctions could facilitate change in South Africa. He believed that there were progressive elements in the white government who wanted to end apartheid, but hesitated for political reasons. Strong sanctions would give them an excuse to do what they thought was right. The mayor recalled negotiations during the civil rights struggles when he and the white officials agreed on what changes needed to be made, but the whites were afraid to risk the next election by going public. Both sides quietly went to the courts and sought changes. Segregation laws were overturned without undermining white political careers. Young contended that sanctions imposed by Congress could serve the same purpose in ending apartheid. He concluded: "In difficult matters of social change, some outside idealistic authority is needed. I think the U.S. Senate in this case becomes that kind of authority . . . to say to the people of South Africa that they must change quickly in order to avoid chaos and bloodshed."[18]

The House approved its version of sanctions in June, and the Senate endorsed a slightly weaker version in early July. Shortly thereafter, Young discussed South Africa in a lengthy interview in the *Atlanta Journal Constitution*. He restated his support for congressional sanctions that would repudiate the old Cold War view that Americans must align with whites in southern Africa against communism. "The only person who can create a force in the black community, who has enough authority to prevent chaos from spreading, is probably Nelson Mandela," he opined.[19] He suggested that religion would play a role in bringing about a settlement, because of the strength of Christianity among Afrikaners. He added that maintaining dialogue with all parties was crucial for bringing reform; if any South Africans wanted to come into his office and see how a multiracial society worked, they would be welcome. He believed white South Africans could continue to prosper under black majority rule, pointing out that it would resemble the situation in Atlanta where blacks controlled politics and whites managed the economy. As the mayor of a city that blended black political power with white economic power, Young's view on South Africa was particularly relevant.

On July 27 a military coup in Uganda temporarily trapped Paula Young in the village of Gulu, where she was working for Habitat for Humanity. She contacted U.S. diplomats in Kampala by radio, who notified her parents that she was safe. The mayor and his wife worried about her nonetheless, until they greeted her at Hartsfield Airport on August 8. "It's good to be back home with my family," she exclaimed. It must have seemed like the understatement of the year to her father, who sat next to her with tears in his eyes. His April introduction of Paula to General Okello, who had seized power in the coup, may well have facilitated her departure. Regardless of his connections in the government, Young did not want his daughter returning to Uganda, which she planned to do. Sounding like a typical parent, the mayor lamented, "None of my children has ever taken my advice anyway."[20]

Samora Machel and Ronald Reagan, White House, September 1985. *Courtesy of Ronald Reagan Library*

Paula Young had returned to Atlanta to be a bridesmaid in the wedding of her oldest sister Andrea on Saturday, August 10. Brother Bo served as a groomsman, and middle sister Lisa joined Paula as a bridesmaid. Both wore necklaces hand-strung by their mother, made from beads that the mayor had acquired in Africa. The festive occasion provided the entire Young family with a welcome respite

from the political fray. Several hundred guests, including come-
dian Eddie Murphy, attended the reception at City Hall, where they
feasted on crabmeat, caviar, and salmon. It was a grand celebration for an impressive couple, who were following in Andrew
Young's footsteps. The mayor's new son-in-law, the Reverend A.
Knighton Stanley, was a Congregational minister in Washington,
and Andrea would be Secretary of African Affairs for the United
Church of Christ. Although he might joke that his children never
took his advice, he must have been very pleased with Andrea's
choices on that day.

In early September, Young's attention once again turned to relations with southern Africa. In Washington, the House and the
Senate had approved different versions of sanctions against South
Africa, and they were near agreement on a compromise. Reagan,
following advice of such hard-liners as Senator Jesse Helms (R–
N.C.), continued to resist comprehensive sanctions. On September 9,
Reagan issued Executive Order 12532, which banned computer sales
and bank loans to South Africa. But Reagan's policy, unlike the congressional version, did not mandate additional economic sanctions
if conditions in South Africa failed to improve. In conjunction with
the president's initiative, Senator Bob Dole (R–Kans.) removed the
sanctions bill from consideration in Congress. The executive order
signified White House concessions to the antiapartheid movement,
while allowing the president to save face and retain control of foreign policy temporarily.

Although critics portrayed the Reagan administration's policy
toward southern Africa, known as "constructive engagement," simply as a racist stance that supported the white minority in South
Africa, it was actually more complex. The architect of constructive
engagement, Assistant Secretary of State for Africa Chester Crocker,
crafted a nuanced approach to southern Africa. Avoiding sanctions
and working with the whites in South Africa were part of Crocker's
policy, but so was supporting the new black governments in Zimbabwe and Mozambique. Therefore, in late September, Reagan
welcomed Mozambique's President Samora Machel to the White
House. The visit boded well for Crocker's efforts to increase American support for Machel's government. After his White House visit,
Machel journeyed to Atlanta. He paid his respects at the tomb of
Martin Luther King and then attended a banquet hosted by Mayor
Young, who had known Machel for nearly ten years. The two breakfasted privately the following morning and discussed potential
economic development and political events in southern Africa.

Between international relations and family affairs, little time remained during the summer of 1985 for Young to campaign for reelection. But since he faced no serious challengers, little time was needed, and he carried 83 percent of the vote. The editors of the *Atlanta Journal Constitution* congratulated Young for his landslide victory and offered general praise. At the same time, the editors rebuked Young for his failure to disclose his personal finances. They pointed, in particular, to his habit of mixing personal and public business when he traveled overseas, but they were careful not to accuse the mayor of corruption. They recognized that Young was not serving as mayor in order to get rich. Indeed, his annual salary of $50,000 paled in comparison to what he had been paid as a speaker between 1979 and 1981. In one year alone during that period, he had earned over $300,000. Instead of pursuing additional riches, however, he had opted for life in City Hall. After his first term he was far from wealthy. His net worth consisted primarily of two modest homes and three well-educated daughters.[21] The editors realized this, but still suggested that Young provide a more thorough accounting of future trips.

As the year ended, Young focused mostly on city business, but also tried to keep his hand in international relations. An early December conversation about foreign affairs with the British media was interrupted by a phone call from twelve-year-old Bo, who was locked out of the house. The mayor calmly took the phone, reminded his son where the family kept the key, and returned to discussing international crises. In mid-December the mayor reminisced about Martin Luther King for a television spot to be included in a series called *Memories of Martin*. The clips were scheduled to air in January and February as part of the first national holiday in King's honor. Young opted to record his piece at Aleck's Barbecue Heaven, where he and King had eaten many meals together. After a heaping barbecued pork sandwich and a Coke, the mayor reminisced: "I remember Martin as a hungry brother who would come in late at night . . . to have what he felt was some of the best barbecue in the world. Here was where he enjoyed the fun and fellowship of the people of Atlanta."[22]

For the mayor and other veterans of the movement, King's struggle for racial justice continued in the fight against apartheid. Young set up a press conference in late December for Stephen Van Zandt, Bruce Springsteen's former guitarist, who had produced the "Sun City" single to raise money for the antiapartheid cause. The song by Artists Against Apartheid, which featured superstars such as Stevie Wonder and Bono of U2, had sold over 250,000 copies. Van Zandt presented $50,000 to Coretta Scott King, a trustee of the fund. She replied that the money would be used to help South African political prisoners and exiles and for educational efforts in the United States.

Helping with this battle against apartheid ranked high on Young's foreign relations agenda as he entered his second term as mayor in January 1986. In response to criticism of his globe-trotting, he replied, "I really don't think I've traveled much at all. Last term, I think I traveled too little." He continued to see international business as the key to Atlanta's prosperity. In his second inaugural address, he pointed to the expansion of Hartsfield International Airport and the new flights from Italy, Japan, and Switzerland as examples of how he had generated business for the city. He envisioned more of the same in Atlanta's future, and took time to underscore the city's progress in race relations. The integration of the inaugural celebration signified remarkable progress. After Dionne Warwick sang the national anthem, Young recalled that it had been only twenty-five years since Harry Belafonte performed before the first integrated audience in the old civic center. "At that time if anybody had said, in 25 years, we're going to have a new civic center, and we're going to swear in a whole bunch of folks and most of them are going to be black . . . nobody, not even me, would have believed it."[23]

Young and his movement compatriots would not have believed that they would see a national holiday for Martin Luther King, either, but, surprisingly, in 1983 Reagan had announced the holiday was to be celebrated in 1986 on the third Monday of January. Atlanta planned ten days of events leading up to the January 20 observance and expected a half million visitors. The mayor was in high demand. On Tuesday, January 14, he participated in a panel with Ralph Abernathy. On the fifteenth, he rose before dawn for a live CBS interview, led a tribute at the state capitol, dedicated a train station in King's name, attended ceremonies at the King Center, and spoke at the Butler Street YMCA. On Saturday, he attended a convocation at Morehouse College, which featured an address by Bill Cosby. On Sunday, he listened to a sermon and keynote talk at the Ebenezer Baptist Church by South African Bishop Desmond Tutu, winner of the 1984 Nobel Peace Prize. Bishop Tutu praised King as an inspiration for the antiapartheid movement and pledged to lead a civil disobedience campaign in South Africa.

Soon after the King festivities concluded, Young and Jimmy Carter embarked on an agricultural mission to Africa. Their first stop was in the Sudan, where they talked with Dinka peoples about better ways to grow wheat. Next, they visited Tanzania, where they discussed peanut farming with their friend President Julius Nyerere. From there the group flew to Zambia to visit President Kenneth Kaunda. Although corn prospered in Zambia, the people imported wheat to make bread. This prompted Young to propose an interesting way to promote cornbread among the Zambians—a television show featuring Rosalynn Carter and Betty Kaunda concocting the southern staple. "Cornbread will be in," he predicted.[24] The group concluded their trip in Ghana, having realized some positive outcomes, such as convincing key officials of the value of hybrid millet seeds that would resist both drought and insects.

In mid-May, the mayor joined a Chamber of Commerce trade mission to Ireland and West Germany. In Limerick he explained that the new Delta flights from Atlanta to Shannon Airport would stimulate commercial activity and tourism. He delivered a similar message in Stuttgart, another new Delta destination. After lunching on a sausage sandwich and a Coke, Young offered his views on Atlanta's success to about sixty German businesspeople. Good race relations and cooperation between the public and private sectors had attracted nearly $30 billion in new investments to Atlanta since 1983, he explained, and the prosperity would continue. Before the group left Stuttgart, a German producer of building materials announced that the firm was opening facilities in Atlanta, which would involve about one hundred new jobs for Georgians.

In Munich, the mayor participated in a trade seminar that attracted over one hundred German businesspeople. The healthy turnout reflected Young's international popularity. According to Dale Slaught, a U.S. Commerce Department official stationed in Munich, the people there considered Young a "civil rights leader" and a "champion of human rights." Several members of the trade delegation commented very favorably on the mayor's central role in the success of the mission. They praised him not only for his ability to articulate the strengths of Atlanta, but also for his skill in adapting to local cultures and thus establishing bonds of friendship. As Young himself observed, "I see my role as making an introduction."[25] It was a role for which he was well suited.

The trade mission had taken place in spite of heightened concerns about terrorism. A few weeks before the trip, the U.S. military had launched strikes against Muammar Qaddafi, the leader of Libya, who was suspected of sponsoring terrorists. In a lengthy column in the June 1, 1986, *Atlanta Journal Constitution*, Young advocated a multinational response to terrorism. He argued presciently that the real threat to American interests was Islamic extremism, not Qaddafi. Young proposed working with other nations of northern Africa and the Middle East both to contain Qaddafi and to address the other nations' concerns. He believed that a coordinated and cautious approach would be a useful step toward stability in the region, whereas continuing to strike unilaterally at Libya could in fact do more harm than good. If Qaddafi should survive the attacks, he would be a hero to Muslim extremists. If he died, he would become a martyr. On the other hand, cooperating with Arab and African states to isolate Libya would injure Qaddafi without adding fuel to the fire. Young concluded that there was no ready solution to the problem of terrorism and that "peace and stability require time and patience and consensus."[26]

In pursuit of his vision of a more cooperative global climate, Young remained involved with his nonprofit group, Young Ideas. Founded to improve relations between the developing world and the United States, the organization produced newsletters and sponsored conferences to promote better communications. In late June the mayor hosted a fundraiser in Washington for Young Ideas, at which guests paid $200 apiece for dinner and a chance to roast Young. As it turned out, most of them praised him instead. Representative Patricia Schroeder (D–Colo.) lauded him for respecting women. Congressman Dick Gephardt (D–Mo.) complimented Young's criticism of American policy in Nicaragua. Walter Fauntroy characterized Young as "a visionary and a genius." Most noteworthy was the presence of Jesse Jackson, in spite of Young's failure to endorse his presidential aspirations. Jackson wrapped the mayor up in a bear hug and exclaimed, "I'm basically here because I love Andy."[27] Even after five years as mayor of Atlanta, Young remained a popular and powerful figure on the national political stage, and many influential Democrats agreed with his ideas about foreign relations.

Back in Atlanta he rejoined the fight against apartheid. In a letter to Bishop Tutu, which appeared in the *New York Times* on July 27, Young advocated an international embargo on commercial flights to South Africa. He argued that it would be a considerable inconvenience for whites, but have virtually no effect on blacks. Furthermore, it was a very specific measure that could be closely monitored and thus be better enforced than broad economic sanctions. He urged Congress to take strong action. He then met in Washington on July 30 with six senators on the Foreign Relations Committee, prodding them to pass a tough sanctions bill. Shortly thereafter, the *Washington Post* published his rationale for an airline embargo, which he described as "more redemptive than punitive, more creative than destructive."[28]

Young also took an interest in policy toward Angola, where the Reagan administration supported the rebel forces of Jonas Savimbi in their fight against the government. At the invitation of Stoney Cooks, his former assistant who had been hired as a lobbyist by the Angolan government, Young flew to Luanda in early August. Young made the trip in spite of a travel warning issued by the State Department and the lack of official diplomatic relations between the countries. The government in Luanda warmly welcomed the mayor, honoring him at a lavish state banquet. Offering a champagne toast, Young decried official American policy as "a tragic mistake."[29] During the five-course meal, the mayor touted the potential for connections between Angola and Atlanta.

After the fancy ceremonies in Luanda, he toured the war-torn southern provinces. He spoke with government soldiers in the bombed-out provincial capital of Ondjiva, only a few miles from South African troops who backed Savimbi's revolt. In the northern province of Cabinda, the mayor inspected an offshore oil rig run jointly by the government and Chevron Oil. He dined on steak with Chevron officials from Texas, who managed the $450-million drilling operation. The American engineers lived comfortably in their air-conditioned complex, which was guarded by some of the thirty thousand Cuban soldiers in Angola supporting the Marxist government. Intent on hearing from all sides, Young visited a captured member of Savimbi's army in prison. The mayor departed from Angola having been sensitized to the extreme complexity of the situation but still certain that funding Savimbi's forces was bad policy, and he imparted that message to members of Congress.

Young's displeasure with American policy toward Angola was soon overshadowed by satisfaction regarding relations with South Africa, when the Senate approved tough sanctions on August 14. In September, the House concurred, and sent the Comprehensive Anti-Apartheid Act (CAAA) to Reagan for his signature. Out of touch with the widespread nature of American activism against apartheid, the president vetoed the bill. Congress quickly overturned his veto, handing him one of the worst setbacks of his presidency. Passage of the CAAA also signified the tremendous increase in African-American political power. Black state and city officials, such as Young, led the nationwide movement that had forced Congress to act. Most important, the CAAA had teeth. It banned private loans, new investments, and computer sales by Americans to South Africa. It blocked the importing of South African steel, uranium, and agricultural products into the United States and withdrew landing rights in the United States for South African planes. Henceforth, the Pretoria regime woud pay a concrete price for maintaining apartheid.

Although his previous excursion, to Angola, generated considerable criticism in Atlanta, Young resumed globe-trotting in late September as the leader of a trade mission to Asia. The first stop was Tokyo, where the Atlantans soon found themselves in the midst of a diplomatic crisis. Prime Minister Yasuhiro Nakasone attributed the high level of education and intelligence in Japan to the homogeneous nature of its society. He contrasted that with a lower level of education and intelligence in the United States, which he blamed on the high number of blacks and Hispanics. An uproar ensued among African-American leaders in Washington, but Young responded calmly. He remarked that the prime minister probably did not know much about American society and should be forgiven for the comments.

Nakasone very quickly issued a formal apology, and on September 29 he met with Young. The mayor praised the prime minister for apologizing, and suggested that contact between Japanese officials and American minorities be increased. "I welcome more dialogue," replied Nakasone.[30] Once again demonstrating his ability as a mediator, Young succeeded in preventing the incident from seriously damaging United States–Japan relations. It was an important example of the intersection of racial issues and foreign policy, and Young was well qualified to handle it. The next day Young discussed a wide range of international issues at the Foreign Correspondents' Club of Japan. He encouraged investment in Atlanta and predicted a rapid rise in commerce due to the new direct flights. Over the next few years, Japanese involvement in Atlanta's economy increased tremendously, fostered by Young's skillful diplomacy.

During the last few months of 1986 the mayor stayed home and focused primarily on local affairs. In October, he participated in the opening ceremonies of the Carter Presidential Center. On Thanksgiving Day he visited with some of the thousands of homeless people who dined at the Atlanta Civic Center. The massive effort was organized by Hosea Williams and funded mostly by corporate donations. Young commented, "One thing you realize is there are some wonderful people out here, homeless, and there, but for the grace of God, go I."[31] The next morning, in spite of feeling ill and with a cold rain falling, the mayor kicked off a campaign for the Children's Wish Foundation. He stood on a streetcorner and collected donations from passing motorists. In a year-ending act of charity inspired by his mother-in-law, the mayor and his family donated the money they would have spent on Christmas gifts to a homeless family for the first month's rent on an apartment.

In January 1987, Young attended a week-long African-American conference in Botswana. Speaking in the capital city of Gaborone, he urged the people of Botswana and neighboring nations to seek help from private corporations such as Coca-Cola. He compared their plight during the Reagan years to that of American cities, which also had failed to receive sufficient federal aid. Like Atlanta, African nations should focus on attracting private investment. He hoped that the governments of the world's wealthy nations would someday make Africa a higher priority, but until then the best solution was through the private sector. The response to his procapitalism message was mixed. He met an ambivalent response a few days later when speaking to rural Botswanans in the village of Molepolole about Martin Luther King and the power of nonviolence. The crowd certainly liked Young, and cheered when he joined kitchen workers in a traditional dance on stage. However, they were not convinced that nonviolence could solve the problems of southern Africa.

From Botswana the mayor flew to Zimbabwe, where his task proved no easier. The State Department had sponsored Young's visit to celebrate the King holiday and perhaps assuage the tensions between Zimbabwe and the United States, which were severe at the time. After a Zimbabwean official lambasted American foreign policy at a July 4th ceremony attended by Jimmy Carter, the Reagan administration cut off aid, withholding some $13 million in payments through the end of 1986. In the same hall where the insulting speech occurred, Young explained that Congress was working to reinstate aid to Zimbabwe. He primarily discussed King's legacy, and how it could be used to fight apartheid and other problems in the region. He delivered a similar message in a sermon before an overflow crowd at a Methodist church, and again during official ceremonies for King at the U.S. Embassy on January 19. His three days in Harare, which also included a meeting with Mugabe, received mixed reviews. As in Botswana, Young himself was popular among Zimbabweans, but his emphases on nonviolence and capitalism were not.

For the next two months Young remained in Atlanta, working on a variety of local and international issues. He spent two days in late January walking the streets disguised as a homeless man, accompanied by a local newscaster whose station was airing a weeklong special on homelessness. The mayor empathized with the plight of the homeless and described his experience in an interview with Peter Jennings on national television. He concluded that a high percentage of the five thousand homeless people in Atlanta worked hard and needed only a little government help to get on their feet. A few weeks later, Young participated in a joyous press conference to announce that the Democratic Party had picked Atlanta for its 1988 national convention. According to the mayor, the decision reflected "the fact that we get along very well in Atlanta."[32] For him, personally, there was some poetic justice in the decision, considering the rough treatment he had received from Jacksonians at the 1984 convention.

In late April, Young headed for Nicaragua, at the invitation of President Daniel Ortega. During his first morning there he breakfasted with Foreign Minister Miguel D'Escoto, a priest and friend from their United Nations days. Following an afternoon conversation with Vice President Sergio Ramirez, Young criticized the Reagan administration's support of the contras in an impromptu press conference. The next morning he talked with U.S. Ambassador Harry Bergold, then attended the wake for Benjamin Linder, the first American casualty of the fighting between the Sandinistas and the contras. A contra attack the day before had killed Linder, an engineer from Oregon, near the tiny village of Bocay. He was surveying for the construction of a hydroelectric plant for the Sandinista government. On his last full day in Nicaragua, Young went to Linder's funeral in the provincial capital of Matagalpa. He then returned to Managua for a state dinner hosted by the vice president, at which he was the guest of honor. Before the banquet he spoke privately with President Ortega for fifteen minutes.

The mayor's brief visit to Nicaragua enlightened him considerably, as he explained to a journalist. He had turned down previous invitations from the Sandinistas as he did not want to become involved in the Nicaraguan war. Now he could not help getting involved, because he had seen firsthand some effects of U.S. policy. The contras were using American tax money "to slaughter innocent people." Upon returning to Georgia, he intended to encourage Congress to curtail the Reagan administration's support for the contras and to urge Democratic presidential candidates to take a similar stance. Young recognized that the Sandinistas had their faults, and he criticized them for closing down the lone opposition newspaper. Still, Reagan's policy was not helping. Instead of supplying weapons, the United States should be exposing Nicaragua to its values and quality of life. Young hoped to see direct flights from Managua to Atlanta and a Nicaraguan trade office there as soon as sanctions were lifted. He believed that American tourism and investment could facilitate the transition of Nicaragua to a healthy social democracy. "But that kind of government is not going to grow out of military intervention," he concluded.[33]

In midsummer, Interior Minister Juan José Rodil of Guatemala invited Young to discuss the possibility of the Atlanta Police Academy's providing training for the Guatemalan police. In Guatemala City in early August, Young visited members of the police force and talked in depth with Rodil. As always, he remembered his friends at the Chamber of Commerce and announced his desire to establish direct flights between Atlanta and Guatemala City. On his final day he met with Nineth Garcia, the president of the Mutual Support Group, a human rights organization consisting primarily of people who had lost family members to government brutality. Young returned to Atlanta intent on working with the Guatemalan police, and an avalanche of criticism from human rights groups ensued. They contended that although Guatemala supposedly had been under civilian rule for over a year, the military, which had killed over fifty thousand civilians since 1978, still exercised considerable power. They believed that helping the Guatemalan government sent a terrible signal. Eventually they convinced the mayor of this, and he dropped his plan to train the police.

In early October, the mayor and his wife attended a Democratic National Convention planning session in Washington, and while they were in town their daughter Andrea gave birth to their first grandchild, Taylor Marie. After basking in the glow of this personal milestone, Young returned to promoting Atlanta's economy. On November 3, he recommended that over $2 million be spent on improvements for the Auburn Avenue area, which he considered a key to attracting tourists. The next day he was there himself, at a benefit screening for the King Center of *Cry Freedom*, a movie about the South African activist Steve Biko, who had been murdered by police in 1977.

In 1988, Young increasingly worked on pursuing the 1996 Olympics for Atlanta, along with attorney Billy Payne, who had initially proposed the idea. During three days in Tokyo in April, the mayor talked with Japan's two representatives on the International Olympic Committee (IOC) about Atlanta's bid for the 1996 games. Back in Atlanta, he hosted a formal dinner for King Carl XVI and Queen Silvia of Sweden. He lobbied Sweden's IOC representative, who was in their entourage. April ended on a high note in Washington, where the U.S. Olympic Committee designated Atlanta as its official nominee for the 1996 Games. Young attended the announcement and escalated his international lobbying campaign. He chatted with diplomats from ten countries, including Communist Cuba and Mozambique. He considered them particularly important, because Belgrade, in Communist Yugoslavia, ranked as one of Atlanta's chief competitors. "We've got to neutralize the Soviet bloc quickly," he remarked. Some members of the press suggested that Young's efforts were futile because the 1984 Games had been held in Los Angeles, precluding another Olympics in the United States so soon. Billy Payne, the leader of Atlanta's quest, countered, "The proven international capabilities of our mayor make us . . . a formidable international competitor."[34]

Although Young continued working on the Olympic bid for the rest of 1988, his main focus was on the presidential election. As the Democratic convention loomed, he temporarily escaped the campaign by biking across the state. In mid-June he peddled his ten-speed over three hundred miles from northern Georgia to the coast, along with one thousand other cyclists. The mayor enjoyed the rare anonymity, which allowed an undercover assessment of the rural political climate as he weighed a run for governor. "Really, what I am trying to do is prove that I'm not getting old," joked the new grandfather.[35] Admittedly, he had hoped the workout would eliminate a few extra pounds before the convention cameras began to roll.

The Democratic National Convention opened on July 18, and Young welcomed the delegates to Atlanta. He briefly recapped some of the highlights in the history of the Democratic Party: Roosevelt's New Deal, Truman's Marshall Plan, Kennedy's "coalition of conscience" with King, Johnson's Great Society, and Carter's inclusion of minorities. The key lesson from all of that, Young implied, was that the widely diverse party could work together and win in 1988. "We need a Democratic president to put together the kind of foreign policy that would mean that Nelson Mandela in South Africa would never have to have another birthday in jail," he exclaimed.[36] He added that American foreign policy should focus on unifying the global economy, particularly by increasing U.S. exports. Three days later the Democrats officially nominated Michael Dukakis of Massachusetts as their candidate. Afterward, Dukakis was joined on stage by Young, Carter, and Jackson. Balloons dropped, flags waved, a Sousa march blared, and the convention concluded.

Soon, all of Young's energy would be focused on campaigning for Dukakis, but first he initiated Atlanta's jostling for the 1996 Games by attending the Seoul Games. During a week in South Korea, Young met with over thirty members of the IOC. Most significant was his forty-five-minute talk with Juan Antonio Samaranch, the group's president. Athens was the odds-on favorite to host the 1996 Games because it had been the site of the first modern Olympics in 1896. Toronto was also frequently mentioned. Atlanta was certainly an underdog, but with Young on the job, it was still a legitimate contender. While in Seoul, he delineated his key arguments in a lengthy editorial in the *Korean Times*, including Atlanta's international population and its positive relations with the Soviet Union.

Young then returned to campaign for Dukakis and against the Republican nominee, George H. W. Bush. In the keynote address before the Southern Governors' Association, he minced no words: "Bush is an imitation Reagan, a poor imitation, and he's got a flake for a vice president."[37] Young's attack on Bush's running mate, Dan Quayle, was possibly a little payback for Quayle's efforts to oust him from his job at the UN ten years before. The bottom line for Young, however, was getting a Democrat back in the White House. Over the next six weeks the mayor tirelessly traversed the country, stumping for Dukakis in about twenty states. In the final week before the election he rallied Democrats in Pennsylvania, Michigan, California, and across the South. Nevertheless, the nation opted for Bush, who received 53 percent of the votes and won forty states.

In spite of the Democratic defeat, Young remained enthusiastic about other challenges, particularly seeking the Olympic bid and running for governor. In December the Atlanta Organizing Committee for the Olympic Games officially appointed Young as chairman of its board of directors. "Andy, both in his capacity as mayor and being the individual most important to our international bid, should be the chairman of the effort," explained the committee's president, Billy Payne. In early January 1989, the mayor concluded his final State of the City address by reaffirming that he was "perhaps most excited about the possibility of the 1996 Olympics."[38] In March he turned down a request from the National Football League that he submit his name as a possible replacement for retiring commissioner Pete Rozelle. He explained that he definitely intended to run for governor and would officially announce his candidacy later in the year.

In his final spring as mayor, he globe-trotted as much as ever. In late May, during ten days in the Soviet Union, he promoted Atlanta both as an Olympic host and as a trading partner. The trip had its somber side. In Tbilisi, Georgia, Atlanta's sister city, he led a group to a cathedral to leave flowers in memory of more than twenty civilians who had been killed in a recent clash with Soviet troops. The visit concluded on a much brighter note, however. In the keynote address at a conference of Soviet and American mayors in Tashkent, Uzbekistan, he called for cooperation between the United States and the Soviet Union. "Together, we will feed the hungry of the world," he exclaimed. His words sparked thunderous applause, and members of the audience swarmed around him afterward with requests for photos and autographs. He gladly complied and handed them pins or buttons emblazoned with "Atlanta 1996."[39]

In late 1989 the mayor tackled his biggest challenges in the quest for the Games. Twenty-nine of the ninety-two IOC members visited Atlanta within a two-week period, beginning with a small group featuring Prince Albert of Monaco. He was glad to see Young, whom he had met before, but he did not hold back on tough questions. He queried the mayor on Atlanta's high crime rate, and Young responded that the statistics were high because the police did such a good job of catching criminals. When the prince inquired about the lowly Braves, the mayor chuckled and countered that amateur sports did much better in Atlanta. The IOC's visits coincided with their annual meeting in Puerto Rico, to which the mayor led an American delegation. Addressing nearly two hundred reporters and IOC members in San Juan, Young emphasized the worldwide influence of Martin Luther King's philosophy and characterized Atlanta as "a capital of the human rights movement."[40] Young kept lobbying right through his last month in office. In Indonesia, in mid-December, he reminded the Olympic Council of Asia that the song "We Shall Overcome" originated in Atlanta and marked the city as a human rights capital.

During his final year as mayor, Young had spent 105 days traveling, and, as before, his journeying received mixed reviews. His successor, Maynard Jackson, joked that the city was probably going to hang a picture of Young in the airport's International Departure Lounge instead of City Hall. The Chamber of Commerce rewarded Young for all his efforts to attract business to the city by giving him two new cars. The National League of Cities named him Municipal Leader of the Year. Yet poor blacks criticized the mayor for neglecting their most pressing concerns, such as affordable housing. As his tenure expired, Atlanta's poverty rate was second-highest among American cities.

Young's eight years of globe-trotting redefined the potential role of a mayor in foreign relations and put Atlanta on the map. His impact showed in many concrete ways. During his tenure, Hartsfield International Airport gained direct flights to Italy, Japan, Switzerland, Ireland, Germany, and France. When the French opened an official consulate in Atlanta in 1989, it brought the number of official consulates there to a record high of sixteen. The total of all consulates, including honorary ones, reached thirty-nine, up from just thirty in 1985. As Young left office, Atlanta boasted fifteen foreign chambers of commerce, compared to two a decade earlier. The most notable new international presence in Atlanta came from Asia. Young's decision to open a trade office in Seoul built economic ties between Georgia and Korea. Korean migration to Atlanta had begun to grow in the late 1970s, and Young's efforts encouraged that trend. By 1988, over fifteen thousand Koreans lived in the metro area, operating more than five hundred small businesses. Japan provided an even more significant economic boost to the area. Between 1981 and 1989, Japanese entrepreneurs invested over $1.2 billion, opened sixty-eight new facilities, and created almost eleven thousand new jobs in Georgia, primarily in metro Atlanta. In the late 1980s, approximately forty thousand Japanese tourists visited Atlanta annually.[41]

During his mayoral tenure, Young did not solve all of Atlanta's problems, but he definitely succeeded in transforming Atlanta into an international city. Although he was leaving office, his work was not done. In the short run, he planned to win the Olympics for his city and to run for governor of Georgia. In the long run, he intended to continue his role on the international stage. He looked forward to carrying on his campaign of spreading King's vision of racial equality and promoting economic growth and free trade. As Young left City Hall and the 1980s behind, he welcomed whatever challenges the 1990s would present. He would tackle them ably, as he had for some twenty years, as one of America's true civil rights ambassadors.

Notes

1. Andrew Young, *A Way Out of No Way: The Spiritual Memoirs of Andrew Young* (Nashville: Thomas Nelson, 1994), 141.
2. Strickland, quoted in Tamar Jacoby, *Someone Else's House: America's Unfinished Struggle for Integration* (New York: Basic Books, 1998), 407.
3. Margaret Allen, quoted in Gary Pomerantz, *Where Peachtree Meets Sweet Auburn: The Saga of Two Families and the Making of Atlanta* (New York: Scribner's, 1996), 482.
4. Young, quoted in Frederick Allen, *Atlanta Rising: The Invention of an International City, 1946–1996* (Marietta, GA: Longstreet Press, 1996), 219. Election statistics are from David Harmon, *Beneath the Image of the Civil Rights Movement and Race Relations* (New York: Garland, 1996), 302.
5. *Atlanta Journal Constitution* (hereafter *AJC*), January 5, 1982, 14A.
6. Ibid., December 19, 1982, 1C.
7. Ibid., March 29, 1983, 1A and 16A.
8. Ibid., April 11, 1983, 8A.
9. Ibid., September 20, 1983.
10. Reagan, quoted in Andrew J. DeRoche, *Black, White, and Chrome: The United States and Zimbabwe, 1953–1998* (Trenton, NJ: Africa World Press, 2001), 322.
11. *AJC*, January 1, 1984, 9A.
12. Ibid., March 25, 1984, 1D.
13. Young, quoted in Jacoby, *Someone Else's House*, 428.
14. *AJC*, March 25, 1984, 18A.
15. Jackson, quoted in Marshall Frady, *Jesse: The Life and Pilgrimage of Jesse Jackson* (New York: Random House, 1996), 371. For a discussion of Young's speech, see Jacoby, *Someone Else's House*, 428–29.
16. *AJC*, March 19, 1985, 28A, and March 21, 1985, 17A.
17. Ibid., June 5, 1985, 2D.
18. Young's testimony in *U.S. Policy toward South Africa*, Hearings before the Committee on Foreign Relations, United States Senate, 99th Cong., 1st sess., April 24, May 2 and 22, 1985 (Washington, DC: U.S. Government Printing Office, 1985), 283.
19. *AJC*, July 21, 1985, 1C.
20. Ibid., August 9, 1985, 2D.
21. Ibid., October 9, 1985, 12A, and October 6, 1985, 1B.
22. Ibid., December 11, 1985, 1C.
23. Ibid., January 5, 1986, 1B, and January 7, 1986, 1C.
24. Ibid., January 30, 1986, 2A.
25. Ibid., May 18, 1986, 2M.
26. Andrew Young, "Only Multinational Effort Can Control Terrorism," ibid., June 1, 1986, 1D.

27. Ibid., June 27, 1986, 3A.

28. Andrew Young, "A Sanction That Would Affect the 'Passive Majority,' " *Washington Post*, August 10, 1986, 28A.

29. *AJC*, August 8, 1986, 14A.

30. Ibid., September 30, 1986, 3E

31. Ibid., November 28, 1986, 1B.

32. Ibid., February 10, 1987, 1E.

33. Ibid., May 1, 1987, 1A.

34. Ibid., April 30, 1988, 10A, and May 3, 1988, 1E.

35. Ibid., June 17, 1988, 13A.

36. Ibid., July 19, 1988, 16C.

37. Ibid., September 27, 1988, 1B.

38. Ibid., December 14, 1988, 5B, and January 4, 1989, 11A.

39. Ibid., June 4, 1989, 6D.

40. Ibid., August 29, 1989, 1A.

41. Ibid., April 3, 1988, 1H; May 22, 1988, 4M; June 3, 1989, 6C; and July 11, 1990, 9A.

7

Private-Sector Diplomat

1990–2000

For Andrew Young, the 1990s brought an incredible range of new challenges and opportunities. In his public life he experienced ups and downs, from losing badly in the 1990 Democratic gubernatorial primary in Georgia to helping host the Olympics in Atlanta in 1996. Personally, he suffered the worst blow of his life when his wife Jean died in 1994. Two years later, joy returned when he married Carolyn Watson in South Africa. No longer in public office, Young labored in the private sector. In the early 1990s he consulted for the Law Companies Group and then, in late 1996, he cofounded GoodWorks International. His dealings occasionally drew criticism, especially when he toiled in the unfamiliar environs of Asia. When he and GoodWorks focused on Africa, they were more successful.

Young's final major project for the decade was playing a key role in the National Summit on Africa. The summit began in 1998 with a series of regional gatherings and culminated in February 2000 with a major conference in Washington. The five-day event provided Young with an ideal forum in which to pronounce his vision for Africa. He explained that his fundamental mission was to promote economic development in Africa by increasing foreign investment, expanding trade, and facilitating cooperation between multinational corporations and African governments. He believed that capitalist prosperity was a key to fostering democracy in Africa and other less-developed areas of the world. He had been working extensively on this project for ten years. Throughout the 1990s, as a private-sector diplomat, Young attempted to sow the seeds of capitalism and democracy, two American institutions that he believed went hand in hand.

Andrew Young took on the challenge of running for governor of Georgia in 1990 with his typical optimism, but he faced several obstacles. His relative lack of wealth was a major handicap. Going into the campaign, his net worth was about $300,000. Two of the other candidates were multimillionaires, and his strongest competitor, Lieutenant Governor Zell Miller, had a net worth of about $750,000. In hopes of making up some of this disparity, Young hired former U.S. Attorney General Griffin Bell to lead his fund-raising efforts. He also accepted a consulting position for the Law Companies Group, an engineering firm. Young knew Law's chairman, R. K. Sehgal, from his days at the United Nations, where India's UN ambassador had introduced them. The two other most significant obstacles were white rural Georgians' distrust of a successful big-city black and poor Atlanta blacks' feeling that Young had neglected them in favor of white business interests. Assuaging two such contradictory attitudes was a daunting task.

George H. W. Bush and Nelson Mandela, Washington, DC, June 1990. *Courtesy of George Bush Library*

In spring 1990, Young focused on courting rural whites. Cruising country roads in his minivan, he logged as many as five hundred miles a day. He shook hands with residents in small towns across the state and attended local festivities such as the Pig Jig in Vienna. Even in rural Georgia, he professed his faith in interna-

tionalism. Throughout the campaign he advocated foreign trade as
a source of wealth and jobs and assured voters he could transform
the governor's role in international affairs just as he had the
mayor's. He told carpet manufacturers in Dalton: "I'd love to be
the governor and take the carpet industry to Japan and Germany. I
bet you all can do a billion dollars worth of business in a couple of
weeks." He pointed out that three hundred foreign companies had
located in Georgia during his mayoralty. His opponents contended
that his impact on Atlanta was actually why he should not be governor. Former Governor Lester Maddox derided Young as "Globe-
trotter Andy," arguing that he had neglected his city and thus
contributed to its problems such as the dramatic rise in crime.[1]

Young finished second among five candidates in the general
Democratic primary, but with just 29 percent of the vote, he lagged
far behind front-runner Zell Miller. Miller, whose campaign was
managed skillfully by James Carville, attracted nearly all the white
rural vote. At the same time, he garnered 20 percent of the black
vote. White turnout was high, and black turnout was low. The results did not bode well for Young, who had only three weeks to
remedy the situation before the August 7 runoff against Miller.
Shifting his strategy, Young aimed his campaigning at the black
community. He spoke on black radio stations, preached in black
churches, and breakfasted with young black professionals, but to
no avail. Participation by African-American voters remained low,
and Miller crushed Young in a landslide, receiving 62 percent of
the ballots to Young's 38 percent. In spite of the surge in participation by rural whites and their nearly unanimous backing of Miller,
Young remained optimistic about race relations. "I haven't had
anybody call me any name. I haven't had anybody shoot me a bird.
And that represents a new day in Georgia," he said. Tamar Jacoby,
renowned scholar of race in American cities, concluded otherwise:
"Young just could not get his message of forgiveness and inclusion
across. The old assumptions about prejudice ran too deep."[2]

In the aftermath of his overwhelming defeat in the primary,
Young had little time to ponder what had gone wrong. He and all
Atlantans waited nervously for the September 18 decision by the
International Olympic Committee (IOC) regarding the location of
the 1996 summer Games. Billions of dollars and an immeasurable
amount of publicity for Atlanta hung in the balance. On the first
ballot, the IOC eliminated Belgrade, with Manchester, Melbourne,
and Toronto removed from contention in turn. In the final showdown, Atlanta triumphed over Athens by a count of 51 to 36.

Maurice Herzog, a French IOC member, attributed the decision in great part to Young's enthusiasm. An *Atlanta Journal Constitution* editorial concurred. The editors characterized Young as "the city's most eloquent and most effective representative on the world stage." They praised him for his efforts that had continued even during the gubernatorial race and concluded that "the impression he made on Olympics officials and others all around the globe was an important factor in the final selection."[3]

Nelson Mandela, Coretta Scott King, and Andrew Young, Atlanta, GA, June 1990. *Courtesy of Carol Muldawer*

Securing the Olympics for Atlanta surely took much of the sting out of the disappointing gubernatorial race. Young indicated as much: "The saying goes that if the Lord closes a door, he opens a window. This time, the Lord closed a window and opened a door."[4] Speculation immediately began that he might capitalize on his Olympic success by running for public office again. He quickly refuted such predictions, explaining that he fully intended to consult for the Law Companies Group for several years, focusing on less-developed countries. Young spent the early 1990s doing just that. He climbed quickly up the company ladder, first to chair of the international branch of Law Engineering, then to vice chair of the entire organization. Initially much of his work dealt with Africa, where the Law Companies Group had many offices.

One of the most exciting stories of the twentieth century unfolded in South Africa in the early 1990s, and Young followed the events closely. In February 1990, after some ten thousand days in prison, Nelson Mandela was released. In June, he toured the United States, including a stop in Atlanta. Young welcomed Mandela when he visited the King Center and laid a wreath on King's grave. In July 1993, Mandela returned to Atlanta in search of backing for his presidential campaign. Young participated in a ceremony in which Mandela received an honorary degree from Clark Atlanta University and he urged his fellow Atlantans to support the South African leader. Young lauded Mandela as "a reason for hope for the future," and added that the "survival of multiracial democracy is on trial in South Africa."[5] Multiracial democracy triumphed in May 1994, when Mandela celebrated his election to the presidency. His victory represented an incredible extension of King's vision of racial equality onto the international stage, a vision for which Young had worked for more than thirty years.

Despite these remarkable developments, the 1990s were the most trying time of Young's life. In July 1991, Andrew and Jean spent three weeks on business in Zimbabwe, then met the rest of their family for a weekend in the Bahamas. Upon returning home, Jean experienced severe stomach pains. Since they had been in Africa where Jean could have been exposed to a parasite or dangerous disease, they decided to go to the hospital for tests. The doctor informed Andrew that Jean had cancer. A tumor was blocking her intestine, and the malignancy had probably spread to her liver. Jean might live only another six months. Overwhelmed by the shocking news, Andrew found the hospital chapel, where he cried and prayed. The thought of losing his wife of forty years was too much. He later recalled his initial feelings: "I could not live without Jean. Her leaving us was a tragedy that no one could consider."[6]

The Youngs pulled together to face this terrible prospect, and it became clear how many friends they had made over the years. Support flooded in from around the country. Dr. Levi Watkins, associate dean of surgery at Johns Hopkins Medical Center, offered to organize a team of specialists to evaluate Jean's condition. Watkins was a movement veteran who had participated with King in the Montgomery bus boycott. Andrew and Jean accepted his offer and went to Johns Hopkins in Baltimore, which was only about forty miles from the homes of two of their daughters in Washington. The doctors suggested six months of chemotherapy, then surgery to remove the tumors from Jean's liver. Throughout the treatment,

Jean demonstrated great courage and faith. At one point she remarked to her husband, "We shouldn't have any complaints, because we've been married almost 40 years and Martin didn't live
to be 40 years."[7]

Jean fought nobly through 1993, but her condition deteriorated.
In spring 1994, Andrew canceled many of his appointments to be
with her. Their son Bo returned from college in May and held her
hand every day all summer. Beginning in August, Jean was rarely
conscious. On September 16, she died. Thousands attended her
funeral, a three-hour ceremony at the Atlanta Civic Center. President Clinton sent a handwritten note of condolence. Maya Angelou
recited a poem. Hank Aaron's wife Billye observed: "Andy and Jean,
like cake and ice cream, they went together well." Coretta King,
who had known Jean since their youth in Alabama, recalled, "She
was Andy's source of comfort and understanding when he needed
it the most." Daughter Lisa, in an extremely powerful eulogy,
summed up their relationship beautifully: "They were best friends.
They were partners."[8]

In the aftermath of his wife's death, Young kept himself busy
as a private-sector diplomat, and he found work somewhat thera-
peutic. In October 1994, President Clinton appointed him to oversee the $100-million Southern Africa Development Fund. Clinton,
who made the announcement during a White House reception for
Nelson Mandela, chose Young because he had "long worked to
improve conditions in the region." He was instructed to find promising small businesses in southern Africa and award them grants
from the fund. Furthermore, Young envisioned the grants serving
as seed money to attract much larger contributions from private
investments. "It's basically to help southern Africans develop business opportunities," he explained.[9]

Although Young welcomed Clinton's appointment as another
way to work on African development, he continued to focus on the
upcoming Olympics. As cochairman of the Atlanta Olympic Organizing Committee, he participated actively in the effort to organize
successful Games. He helped coordinate a program enabling foreign
athletes to spend time training in Georgia before the Olympics to
acclimatize to the heat and humidity. About fifty communities
opened their doors to the competitors. LaGrange, a town Young
had avoided in the 1960s because of its racist reputation, hosted
over four hundred athletes from fourteen different countries, including South Africa, Mozambique, Zambia, Brazil, and Saudi
Arabia. The athletes in LaGrange not only trained, but also took

college courses and visited elementary schools. They befriended locals through an adopt-an-athlete program, and these hosts took them to church dinners and high-school football games. The hospitality thrilled Young, who commented: "People in L.A. and New York will never believe this happens in the South."[10] Clearly the benefits of hosting the Olympics expanded beyond monetary considerations.

In addition to his Olympic work and consulting for the Law Companies Group, Young became the chair of the Atlanta Chamber of Commerce in December 1995. His ascension to the post signified once again how much had changed in the South. When he moved to Atlanta in the 1960s, the chamber would not accept black members. During his first run for mayor in 1981, the chamber had vigorously opposed his candidacy. By the mid-1990s, he was welcomed as the organization's leader. Bill Dahlberg, the previous chair, expected Young to provide a global vision for Atlanta. Young planned to do just that and emphasized the unprecedented opportunity afforded by the Olympics, when people from nearly two hundred nations would visit Atlanta.

His personal life also took a turn for the better as Young found a friend in neighbor Carolyn Watson. They developed a strong bond in the two years following Jean's death. In March 1996, Young asked Carolyn to accompany him on a journey to South Africa, where he would be working on the Southern Africa Development Fund and Olympic issues. Both felt they should get married before taking a trip together. "She's superintendent of a Sunday school and a fifth-grade teacher," said Young. "How is she to explain to her fifth-grade class that she's traveling around the world with somebody she's not married to?" Their wedding was a simple ceremony on March 24 at the Cape Town residence of U.S. Ambassador James Joseph, an old friend of Young's from the Carter administration. Joseph served as best man and Bishop Desmond Tutu offered a blessing. At the reception, Young joyfully toasted his bride: "I just want to thank God for this woman."[11] The newlyweds stayed a few days in Cape Town, and then visited wild game reserves and the Sun City resort.

Back in Atlanta after their honeymoon, Young helped with final preparations for the Olympics. He and some seventy thousand other workers geared up for the onslaught: more than ten thousand athletes, fifteen thousand journalists, and two million spectators from two hundred countries. Festivities began on July 19, when the Olympic torch toured the city, first visiting landmarks such as the Varsity Restaurant, Centennial Park, and Underground Atlanta. In midafternoon, Coretta Scott King carried the flame past the Martin Luther King Jr. Chapel and then passed it to her son Dexter. From there, the Olympic symbol went to City Hall. Maynard Jackson handed it off to Mayor Bill Campbell. Young pronounced the official welcome. After a few hours on display at City Hall, the flame made one last stop at King's grave and was then transported to the Olympic Stadium for the opening ceremony. Kicking off the Games in a poignant moment, Muhammad Ali lit the giant torch.

The 1996 Olympics in Atlanta had gotten off to a spectacular start, but tragedy struck early on the morning of Saturday, July 27. A pipe bomb exploded in Centennial Park, killing two people and wounding over one hundred. Shrapnel from the blast killed Alice Hawthorne of Albany, and a Turkish journalist named Melih Uzunyol died of a heart attack caused by the shock. The park reopened three days later, when Young preached to tens of thousands at a memorial service for the victims: "We want everyone to know there's no need to feel alienated from this loving community. There's nothing keeping you out."[12] The crowd responded to Young's sermon with tears and applause and then honored the victims with a moment of silence. Afterward, a gospel choir sang "Hallelujah," and Billy Payne declared the park officially reopened.

Fortunately, the 1996 Olympics concluded a week later without further incident. In the aftermath, members of the IOC criticized the Atlanta Games arrangements for inconvenient transportation, lax security, and overcommercialization. Young agreed that there were too many vendors and acknowledged that the capitalist display was probably overwhelming to visitors from socialist or formerly socialist countries. He noted, however, that without public funding the Games were entirely dependent on free enterprise; therefore, trying to limit merchandising was problematic. He praised the unprecedented extent of participation that featured more nations, journalists, and spectators than ever before. "The IOC has formerly been elitist. It can no longer be that way," he observed. He downplayed the fact that IOC President Juan Antonio Samaranch had not pronounced the Games the greatest ever, which he had done after previous Olympics. With the horrible exception of the bombing, the 1996 summer Olympics were successful. "We know we did our best," Young concluded.[13]

Young's positive reputation in Africa and his links to the world of corporate capitalism were key reasons that Atlanta had been selected for the site of the 1996 Games. In late 1996, he decided to make further use of these attributes. Along with Hamilton Jordan, former chief of staff for President Carter, and Carl Masters, a bank executive from Canada, Young formed a consulting firm called GoodWorks International. Officially opening its doors in January 1997, GoodWorks planned to build bridges among governments, large corporations, and local businesses. Young and his associates billed themselves as "global advocates" and "visionary capitalists," who could link "fast-growing countries" with "forward-thinking multinational companies."[14] Headquartered in Atlanta, GoodWorks intended to focus primarily on facilitating development in Africa and the Caribbean. As fate would have it, however, their first major project was in Asia investigating conditions in Nike factories.

In early 1997, Nike faced a serious public relations problem. Workers in Vietnam staged walkouts over poor conditions, and laborers in Indonesia rioted over low pay. In New York, Seattle, and Los Angeles, activists excoriated Nike for exploiting its Asian workforce. On February 22, hundreds of demonstrators picketed the opening of the Niketown store in San Francisco. Phil Knight, the CEO of Nike, reacted quickly and explained to the media on February 24 that he had hired GoodWorks to determine if Nike's Code of Conduct was being upheld in its facilities in Asia. Young accepted the assignment reluctantly, and with conditions. He insisted that Nike allow him open access to all areas and people in the factories. Knight agreed and in writing promised "blanket authority" for Young to "go anywhere, see anything and talk with anybody in the Nike family."[15] It was a perilous undertaking, but GoodWorks seemed to be handling it carefully.

For fifteen days in spring 1997, Young examined the conditions in twelve Nike factories in Vietnam, China, and Indonesia. Unable to speak the local languages, Young communicated with workers through translators provided by Nike. Young and GoodWorks made their first mistake—they should have hired their own intermediaries. The Belgrade Minimal Rules, established in 1980 by the International Law Association to standardize factory inspections, stipulate that "analysts should provide all of their own experts." The GoodWorks team toured each factory for just three or four hours, which represented their second mistake. Veteran inspectors suggest at least ten separate visits of several hours' duration for each factory. Upon first returning from Asia, Young himself questioned the validity of his findings. In a May 14 discussion with labor experts in Washington, he told them that he felt "snowed" by the Nike officials in China.[16]

In contrast, the official report he released on June 24 made no mention of being "snowed." He did recommend five improvements for Nike in Asia: (1) clearer communication of the Code of Conduct to managers; (2) development of worker representatives; (3) improvement of the grievance system; (4) a closer relationship with human rights organizations; and (5) an ongoing external monitoring system. Nevertheless, his overall assessment was positive. "We found Nike to be in the forefront of a global economy. Factories we visited that produce Nike goods were clean, organized, adequately ventilated and well lit," he wrote. "It is my sincere belief that Nike is doing a good job in the application of its Code of Conduct," he concluded, "but Nike can and should do better."[17] Phil Knight immediately placed full-page advertisements in the major papers trumpeting Young's report and promising to do better in the future.

Simultaneously, human rights groups blasted Young for his shoddy methodology—particularly the quick visits and the reliance on Nike's translators. In the most visible attack, columnist Bob Herbert lambasted Young, primarily because his report made no mention of pay. Herbert contended that workers in the Nike plants in Vietnam were not receiving even a subsistence wage. "The kindest thing that can be said at this point is that Mr. Young was naive," he wrote. A few days later Young responded: "I have been through too many human rights battles to be called naive." He explained that he and his fledgling firm, GoodWorks, were not qualified to judge wages in Asia. He stood by his report and concluded, "The United States and the world need a globally integrated economy." Young's stance defending his work for Nike put him in the crosshairs, along with other big names such as Michael Jordan, of all those who opposed globalization. Most notably, journalist Stephen Glass berated Young in a fall issue of the *New Republic*. Glass argued that Young had given Nike a clean bill of health in order to drum up more powerful clients for GoodWorks.[18]

Glass suggested that Young was motivated by greed and ambition, but less cynical interpretations are possible. Young undoubtedly considered the jobs in the Nike plants better than no jobs at all. Having spent much of his life in less-developed areas of the world that were plagued by poverty and unemployment, he believed that Nike offered people in Southeast Asia steady work in safe conditions. Throughout his career, he had worked with business leaders in Birmingham, Charleston, and Atlanta in order to bring opportunity to people of color, and he considered this a similar situation. In his consulting for Nike he made mistakes, but he was willing to learn from them. The most important lesson from the Nike assignment was that GoodWorks should focus on projects in Africa and the Carribean where Young and his colleagues were more at home and would not need translators.

During the next two years, Young and his GoodWorks staff helped plan the National Summit on Africa, which grew out of a Ford Foundation project. The National Summit, a nongovernmental and nonprofit program, aimed to educate all Americans about Africa and thus mobilize a constituency to influence U.S. relations with Africa. Young and the other organizers planned a series of regional conferences, which would build momentum for a national gathering in Washington in 2000. The first meeting convened in Atlanta in May 1998. Young and Jimmy Carter spoke during the opening ceremony, when Young exclaimed, with some exaggeration, "I believe that the National Summit on Africa is the most important movement to come along since the Civil Rights movement."[19] The festivities featured a convocation to honor Julius Nyerere, former president of Tanzania, and a presentation by Dikembe Mutombo, the Atlanta Hawks center who grew up in Zaire. The summit's work occurred in break-out sessions on security, economic development, education, the environment, and democracy. Participants began crafting policy recommendations to bring to Washington. Over the following two years, this process was replicated at similar regional summits around the country.[20]

Contributing to the National Summit on Africa helped Young get back on his feet after the controversy over his consulting for Nike, and an opportunity offered by Ted Turner had a similar effect. In June 1998, Turner appointed a board of directors to manage the $1-billion gift he had given to the United Nations. He named Tim Wirth, a former U.S. senator and diplomat, as president. Young was the most prominent among the other seven members of the board. In an article assessing Turner's team, columnist Stephanie Salter approved of the choice and observed that Young generally was "on the right and humane side of global politics and business." Another noteworthy member named to the board was Graca Machel, former wife of the late Samora Machel and future wife of Nelson Mandela. Inclusion on Turner's "United Nations all-star team" was an honor for Young that further mitigated the criticism over his Nike project.[21]

Within a few months, Young stepped back into the spotlight of media scrutiny after a visit to China as part of a National Council of Churches (NCC) delegation. In October 1998, Young and five other ministers spent six days in China, assessing the status of church–state relations. During their stay they discussed with Chinese officials the International Religious Freedom Act, recently passed by Congress, which authorized sanctions against any nation practicing religious persecution. Personally, Young opposed the bill and hoped Clinton would veto it. In any case, he did not think it should apply to China because he and his colleagues had found "no religious repression nor active persecution."[22] Although he recognized that Chinese citizens did not have religious freedom in the sense that Americans did, he found no official policy of persecution. He and the other delegates celebrated the fact that some ten million Protestants openly practiced Christianity in China.

Journalist Jeff Jacoby downplayed the significance of these ten million Protestants praying publicly in China. Instead, he focused on the fate of about one hundred people who had been arrested for worshiping in underground churches. He harshly condemned Young and the NCC for not speaking out regarding such injustices. He compared Young's trip to Beijing to Neville Chamberlain's meeting with Hitler in Munich. He contended that "Young and the NCC leadership, blind to the suffering of their fellow Christians, give their seal of approval to the world's largest dictatorship." Jacoby took his criticism of Young a step further, stating, "the moral stature Young acquired in his youth he seems willing to squander as he approaches old age."[23] Jacoby's strident language reflected the intense political nature of the debate over religious persecution.

On October 27, shortly after Young and his colleagues returned from China, President Clinton signed the International Religious Freedom Act into law. Members of the religious right, such as Charles Colson, a former Nixon aide, had been the strongest supporters of the bill, and they lambasted Clinton early in 1999 for his failure to request funds for its enforcement. They also criticized the president for being slow to make appointments to the U.S. Commission on International Religious Freedom, which the new law had created. Clinton made his three appointments in May, and the group convened in June to begin its work. As expected, China was high on their agenda, soon to be joined by Vietnam and North Korea. In part, the movement against religious persecution was an effort to resuscitate the Cold War and frustrate Clinton's vision for globalization and free trade. In visiting China with the NCC, Young had walked into another political minefield, which primarily involved Asia.

Young returned his focus to Africa again in 1999 and 2000, and his efforts there were less controversial and more successful. He and his team at GoodWorks expanded their activities, mainly in Africa but also in the Caribbean. In March 1999, they coordinated a banquet in Atlanta for Olusegun Obasanjo, who had just been elected president of Nigeria. Working in conjunction with Chevron, GoodWorks hosted Obasanjo again at a Washington dinner in October, and Young delivered a speech welcoming the Nigerian leader. Obasanjo, who was in the nation's capital for a meeting with Clinton, called on the audience to lobby for passage of the Africa Growth and Opportunity Act. The bill, nicknamed "NAFTA for Africa," was being debated in Congress. Young agreed wholeheartedly with Obasanjo's advocacy of the legislation and saw it as key to promoting prosperity in Africa.

In addition to developing ties with Nigeria in 1999, Young and GoodWorks were involved in the establishment of daily nonstop Delta flights between Atlanta and Johannesburg, which began in late fall. In the succeeding years, GoodWorks joined with corporations such as Chevron, Coca-Cola, South Africa Airways, and Southwestern Bell to facilitate improvements in telecommunications and infrastructure in southern Africa. Late summer of 1999 also brought Young a remarkable honor, when Georgia State University in Atlanta announced it was naming its School of Policy Studies after him. The editors of the *Atlanta Journal Constitution* hailed the decision, praising Young as the suitable namesake because of his belief that "capitalism represents the best hope for global democratic and social reform."[24] The Andrew Young School of Policy Studies includes several departments and programs, most notably Economics and International Studies.

In November 1999 the National Council of Churches celebrated its fiftieth anniversary in Cleveland. The council inaugurated Young as its new president, and old friends such as Jesse Jackson offered their congratulations. Young had worked for the ecumenical group in its early days, during the 1950s, and had seen it grow to include thirty-five denominations and more than fifty million members. He accepted the position, which was unpaid and would last two years, with a mix of optimism and realism about the challenges ahead. The NCC's budget shortfalls did not worry him particularly. Of more concern was the flagging faith of America's Protestants. He considered the state of American Protestantism to be at a "crisis moment," because so many people were "losing interest in their own denominations and in the mainstream local churches." American Protestantism needed a boost, and he was enthusiastic about having the opportunity to contribute as head of the NCC. "Nothing could be more exciting than to be president," he said.[25]

Obviously, Young was not slowing down, in spite of being almost sixty-eight and facing surgery for prostate cancer. He publicized his condition, which had been diagnosed in September, in order to encourage middle-aged men to have regular exams. He was fortunate in that his illness had been detected early, and doctors at Emory University Hospital removed his prostate in mid-December. Instead of flowers, he requested that well-wishers purchase moringa tree seedlings, which would be planted in Africa. Malnourished African children would benefit from the fruit of the moringa trees, which are rich in vitamins and minerals. Even in the midst of personal health problems, Africa was on his mind.

He recovered quickly from the surgery and prepared to serve as the Master of Ceremonies at the five-day National Summit on Africa, scheduled for February in Washington. In his letter of welcome to several thousand participants, he characterized the summit as "an opportunity for the American people to come together and share their thoughts and dreams about building a bridge to the future broad enough for both Africans and Americans." He contended that Americans were well qualified to help Africans face the challenges of hunger, disease, and infrastructure development. The success of democracy in America was in great part due to its economic strength, and both traditions needed to be nurtured in Africa. "Together, we can forge a vision and a plan that will enable the countries of Africa to share in the benefits of both democracy and prosperity," he proclaimed.[26]

Young's first major task at the National Summit was to introduce President Bill Clinton, who addressed a crowd of over two thousand at the opening session on February 17. Young welcomed the president and praised him for his interest in Africa. Clinton responded, "Africa never had a better friend in America than Andrew Young." Clinton then launched into an impassioned speech. He pointed out some of the positive developments in Africa, such as the massive peacekeeping efforts by Nigeria. At the same time, he pulled no punches regarding Africa's problems, and he singled out AIDS as the number-one concern. He warned that the epidemic would "reduce the life expectancy in Africa by 20 years." The horrible consequences included the rapidly increasing number of orphans who had lost their parents to AIDS. The president closed with a plea for Americans to "do something about this." Clinton's speech impressed the crowd, including Nigerian Vice President Atiku Abubakar, who commented afterward that Clinton's words "filled us with tremendous hope."[27]

On her way to the stage to deliver the second speech of the opening session, Secretary of State Madeleine Albright ran into Abubakar. She spoke with him and listened to his concerns. Young, as Master of Ceremonies, found himself in front of two thousand people with an indeterminate amount of time to fill. He explained that there would be a slight delay while Albright met with Abubakar and praised the secretary of state for talking with the vice president. Young then commended Albright's efforts on behalf of Africa, in particular her role in facilitating Kofi Annan's ascendency to the Secretary Generalship of the UN. He lauded her for utilizing America's most recent turn as chair of the Security Council to investigate African problems. Young had used up his introductory material, and there was still no sign of Albright. He did not miss a beat and began to reminisce about their days together in the Carter administration. He then discussed the upcoming elections, urging the crowd to canvass candidates regarding African issues. Finally, he offered some humorous insight into Clinton's similarity to Franklin Roosevelt: each had made the wise choice of marrying a woman who was more intelligent than he. The laughter throughout the crowd suggested that they enjoyed Young's impromptu remarks.[28] Few people could have entertained and enlightened the audience with Young's combination of history, foreign-policy analysis, and stand-up comedy.

Secretary Albright thanked Young for his warm introduction and praised him for his ability to ad-lib. She jokingly complained that it was difficult to follow speakers like Young and Clinton even on a good day, but, she explained, to make matters worse she was feeling ill to boot. She then provided a clear and engaging overview of U.S. policy toward South Africa and Nigeria, illuminating them as focal points of American relations with Africa. Her speech concluded the first morning's activities. In the afternoon and throughout the second day, smaller break-out sessions were held. These panel discussions provided the audience with opportunities to ask questions and served as educational forums to help the summit participants produce policy suggestions. For example, former UN ambassador Donald McHenry and former assistant secretary of state Chester Crocker headlined the session on peacemaking in Africa. Crocker emphasized the importance of U.S. leadership.

McHenry contended that preventing wars everywhere was in the best interests of the United States. An animated question-and-answer session followed, touching on a range of African crises, including those in Zimbabwe, Ethiopia, Rwanda, and the Sudan.[29]

On the second night of the summit, Young delivered the keynote address at the official banquet. The dinner had started late and several of the preceding speakers ran long, so it was nearly 11 P.M. by the time Young took the stage. By then the crowd had dwindled somewhat, and he wisely opted to shorten his remarks. He first lauded the long tradition of African-American interest in Africa and singled out Ralph Bunche for his scholarship and diplomacy. He then explained how the success of the summit derived in great part from cooperation among governments and corporations such as Coca-Cola and Chevron. Joint efforts by the public and private sector, he argued, were a key to future relations with Africa.

Next, Young optimistically praised the new generation of African leaders, young men and women who had been educated by Mandela, Nyerere, and Obasanjo. He called on Congress to pass the Africa Growth and Opportunity Act and grasp the "opportunity to open a door of trade." He urged Africans living in the United States to invest in their native countries and he encouraged African leaders to court investment and tourism by African Americans. He estimated that blacks in the United States represented a market of over $500 billion, and that they spent $20 billion annually on conventions alone. With direct flights from New York to Ghana and Atlanta to Johannesburg, some of those lucrative gatherings could easily be held in Africa. He ended with a positive vision of collaboration among African-American politicians, young black executives working for Coca-Cola or Chevron, and the new generation of African leaders. "When we put all of this together, there is no way that we can't solve the problems of Africa. But there is no single solution, and we all need to take a problem and take some time to learn about it, and then pass that knowledge on," he concluded.[30]

The final two days of the National Summit consisted of speeches by Colin Powell and Jesse Jackson and drafting sessions that produced a final document with over two hundred recommendations for future policy toward Africa. Although the concrete impact of such a broad proclamation was probably minimal in the short run, the summit succeeded in terms of communication and education. Several thousand people from all walks of life and all parts of the United States and Africa talked, listened, and generally paid positive attention to a continent often associated only with wars and disease. Reflecting Young's collaborative vision, the summit combined grassroots input with the thoughts of high-ranking government officials and linked the public and private sectors.

At least one of Young's concrete goals, passage of the Africa Growth and Opportunity Act (AGOA), was within reach as the summit concluded. After a few more months of debate and revision, Congress approved the bill. On May 18, 2000, Clinton signed the legislation, which was the first major trade initiative in five years. The AGOA focused on stimulating the textile industy in sub-Saharan Africa by eliminating quotas and duties on imports of African cloth. To be eligible, countries had to demonstrate progress in several areas: a market-based economy, the rule of law, reduction of barriers to U.S. investment, antipoverty programs, and protection of workers' rights. The bill thus linked corporate capitalism with human rights. Critics contended that the AGOA would benefit only multinational corporations, but Young believed those corporations could greatly benefit Africa.

Helping to host the National Summit on Africa and contributing to the passage of the Africa Growth and Opportunity Act served as very fitting codas to Andrew Young's endeavors in the 1990s. Both exemplified his vision for promoting capitalism and democracy in less-developed regions of the world. Both applied specifically to Africa, where he felt more at home than in other foreign areas and where he had had many of his best moments during the decade. Also, the summit and the AGOA both attracted criticism for benefiting multinational corporations, as had much of his work in the 1990s. Andrew Young truly believed that spreading capitalism was a good idea, however, and worked hard to do so throughout the decade. As a private-sector diplomat he succeeded in building bridges between American companies and African governments, which he contended was a key to fostering prosperity and democracy.

Throughout Young's career, links between capitalism and opportunity for people of color had always been important. In a variety of ways, Young had often worked with the capitalist system to promote democracy and racial justice. In the early 1960s, he had negotiated with business leaders in cities such as Birmingham, and those concessions had been important in opening doors for blacks in the South. In the late 1960s, the civil rights movement focused increasingly on improving the economic condition of African Americans, and Young was central to efforts such as the Poor People's Campaign. Their goal was not to replace capitalism, but rather to use boycotts and demonstrations to get a fair share of its benefits for blacks. While in Congress, he had championed U.S. participation in the African Development Fund, which facilitated investment in Africa. As mayor of Atlanta in the 1980s, he had courted foreign investment, and, through affirmative action, assured that a large percentage of the new jobs went to blacks. As a private-sector diplomat in the 1990s he worked to bring development and opportunity to Africa, and this was not a new effort. During his four decades as a civil rights ambassador, he consistently worked with the capitalist system to spread democracy and racial justice.

Notes

1. Young quoted in the *Atlanta Journal Constitution* (hereafter *AJC*), October 26, 1989, 4D; Maddox quoted in *Time*, July 16, 1990, 66.
2. Young and Jacoby quotes are from Tamar Jacoby, *Someone Else's House: America's Unfinished Struggle for Integration* (New York: Basic Books, 1998), 520.
3. *AJC*, September 19, 1990, 10A.
4. Ibid., September 20, 1990, 1A.
5. Ibid., July 11, 1993, 1A.
6. Andrew Young, *A Way Out of No Way: The Spiritual Memoirs of Andrew Young* (Nashville: Thomas Nelson, 1994), 164.
7. *AJC*, November 13, 1994, 1A.
8. Ibid., September 20, 1994, 1D.
9. Ibid., October 6, 1994, 1E.
10. *New York Times*, October 11, 1995, B9 and B11.
11. *People*, February 10, 1997; *AJC*, March 29, 1996, 3E.
12. *AJC*, July 31, 1996, 34S.
13. Ibid., August 6, 1996, 21S.
14. Http://GoodWorksIntl.com/latestnews.html.
15. *AJC*, June 24, 1997, 3E.
16. Stephen Glass, "The Young and the Feckless: Andrew Young, Nike and the Reputation Racket," *New Republic*, September 8 and 15, 1997, 24 and 26.
17. *New York Times*, June 25, 1997, C2; *AJC*, June 24, 1997, 1A.
18. Bob Herbert, "Mr. Young Gets It Wrong," *New York Times*, June 27, 1997, A29; Young to the editor, July 6, 1997, ibid.; Walter LaFeber, *Michael Jordan and the New Global Capitalism* (New York: Norton, 1999), 149; Glass, "The Young and the Feckless," 26.
19. The National Summit on Africa, "Africa and America: Partners in the New Millennium," February 16–20, 2000, Washington, DC, *Commemorative Book*, 8.
20. The author participated in the Mountain–Southwest Regional Summit in Denver on September 24, 1999.
21. Stephanie Salter, "Turner's United Nations All-Star Team," *Rocky Mountain News*, June 7, 1998, 5B.
22. *AJC*, October 15, 1998, A17.

23. Jeff Jacoby, "Deaf Ear Turned to Persecution," *Rocky Mountain News* (Denver, CO), December 26, 1998.

24. *AJC*, August 5, 1999, A22.

25. Jeffrey Sheler, "Christians, Unite!" *U.S. News & World Report*, November 15, 1999, 100; *AJC*, November 12, 1999, A3.

26. Andrew Young, letter of welcome to participants, January 26, 2000, National Summit on Africa, *Commemorative Book*, 1.

27. President Bill Clinton's address at the National Summit on Africa, Washington, DC, February 17, 2000, author's personal typescript and tape recording; Nora Boustany, "U.S. Ties Key, Say Africans," *Washington Post*, February 19, 2000.

28. Young's improvised remarks at the National Summit, February 17, 2000, author's personal typescript and tape recording.

29. Deliberative Process, "Peacekeeping Session," February 18, 2000, National Summit, author's personal notes.

30. Young's keynote address at the National Summit on Africa, February 18, 2000, author's personal typescript and tape recording.

Conclusion

Andrew Young's parents instilled in him a devout faith in Christianity and a strong work ethic. Growing up in New Orleans exposed him to many different races and ethnicities, and his father demonstrated how to get along with all sorts of people. At Howard University, he learned more from fellow students, especially one from Nigeria, than he did in the classroom. During his postgraduate summer, he became interested in Gandhi's philosophy of nonviolence. Young also began to realize how much his Christian faith meant to him, and taking religion courses at the Hartford Seminary reinforced that judgment. After receiving his divinity degree in 1955, he and his new wife Jean moved to southern Georgia, where Young had his first pulpit. During their two years in Georgia, they became involved in voter registration drives. In 1957 they moved to New York, where Young worked in the Youth Division of the National Council of Churches (NCC). Impressed by the determination of students staging sit-ins across the South, in 1961 the Youngs returned to Georgia to participate in the civil rights revolution.

Initially, Young oversaw a Voter Education Program funded by the NCC, but he worked more and more closely with King's Southern Christian Leadership Conference (SCLC). He played a key role during the protests in Albany, Georgia, demonstrating his skill in communicating with white officials. King asked him to serve as the SCLC's negotiator with the white leadership in Birmingham, Alabama, where a major campaign began in the spring of 1963. Young's mediation helped the SCLC reach a successful resolution, and the conflict in Birmingham influenced President John Kennedy to call for a civil rights bill. Next, Young and the SCLC confronted the Ku Klux Klan in St. Augustine, Florida, which prompted Congress to approve the Civil Rights Act in the summer of 1964. Young marched from Selma to Montgomery in spring 1965, a seminal event that led to passage of the Voting Rights Act in August.

During these dramatic days, King showed Young that the civil rights struggle was linked to the struggles for racial justice around the globe. King's winning the Nobel Peace Prize in 1964 underscored the fact that he was not just a leader of African Americans, but an important presence in the international arena. King explicitly linked the movement for racial equality in the United States to the battles against colonialism and apartheid in Africa. In the mid-1960s, all U.S. foreign relations were overshadowed by the escalating conflict in Vietnam. Young and other SCLC leaders criticized the war in private, but hesitated to challenge President Lyndon Johnson publicly, because he had been such an important ally of their movement. Finally, in 1967, King decided he could no longer remain silent. In April he delivered "Beyond Vietnam," a powerful condemnation of the American intervention that Young helped him write. Its antiwar stance ignited a firestorm of criticism, but King would not renounce what he considered to be the only morally acceptable position, and his determination deeply impressed Young.

In the late 1960s, King increasingly decried economic injustice, both at home in cities such as Chicago and abroad in former African colonies. He believed people could not truly be free until they escaped the chains of poverty. He initiated the Poor People's Campaign in 1968, but was assassinated before it got off the ground. Young attempted to carry on the fight by coordinating a tent city and a series of protests in Washington, DC, but the campaign failed to bring about any concrete progress. In his last major SCLC action in 1969, Young helped to resolve a hospital workers' strike in Charleston, South Carolina, but he had learned that solving problems of economic inequality was extremely difficult.

Young believed that entering the political realm was a natural extension of the voter-registration work he had done. After an unsuccessful first attempt in 1970, he won a seat in the U.S. Congress in 1972, representing Atlanta. He was the first black elected to Congress from the Deep South since 1901, and he personified the positive impact of the Voting Rights Act. During four years as a member of the House of Representatives, Young continued King's fight for peace and racial justice around the world. He advocated economic sanctions against the white minority regime in Rhodesia, espoused an end to the Vietnam War, and crafted an amendment that prohibited Portugal from using U.S. aid to suppress its African colonies. He visited South Africa with Arthur Ashe and befriended the black activist Robert Sobukwe. He opened his home to Sobukwe's children while they attended college in Atlanta, demonstrating on a personal level the new aproach he brought to U.S. foreign relations. In 1976, Young played an instrumental role in the formation of TransAfrica, which would lobby for progressive policies in Africa and the Caribbean.

After Jimmy Carter was elected to the presidency, he asked Young to serve as his ambassador to the United Nations. He intended to improve relations with Africa and hoped that Young's past association with Martin Luther King would help convince people that the Carter administration was serious about championing human rights worldwide. Young accepted this opportunity to take King's vision onto the international stage. In the first two years, he was very successful, helping to impose sanctions against Rhodesia, fostering better relations with Nigeria, and improving the U.S. image in Latin America. In his final year, he continued to battle racism around the globe, most notably in Africa but also in Australia. His willingness to speak his mind sparked controversy on numerous occasions. Finally, Young's meeting with a representative of the Palestine Liberation Organization in the summer of 1979 ended his tenure at the UN. Carter continued positive relations with Africa even after Young's departure. Ultimately, the policy toward Rhodesia that Young had helped craft and implement contributed to a settlement that brought peace, majority rule, and independence to the country renamed Zimbabwe in 1980.

Young returned once again to Georgia, and in 1981 was elected mayor of Atlanta. During his eight years in office, he transformed Atlanta into an international city and redefined the role of mayors in foreign relations. He emerged as a leading critic of Ronald Reagan's foreign policy and played a key part in the antiapartheid movement that culminated in the passage of a tough sanctions bill in 1986. Just as Young's involvement with the civil rights movement shaped his participation in foreign affairs, Atlanta's close connections with the fight against racism defined it as a progressive, multicultural city. As mayor, Young capitalized on this aspect of his city to attract foreign investment, trade, and tourism. During his last years in office, he spearheaded the effort to have the 1996 Olympic Games held in Atlanta, and in doing so he emphasized the legacy of King.

After a failed bid for the governorship of Georgia in 1990, Young settled into the position of private-sector diplomat. He served as a consultant for the Law Companies Group, an international engineering firm. Atlanta's successful bid for the summer Olympics was a great triumph for Young and his goal to connect Atlanta to the world. He remained very active in the planning and staging of the spectacle. In 1997, he founded GoodWorks, aimed at promoting economic development by serving as a link between multinational corporations and governments. His efforts drew some criticism, particularly after he inspected Nike plants in Southeast Asia and issued a relatively positive report. His primary focus remained on southern Africa, and his efforts to build bridges to that troubled region were much more fruitful. He supported the efforts of Nelson Mandela to bring multiracial democracy to South Africa, managed the Clinton administration's Southern Africa Development Fund, and helped organize the National Summit on Africa. That endeavor featured a series of regional summits to discuss policy proposals, leading up to a final conference in Washington, DC, in February 2000. Young served as master of ceremonies, a fitting end to a decade in which he had worked tirelessly to foster democracy and economic development in Africa. Nearly forty years after joining Martin Luther King's movement in the South, Young continued to champion King's global vision. Throughout his career as an activist, politician, and diplomat, he believed U.S. foreign relations should promote racial justice around the world. For four decades, Andrew Young served as an influential and effective civil rights ambassador for the United States.

What is the significance of Andrew Young's long career as a civil rights ambassador? What is Young's legacy? What lasting impact has he made on U.S. foreign policy? The answer is quite simple. Andrew Young helped widen the scope of American foreign relations. He assisted in adding new issues to the agenda, championing racial equality, and fighting hunger and poverty. He focused on previously neglected regions of the world, most notably southern Africa. He spoke for the increasingly influential African-American community, as racial minorities and women gained access to the foreign policy establishment. Young facilitated participation in international affairs by a host of institutions beyond the White House and State Department such as Congress, the United Nations, churches, and private corporations. He expanded the definition of foreign relations to include cultural events such as the Olympic Games and the National Summit of Africa. He demonstrated the potential role of mayors and city governments on the international stage. In all of these ways, Andrew Young broadened the playing field of American foreign relations to allow participation by the diverse and pluralistic society of the United States.

Bibliographical Essay

The most important sources on Andrew Young's youth and early adulthood in the 1950s are his two autobiographies, *An Easy Burden: The Civil Rights Movement and the Transformation of America* (New York: HarperCollins, 1996) and *A Way Out of No Way: The Spiritual Memoirs of Andrew Young* (Nashville: Thomas Nelson, 1994). *An Easy Burden* is by far the more comprehensive of the two, but *A Way Out of No Way* provides some very useful insights into the development of Young's Christian faith.

On the beginnings of the African-American civil rights movement in the 1950s, see Taylor Branch, *Parting the Waters: America in the King Years, 1954–63* (New York: Simon & Schuster, 1988); Stephen Oates, *Let the Trumpet Sound: The Life of Martin Luther King, Jr.* (New York: Harper & Row, 1982); and David Garrow, *Bearing the Cross: Martin Luther King, Jr., and the Southern Christian Leadership Conference* (New York: Vintage Books, 1986). For an overview of the Eisenhower administration's handling of civil rights, see Robert Burk, *The Eisenhower Administration and Black Civil Rights* (Knoxville: University of Tennessee Press, 1984). In *Cold War Civil Rights: Race and the Image of American Democracy* (Princeton: Princeton University Press, 2000), Mary Dudziak provides a thoughtful analysis of how the Cold War influenced civil rights. For a discussion of the impact on foreign relations of the Little Rock crisis, consult Cary Fraser, "Crossing the Color Line in Little Rock: The Eisenhower Administration and the Dilemma of Race for U.S. Foreign Policy," *Diplomatic History* 24 (Spring 2000): 233–64.

For general assessments of the Eisenhower administration's foreign policy, see Stephen Ambrose, *Eisenhower: The President* (New York: Simon & Schuster, 1984), and idem, *Nixon: The Education of a Politician, 1913–62* (New York: Simon & Schuster, 1987). For the role of Secretary of State John Foster Dulles, start with Richard Immerman, *John Foster Dulles: Piety, Pragmatism, and Power in U.S. Foreign Policy* (Wilmington, DE: Scholarly Resources, 1999), and for more specialized essays, follow that with Richard Immerman, ed.,

John Foster Dulles and the Diplomacy of the Cold War (Princeton: Princeton University Press, 1990).

One of the most important reasons for studying Andrew Young's career is what it demonstrates about the increasing importance of race in U.S. foreign relations. In order to grasp the significance of his work in the 1970s and 1980s, it is necessary to understand how little consideration policymakers in the 1950s gave to fostering racial equality both at home and abroad. Among a growing body of literature, the best works are Michael Krenn, *Black Diplomacy: African Americans and the State Department* (Armonk, NY: M. E. Sharpe, 1999); idem, " 'Unfinished Business': Segregation and U.S. Diplomacy at the 1958 World's Fair," *Diplomatic History* 20 (Fall 1996): 591–612; Paul Gordon Lauren, *Power and Prejudice: The Politics and Diplomacy of Racial Discrimination,* 2d ed. (Boulder, CO: Westview Press, 1996); Brenda Gayle Plummer, *Rising Wind: Black Americans and U.S. Foreign Affairs, 1935–1960* (Chapel Hill: University of North Carolina Press, 1996); and Penny Von Eschen, *Race against Empire: Black Americans and Anticolonialism, 1937–1957* (Ithaca, NY: Cornell University Press, 1997).

Another central aspect of Young's contribution to U.S. foreign policy was his success in making relations with Africa a higher priority. Once again, to appreciate the extent of his impact, it is imperative to look at the period when Africa was scarcely even on the radar screen of the American foreign policy establishment. For useful studies of relations with Africa in the 1950s, see Thomas Borstelmann, *Apartheid's Reluctant Uncle: The United States and Southern Africa in the Early Cold War* (New York: Oxford University Press, 1993); Andrew J. DeRoche, "Establishing the Centrality of Race: Relations between the U.S. and the Rhodesian Federation, 1953–1963," *Zambezia* 25 (1998): 209–30; William Minter, *King Solomon's Mines Revisited: Western Interests and the Burdened History of Southern Africa* (New York: Basic Books, 1986); and, most important, Thomas Noer, *Cold War and Black Liberation: The United States and White Rule in Africa, 1948–1968* (Columbia: University of Missouri Press, 1985).

For primary sources on the relevant events of the 1960s, both international and domestic, the presidential archives are beyond compare. Both the John F. Kennedy Library in Boston and the Lyndon B. Johnson Library in Austin feature a wealth of material and helpful staffs. For the civil rights movement, there are many important collections in the Martin Luther King, Jr., Library in Atlanta. Most valuable among them for studying Young's role in the movement are the papers of the Southern Christian Leadership Conference.

The most thorough discussion of Young's activities in the 1960s is his *An Easy Burden*. For a carefully researched treatment of the crucial civil rights events of 1963 to 1965 that illustrates Young's role, consult Taylor Branch, *Pillar of Fire: America in the King Years, 1963–65* (New York: Simon & Schuster, 1998). Other important studies of the movement that shed light on Young's contributions are David Garrow, *Bearing the Cross*, and Adam Fairclough, *To Redeem the Soul of America: The Southern Christian Leadership Conference and Martin Luther King, Jr.* (Athens: University of Georgia Press, 1987). For an analysis of the development of Young's philosophy in the 1960s, see Andrew DeRoche, "A Cosmopolitan Christian: Andrew Young and the Southern Christian Leadership Conference, 1964–68," *Journal of Religious Thought* 51 (Summer–Fall 1994): 67–80.

In the 1960s, the civil rights movement became intertwined with foreign relations to a much greater degree than it had been. The best study of this dynamic is Thomas Borstelmann's *The Cold War and the Color Line: American Race Relations in the Global Arena* (Cambridge: Harvard University Press, 2001). Also see his " 'Hedging Our Bets and Buying Time': John Kennedy and Racial Revolutions in the American South and Southern Africa," *Diplomatic History* 24 (Summer 2000): 435–63. Mary Dudziak explains how the Cold War prompted progress at home during the 1960s in *Cold War Civil Rights*. The frustrations of blacks in their endeavors to have significant influence at the State Department during this period are demonstrated in Michael Krenn, *Black Diplomacy*. An excellent analysis of black and white Southerners' impact on 1960s foreign policy can be found in Joseph Fry, *Dixie Looks Abroad: The South and U.S. Foreign Relations, 1789–1973* (Baton Rouge: Louisiana State University Press, 2002).

Africa was a somewhat higher priority for the Kennedy and Johnson administrations than it had been for Eisenhower's. The best overview of American policies toward Africa in the 1960s remains Thomas Noer, *Cold War and Black Liberation*. For a thorough examination of relations with South Africa, see Robert Massie, *Loosing the Bonds: The United States and South Africa in the Apartheid Years* (New York: Doubleday, 1997). Policies toward Zambia and Zimbabwe are detailed in Andrew J. DeRoche, *Black, White, and Chrome: The United States and Zimbabwe, 1953–1998* (Trenton, NJ: Africa World Press, 2001). The crucial act of Kennedy's intervention in the Congo crisis is best explained in David Gibbs, *The Political*

Economy of Third World Intervention: Mines, Money, and the U.S. Policy in the Congo Crisis (Chicago: University of Chicago Press, 1991). For Johnson's Congo intervention, see the masterpiece by Piero Gleijeses, " 'Flee! The White Giants Are Coming!': The United States, the Mercenaries, and the Congo, 1964–65," *Diplomatic History* 18 (Spring 1994): 207–37.

All other U.S. foreign relations in the 1960s were overwhelmed by the events in Vietnam. The classic introduction to the subject is George Herring, *America's Longest War: The United States and Vietnam, 1950–1975*, 3d ed. (New York: McGraw-Hill, 1996). Other major studies include George Kahin, *Intervention: How America Became Involved in Vietnam* (New York: Doubleday, 1986); Robert Schulzinger, *A Time for War: The United States and Vietnam, 1941–1975* (New York: Oxford University Press, 1997); and Marilyn Young, *The Vietnam Wars, 1945–1990* (New York: HarperCollins, 1991). A concise study of the role of Kennedy and Johnson's secretary of state can be found in Thomas Zeiler, *Dean Rusk: Defending the American Mission Abroad* (Wilmington, DE: Scholarly Resources, 2000). For insightful analysis of Martin Luther King's difficult decision to oppose the Vietnam War and Young's contributions to the debate, see Fairclough, *To Redeem the Soul of America*.

By far the best source for Young's work in Congress in the 1970s is the *Congressional Record*. Other important primary sources either by or about Young can be found in the Gerald Ford Library and in the papers of Charles Diggs at Howard University. Two early biographies, James Haskins, *Andrew Young: A Man with a Mission* (New York: Lothrop, Lee, and Shepard, 1979), and Carl Gardner, *Andrew Young: A Biography* (New York: Drake, 1978), contain important details regarding Young's congressional years. For a description of the formation and early years of the Congressional Black Caucus, including Young's role, see William Clay, *Just Permanent Interests: Black Americans in Congress, 1870–1992*, rev. ed. (New York: Amistad, 1993).

Most of Young's contributions to American foreign relations while a U.S. Representative dealt with Africa. Scholars interested in early 1970s policies toward Africa in general should peruse the Diggs Papers at Howard. In his *Uncertain Greatness: Henry Kissinger and American Foreign Policy*, former Kissinger staffer Roger Morris reveals the stunning ignorance about Africa that existed in the Nixon White House. For the contentious debates over Rhodesian chrome imports, start with Anthony Lake, *The "Tar Baby" Option: American Policy toward Southern Rhodesia* (New York: Columbia

University Press, 1976); and also see DeRoche, *Black, White, and Chrome*. For relations with South Africa, consult Steven Metz, "Congress, the Antiapartheid Movement, and Nixon," *Diplomatic History* 12 (Spring 1988); and Massie, *Loosing the Bonds*. For dealings with Nigeria, see Robert Shepard, *Nigeria, Africa, and the United States: From Kennedy to Reagan* (Bloomington: Indiana University Press, 1991). The most important American policy toward Africa in the mid-1970s—and arguably the most tragic one—involved Angola. By far the best discussion of this case is in Piero Gleijeses, *Conflicting Missions: Havana, Washington, and Africa, 1959–1976* (Chapel Hill: University of North Carolina Press, 2002).

For an overview of the Nixon administration, see Melvin Small, *The Presidency of Richard Nixon* (Lawrence: University Press of Kansas, 1999). Jeffrey Kimball details the ongoing focus on Vietnam in *Nixon's Vietnam War* (Lawrence: University Press of Kansas, 1998). Nixon's approach to civil rights is analyzed in Hugh Graham's "Richard Nixon and Civil Rights: Explaining an Enigma," *Presidential Studies Quarterly* 26 (Winter 1996). The best general works on Kissinger are Walter Isaacson, *Kissinger: A Biography* (New York: Simon & Schuster, 1992); and Robert Schulzinger, *Henry Kissinger: Doctor of Diplomacy* (New York: Columbia University Press, 1989). John Greene examines the Ford administration in his *Presidency of Gerald R. Ford* (Lawrence: University Press of Kansas, 1995). For relations with the Soviet Union, see Raymond Garthoff, *Detente and Confrontation: American–Soviet Relations from Nixon to Reagan* (Washington, DC: Brookings Institution, 1994).

Primary sources for Young's stint as UN ambassador abound. The best archival collection is at the Jimmy Carter Library in Atlanta. Other valuable documents can be found in the Harry Byrd Jr. Collection at the University of Virginia and the Diggs Papers at Howard University. Young testified numerous times before Congress and those hearings, available in government document sections of all major libraries, contain a wealth of information. Both the *Washington Post* and the *New York Times* feature a great number of useful articles on Ambassador Young.

Young's major speeches from his first two years at the UN are published in Lee Clement, ed., *Andrew Young at the United Nations* (Salisbury, MD: Documentary Publications, 1978). Bartlett C. Jones provided a thoroughly detailed study of this period in *Flawed Triumphs: Andy Young at the United Nations* (Lanham, MD: University Press of America, 1996). Much insightful information and analysis can also be found in Seymour Finger, *American Ambassadors at the*

UN: People, Politics, and Bureaucracy in Making Foreign Policy (New York: Holmes and Meier, 1988).

Andrew DeRoche assesses the crucial example of U.S. relations with Zimbabwe in his "Standing Firm for Principles: Jimmy Carter and Zimbabwe," *Diplomatic History* 23 (Fall 1999): 657–85. For an analysis more critical of Carter, see Stephen Stedman, *Peacemaking in Civil War: International Mediation in Zimbabwe, 1974–80* (Boulder, CO: Rienner, 1991). A valuable insider's perspective from a former U.S. ambassador to Zambia is provided by Stephen Low, "The Zimbabwe Settlement, 1976–79," in Saadia Touval and William Zartman, eds., *International Mediation in Theory and Practice* (Boulder, CO: Westview, 1985). For two very different African perspectives on Zimbabwe, consult Ian Smith, *The Great Betrayal: The Memoirs of Africa's Most Controversial Leader* (London: Blake, 1997); and Joshua Nkomo, *Nkomo: The Story of My Life* (London: Methuen, 1984).

For Carter's policies toward Africa more generally, the best discussion may be found in Peter Schraeder, *United States Foreign Policy toward Africa: Incrementalism, Crisis, and Change* (Cambridge: Cambridge University Press, 1994). For South Africa, start with Massie, *Loosing the Bonds*, and for Nigeria, see Shepard, *Nigeria, Africa, and the United States*. Discussion of several other hot spots, as well as analysis regarding the rising influence of Americans concerned about Africa in the late 1970s, can be found in Andrew Young, "The United States and Africa: Victory for Diplomacy," *Foreign Affairs* 59 (Spring 1981). The interaction of domestic race relations and American policy regarding Africa is insightfully examined in Borstelmann, *The Cold War and the Color Line*.

The best comprehensive look at the Carter administration is John Dumbrell, *The Carter Presidency: A Re-Evaluation*, 2d ed. (Manchester, England: Manchester University Press, 1995). Also useful is Burton Kaufman, *The Presidency of James Earl Carter, Jr.* (Lawrence: University Press of Kansas, 1993). Gaddis Smith explains Carter's foreign policy successes and failures clearly and concisely in *Morality, Reason and Power: American Diplomacy in the Carter Years* (New York: Hill & Wang, 1986). For the actors' own explanations of events, see Jimmy Carter, *Keeping Faith: Memoirs of a President* (New York: Bantam Books, 1982); Cyrus Vance, *Hard Choices: Critical Years in America's Foreign Policy* (New York: Simon & Schuster, 1983); and Zbigniew Brzezinski, *Power and Principle* (London: Weidenfeld and Nicholson, 1983).

Andrew Young's two terms as mayor of Atlanta are chronicled in the pages of the *Atlanta Journal Constitution*, and there are several important articles in the *Washington Post* and *New York Times* as well. Young's testimony in *U.S. Policy toward South Africa*, a hearing before the Senate Foreign Relations Committee in May 1985, is an in-depth example of his ideas about the value of sanctions. For analyses of Young's performance as mayor, see Alton Hornsby, "Andrew Jackson Young: Mayor of Atlanta, 1982–1990," *Journal of Negro History* 77 (Summer 1992): 159–82; and Ronald Bayor, "African-American Mayors and Governance in Atlanta," in *African-American Mayors: Race, Politics, and the American City*, ed. David Colburn and Jeffrey Adler (Urbana: University of Illinois Press, 2001), 178–99.

For additional insights into Young's mayoral tenure, and for the story of Atlanta in the 1980s more generally, there are several excellent books. The most literary is Gary Pomerantz, *Where Peachtree Meets Sweet Auburn: The Saga of Two Families and the Making of Atlanta* (New York: Scribner's, 1996). Tamar Jacoby provides the best discussion of racial issues in her *Someone Else's House: America's Unfinished Struggle for Integration* (New York: Basic Books, 1998). Atlanta politics are described by Clarence Stone in *Regime Politics: Governing Atlanta, 1946–1988* (Lawrence: University Press of Kansas, 1989). Also valuable is Frederick Allen, *Atlanta Rising: The Invention of an International City, 1946–1996* (Marietta, GA: Longstreet Press, 1996).

In the heated debates over American policy toward South Africa in the 1980s, TransAfrica President Randall Robinson often squared off against Assistant Secretary of State for Africa Chester Crocker. Crocker's *High Noon in Southern Africa: Making Peace in a Rough Neighborhood* (New York: Norton, 1992) provides a wealth of details on U.S. diplomacy in the region. Robinson's *Defending the Spirit: A Black Life in America* (New York: Penguin, 1998) offers a forceful critique of American relations with Africa and the Caribbean. The best study of U.S. relations with South Africa is Massie's *Loosing the Bonds*, and Schraeder's *United States Foreign Policy toward Africa* is also insightful. The perspective of the most important South African citizen is wonderfully presented in Nelson Mandela, *Long Walk to Freedom: The Autobiography of Nelson Mandela* (Boston: Little, Brown, 1994). For details of Jimmy Carter's ongoing involvement with Africa, see Douglas Brinkley, *The Unfinished Presidency: Jimmy Carter's Journey beyond the White House* (New York: Viking, 1998).

The best source for Andrew Young's activities in the 1990s can be found in the *Atlanta Journal Constitution*. Key personal details from the early 1990s are found in Young's *A Way Out of No Way*. His projects after 1996 are described on his consulting firm's website at GoodWorksIntl.com. For an interesting discussion of globalization, which includes some analysis of Young's work for Nike, see Walter LaFeber, *Michael Jordan and the New Global Capitalism* (New York: Norton, 1999). Michael Dyson provides thoughtful commentary on the legacies of Martin Luther King, including Young's support for corporate capitalism in the 1990s, in *I May Not Get There with You: The True Martin Luther King, Jr.* (New York: Free Press, 2000). Haynes Johnson identifies important developments of the 1990s in his *The Best of Times: America in the Clinton Years* (New York: Harcourt, 2001). For a thorough overview of the decade's foreign relations, consult Robert Schulzinger, *U.S. Diplomacy since 1900*, 5th ed. (New York: Oxford University Press, 2001).

Index

Aaron, Billye, 156
Aaron, Hank, 50, 156
Abernathy, Ralph, 16, 23–24, 25, 26, 36, 136
Abubakar, Atiku, 165
Affirmative action, 114, 168
Africa: AIDS in, 164; and civil rights movement in United States, 10–11, 13, 18–19, 20, 24, 25, 28, 30–31, 54, 72, 79, 82, 83, 92, 104, 167, 172; colonialism in, 9, 10–11, 12–13, 17–19, 46–47, 50, 57, 172. *See also by country*
Africa Growth and Opportunity Act, 163, 166, 167
African Development Fund (ADF), 59–60, 168
African National Congress, 12, 25, 53–54
Agnew, Spiro, 47
Albany, Ga., 16, 171
Albert, Prince, of Monaco, 146
Albright, Madeleine, 165
Algeria, 124
Ali, Muhammad, 158
Allen, Ivan, 44
Allen, Ivan, III, 122
Allende, Salvador, 54–55
Alston, Philip, 108–9
American Civil Liberties Union, 52
American Jewish Congress, 114
American Negro Leadership Conference on Africa (ANLCA), 18
Amin, Idi, 60, 86
Angelou, Maya, 156
Angola, 33, 121; CIA involvement in, 17–18, 55, 60, 61–62, 68; civil war in, 55, 60–62, 76–77, 98,

102, 139; Cuban intervention in, 60–61, 62, 76–77, 80–81, 84, 86, 102, 139; FNLA in, 60–61, 62; MPLA in, 60–62; Portuguese policies in, 17–18, 46–47, 50, 57, 172; relations with South Africa, 61, 77; UNITA in, 18, 60–61; and Young, 46–47, 61–62, 68, 76–77, 84, 139, 140
Annan, Kofi, 165
Arafat, Yasir, 111
Arbenz Guzmán, Jacobo, 21
Argentina, 62
Ashe, Arthur, 53, 80, 172
Atlanta: Atlanta Council of International Organizations, 126; Chamber of Commerce, 157; Community Relations Commission, 42; Edgewood Redevelopment Project in, 56; Hartsfield Airport, 56, 126, 136; Olympic Games in, 121, 144, 145–47, 151, 153–54, 156–58, 173–74; race relations in, 121, 122–23, 137, 146–47, 173. *See also* Young, Andrew, as mayor of Atlanta
Australia, 108–9, 118, 173; Aborigines in, 97, 108

Bahamas, 127
Bailey, Pearl, 50
Bakhtiar, Shahpur, 106
Baptist Church, 1, 8, 11, 15, 24, 31
Barletta, Nick, 49
Barry, Marion, 123
Belafonte, Harry, 42, 43, 122, 136
Bell, Griffin, 152
Bellanger, Serge, 131
Bennet, Charles, 58

ISBN 0-8420-2956-7

90000 >